Classroom Management and Teaching

Classroom Management and Teaching:

persistent problems and rational solutions

CHARLOTTE EPSTEIN
Temple University

Reston Publishing Company, Inc.
A Prentice-Hall Company
Reston, Virginia

Library of Congress Cataloging in Publication Data

Epstein, Charlotte.
　Classroom management and teaching.

　Includes index.
　　1. Classroom management.　2. Teacher-student
relationships.　I. Title.
LB3013.E67　　　　372.1'1'02　　　　78-27124
ISBN 0-8359-0824-0

10　9　8　7　6　5　4　3　2

Printed in the United States of America

For Paula and Paulette, my favorite teachers

Contents

Chapter 8

FATE CONTROL FOR THE TEACHER, 281

Preface

The books on classroom management and discipline have all been written. The behavior modification approaches, the mental health approaches, the tricks, and the dos and don'ts fill up a twelve-foot shelf. The question is, "What can another book add to help teachers who are still searching for the magic formula for maintaining order in the classroom?"

The chances are that if each teacher were assigned to a class that had had no previous school experience, she would be able to establish some kind of relationship with the children and an atmosphere in the class that would be adequate for insuring a reasonable process of learning. Some teachers would be more authoritarian, some less. Some would be volatile, others would be calm and quiet. Some would provide marvelous opportunities for growth and development; others would at least not prevent most of the children from learning. The point is that most students of education learn enough in their professional courses to do a job of teaching the children.

Unfortunately, however, by the time most teachers meet their classes, the children have already had a variety of experiences, the cumulative effect of which seems to have reduced the force of curiosity, encouraged apathy, impeded the development of independence, and damaged self-concept. No one teacher has caused any of this, but somehow the school-life experience of the child has resulted in all of this. Almost inevitably—these children are "discipline" problems. They create noise and confusion, they resist teaching and fear learning, they express hostility to adults, and they become involved in conflict with each other. To resolve classroom management problems, we need to teach children that they can be seen, can be heard, and can be appreciated without calling attention to themselves with behavior that drives adults up the wall. We need to permit children to appreciate themselves so they can afford to appreciate others. We must give children time and opportunity to be thoughtful about their own behavior—to consider how their behavior affects the behavior of the significant others in their lives.

Nor do these observations concern only urban children or only inner-city (read Black and Puerto Rican) children. Wherever the contingencies occur, the results occur. If children never know who the teacher will be that day, if they are "taught" disconnected lessons that have no relation to their concerns or their interests, if the school is dirty or falling down around their ears, if they are expected to score low on achievement tests, then their behavior will be self- or other-destructive or defensive. Perhaps a child who is poor has a lower tolerance to some of the debilitating experiences to which he is exposed, so his resulting disruptive or destructive behavior will be apparent more quickly than is the case with children who are more comfortable physically. But no child is immune to a succession of substitutes, fragmented teaching, low adult expectations, and uncomfortable physical surroundings. When these things occur in the suburbs or the country with the frequency and intensity with which they occur in the city, the behavior of all the children looks pretty much the same.

What I am trying to do here is to identify those *human* problems that arise in a specific setting: the classroom. These are not problems experienced by teachers of inner-city children, or teachers of middle class children; teachers of Black children or white children; Native American, Puerto Rican, or Chicano children. They are problems faced by teachers of children whoever and wherever they are. Given certain contingencies, certain consequences, certain common behaviors appear. With some children, these behaviors may appear more quickly. They may last longer and be more resistent to extinction. But, given the same contingencies, we will see the same behaviors.

Because certain contingencies obtain more frequently in urban schools, we may get more frequent behaviors of certain kinds. But it is a matter of frequency, not kind. That is, urban and suburban children do not respond differently to the education situation; it is just that the different behaviors appear with greater or lesser frequency in the urban or suburban setting. It is the causes and the reinforcing factors of the various behaviors that are the keys to dealing with them effectively.

If children respond to sudden and drastic change in their lives with fear, anxiety, and an inability to concentrate on school work, we need to educate them to deal effectively with change. Whether the changes are occurring in the lives of city children or suburban children is not the prime factor in our lesson planning.

If children act out their boredom with whining irritability and argumentativeness, they are *bored*; the fact that they live in the city or in the mountains of Appalachia is not of primary relevance to the educational remedy.

If children solve all their problems of confrontation by fighting, what does it matter that they learned this response on a city street or in front of a television set? The point of educational relevance is that they need to learn alternatives to fighting.

What I have tried to do is draw together what we know in our profession about changing behavior, synthesize it, and apply it to specific classroom problems. It is, above all, I hope, a rational approach to classroom interaction. If there are errors of thinking here, they can be easily routed by some rethinking and more careful use of logical principles. The errors of fact must wait on a more accurate science of behavior.

The reader is probably familiar with education textbooks—with the carefully laid-out principles and the "approved" practices. The tone here is a more immediate one, I hope, conjuring up the atmosphere of the teacher's room during "prep" time or the supervising teacher's office during "I'm at the end-of-my-rope time." Nobody's blaming you for the problems you are having with the children. Rather, you are to be commended for caring enough about the children to be disturbed about having the problem and to ask everywhere for help in solving it.

As teachers, this is where our strength lies: in our ability to identify educational problems and bring teaching strategies to bear on solving them. For some time now, our strength has been subverted by a number of factors, and, like other victims of subversion, we have begun to believe that we are truly powerless to do what we have been educated to do. Ex-teachers have told us that we haven't a chance against administrative and social odds; reporters have told us that we don't know how to teach; and academics have told us that we perpetuate the socioeconomic status quo. We have been condemned, advised, and wished into oblivion with such frequency and intensity that many of us have been paralyzed into virtual professional immobility.

Already some teachers are proclaiming, "All that humanism stuff isn't working." Before it ever really gets off the ground, it's being neatly balanced by "back to basics." One would think that humanistic education were really an innovation in teaching. Remember Dewey? What was he advocating, if not honesty, independence, decision making, and other "humanistic" factors. But it is an idea whose time has *still* not come. The pendulum is swinging the wrong way, and what's in is dress codes and corporal punishment. Just as an example of how divided our profession is, compare the items in the columns below and recall the colleagues who line up on each side:

Humanistic	*Basic*
1. One way to establish pleasant relations is to smile when you feel friendly.	1. Don't smile too much. The kids will think you're easy and take advantage of you.

2. Don't force people into humiliating and/or frightening situations. It doesn't make them friendly or help them learn.

2. If you told them to study something, call on them to answer, especially when they look as if they're not prepared. If they're humiliated in the process, it's their own fault for not being prepared.

3. Let the children participate in making decisions about what they are to learn and how they are to learn it. Not only does it help them become skillful at decision making and encourage independence; but it makes them feel worthwhile and in control of their own lives, both facets of academic success.

3. You know what's important for children to learn. You teach them what they need and one day they'll appreciate it.

Similarly, behavior modification approaches are being abandoned before they have been adequately tested. "I was in a school that was all behavior mod," one teacher tells me. "But it didn't work with those kids. So the teachers would look out through a peephole in the door and when they saw the principal or someone else coming, they would start giving out tokens. But the rest of the time, they just didn't bother. It was a behavior mod school, but it wasn't working."

Thus, behavior modification becomes a token approach—no pun intended. And whatever efficacy is intrinsic to the approach is systematically subverted.

I am reminded of one of my students who assures me that behavior modification does not work. "What exactly," I ask her, "have you seen that doesn't work?"

"Well, the teacher gave tokens for all kinds of things. But the kids were only interested in getting tokens; they didn't care about doing the work."

I was in that class too," another young woman interjects.

"The kids traded tokens and even sold them. It was a mess."

"They got tokens for completing certain work?" I ask.

"Yes. And they got them for good behavior and things like that. The teacher even took back tokens when they didn't behave. She was always threatening them, threatening to take the tokens away, because they were fighting over them. It just didn't work."

What was happening certainly didn't work. But it wasn't behavior modification, either.

Multiply these experiences by the total number of teachers who "tried behavior mod" before they abandoned it; and add the opinions of the students who watched it all disintegrate into chaos and frustration, and you have an idea of what has happened to most innovations in the history of teaching.

Faced with this onslaught of advice, attack and distortion, we have sometimes been stampeded into rejecting out of hand many approaches to teaching that, fairly tried, may solve some of our persistent problems. Sweeping, unequivocal renunciations of complex ideas and strategies make me suspicious. They call to mind the fate of "progressive education," which didn't work: that gross distortion of progressive education that encompassed everything from never voicing an opinion in the presence of children to interacting with the children as if there were no differences between them and adults.

The purpose of this book is to jog some memories of those of us who, surrounded by the scrapheaps of strategies and philosophies that "didn't work," may have forgotten how much we know and how skillful we are. This is not a "bag of tricks" approach. Such an approach leaves the teacher without alternatives when a trick does not work. This is a reasoned approach to living with children for a large part of the day and helping them become everything they are capable of.

So down with the barricades and on with the job!

CHARLOTTE EPSTEIN

chapter 1

Solutions Based on Physical Management

Problem 1
A MATTER OF SEATING

Mr. Smith teaches a class of twenty-eight fourth-graders. Before he ever saw them he already knew they were trouble. They did not pay attention, they were noisy and always out of their seats on one pretext or another, and they picked on each other and got into fights right in the classroom. There was no question in his mind about their learning ability—they just didn't have what it took.

The principal promised Mr. Smith that he would do all he could to help him manage his class, because he realized that no teacher could do very much with them unaided. Consequently, he saw to it that there were always at least two other adults in the room with the teacher: one a senior education student doing his practice teaching, and the other a special aide who was hired by the school system while he completed his college studies.

Mr. Smith was determined that he would expose these

1

children to every aspect of the curriculum just as he would have done with any other class. For one thing, one or two of them might be motivated a little and perhaps make some progress. For another, he did not ever want to be accused of depriving these children of any opportunity.

Each afternoon for a week, after school was out, Mr. Smith and the two students planned a science lesson that was designed to involve the children in activities that were interesting and that would give them some information and a chance to develop some basic skills. For each child, they prepared a small kit of materials with different textures, odors, colors, sizes, and shapes. The plan was to explain the procedure to the children, then give them time to feel, taste, and smell the various materials and answer questions about their experiences: How would you describe the odor of this? How does the feel of this compare with the feel of that? The questions were to be asked of individual children or small groups by the adults as they circulated around the room.

The children in Mr. Smith's room sat in groups of four all the time. Four desks were pushed together to form an oblong table. Two children sat on one side and two others sat facing them. The chalkboard was on the wall considered the front of the room; no child faced it when he was seated at the table. Each child had to turn his head either to the right or the left to see the board—or to look at the teacher when he spoke to them from the front of the room.

On the day appointed for the science lesson, the children sat in their accustomed groups. They had heard enticing hints from Mr. Smith and the student teachers that they had something interesting in store for them, and the crackling excitement actually acted to put a damper on their customary behavior. They had come into the room after lunch and sat down immediately, not waiting to play out the usual hassle about coming to order. Even Johnny, usually the last one to amble in—when he came at all—was in his seat. Of course, he could not refrain completely from the usual behavior pattern, so he sat energetically poking Frederick in the ribs. Frederick's anticipation acted as a shield, however. Absentmindedly, he kept batting at Johnny's hand, as one would at an annoying fly.

Mr. Smith and the two students quickly began to place some kits in front of each child. You can imagine with what enthusiasm each child pounced on the kit and proceeded to open it! As soon as Mr. Smith saw this, he signaled to the students to stop handing out kits, and he called for everyone's attention.

"Just a minute, please! Stop what you're doing! Wait for directions!"

Though one or two of the children's hands hovered over the kits in front of them, most of the children paid no attention at all. They were too involved in examining each item and talking about it to the other people in the group.

"Be quiet! Let me tell you what you are to do!"

The children's voices just rose to make themselves heard over Mr. Smith's shouting. They were enjoying touching, smelling, and describing the objects in the kits. One would have thought that the educational objective of the lesson was being admirably achieved. One would have thought so, that is, if one were not witnessing Mr. Smith's anguish and anger.

As the two student teachers watched the escalating temper of the experienced teacher, they too began to feel disturbed. Soon they were swooping down on the children, admonishing, shushing, even shaking some of them to make them respond to Mr. Smith's demands for silence and attention. But it was all in vain. The children were too caught up in the fascination of the materials in the kit and were obviously unable to pull themselves away.

Finally, the teacher gave up, in disgust.

"You don't know how to behave!" he shouted. "It's no use trying to teach children like you! You're disorderly. You just don't want to learn!"

Calling to the students, he instructed them to collect the kits. They did so, sometimes having to pry them loose from the clutching hands of the children.

"Maybe we'll try again another time," Mr. Smith said. But the hopeless tone of his voice and the discouraged stance of his body made it clear what he thought of his chances of getting these children to respond appropriately to sincere attempts to teach them. What all the other teachers had said about them was obviously true.

The Modification Target

Though there can be no doubt that this group of children presents the classroom teacher with many problems, it is also clear that the behavior described here was inevitably precipitated by teacher error. Children seated facing each other were in ideal position to interact concerning everything that interested them at the moment. This was quite consistent with the teacher's lesson objective: the children were to communicate with each other their feelings and sensations about the variety of interesting materials they would manipulate. The message the teacher was giving them was clear: talk to each other. The second message, however, contradicted the first: talk to each other, but not yet.

Perhaps there are children—and adults, too—who can withstand the temptation to respond to a new and exciting experience without putting voice to it to others in close proximity who are having the same experience. However, it requires an enormous amount of control by all but the most laconic of individuals. Here we had children who had a history of short fuses, short attention spans, and apparent inability to respond in orderly fashion. Yet the teacher had presented them with a demand for order that other more disciplined individuals would have had difficulty obeying. By his seating arrangement, Mr. Smith had set these children up for failure; it was impossible for them to succeed.

Better to have seated them, at first, in a close group facing the teacher, if he felt it was necessary to give them directions. (Though it would seem to even the casual observer that directions at that moment were really superfluous.)

Of course, he may have felt that it was too much trouble to move the desks first one way and then another for one rather short lesson. The time needed to do this would be prohibitive, leaving too little time for other things. This is usually the reason for arranging desks in one way and keeping them that way permanently. Some lip service is also given to the children's need for security, their need to know where they belong in a room. There is a feeling extant that constantly moving the furniture around in a classroom encourages a feeling of transiency and results in chronic disorder.

In this case, if he believed all this, Mr. Smith might just have gathered the children around him in front of the room and they could have remained standing for the minute or two he needed to explain the lesson. It might have been a pleasant relief from sitting at the same desks all the time.

Seating and Security

It might be worthwhile to examine our ideas about seating arrangements a little more closely. While it is true that children may be upset at sudden, unexpected changes in process and routine, it is also clear that any process that facilitates the achievement of objectives that the children have identified and agreed to is generally acceptable to them. If Mr. Smith had gathered the children around him for a moment or two at the chalkboard *before distributing the kits*, and given them a sentence or two of instructions, the children would probably have listened and then eagerly gone back to their desks in excited anticipation. They would have maintained the security of their permanent places and still experienced a logical arrangement for the lesson.

But it seems to me that this insistence on the necessity for permanent furniture arrangement in order for the children to feel secure is a distortion of both the need and the appropriate way to satisfy it. It would seem that the confusion in children, the feelings of apprehension and discomfort, with the resultant disorder in the classroom, is not a simple function of a desk in the same or in a different place. In their homes, children sit around a table for dinner, in a semicircle to watch television, and singly or in twos when they are working alone or speaking to another person. They are very clear about the functional relevance of those different seating arrangements, even when they make appropriate seating changes in order to combine two or more functions—as when they eat on a tray facing the TV. Is there some psychological explanation for expecting that they cannot understand the functions of variable seating arrangements in the classroom?

Oh, you may say, the home is not the classroom! There are twenty-five of them in the classroom, and you cannot leave them to arrange themselves in an orderly fashion! But I cannot accept numbers as a deterrent to functional seating! At a birthday party, the announcement that ice cream is served will bring twenty or thirty children to the chairs around a table; the entrance of a clown will cause them to cluster on the floor facing him; and a suggestion to play hide-and-seek will send them scattering throughout the house.

The essential point is that the children know *what is expected*; they have experienced the logic of a particular physical arrangement in terms of *their own immediate goals*, so there is no feeling of insecurity in changing from one arrangement to another. As long as they are clear about the goals and have adopted them as their own, and as long as they have experienced the relationship between the goal and a particular seating arrangement, they will naturally fall into it. Anything else would be as unthinkable as their seating themselves around the dinner table when they want to play hide-and-seek!

Seating and Understanding Objectives

What happens in most classrooms is that children

1. are not clear about the goals of a particular activity;

2. have certainly not adopted those goals as their own; and

3. have had little or no opportunity to learn how a particular seating arrangement makes the activity pleasurable and helps them to feel successful at it.

If the children have been involved in making the work plan for the day, at appropriate points these questions should be raised:

1. In which part of the room should this work be done?

2. Is it better to work on it alone or with others? How many others?

3. Do we need to talk to each other? If yes, how can we talk to each other without interfering with the work of other people?

4. How should the seats be arranged to facilitate this working alone or together?

The children must be very young indeed to be unable to respond thoughtfully and sensibly to these questions. I suggest that, if they are able to speak, they are able to consider appropriate seating arrangements.

I am not suggesting that after the first such discussion there will be no seating problems to be solved. However, unless this kind of consciousness raising and problem solving is undertaken by the children, they are forever doomed to be arranged by the teacher and to balk at any threat to their accustomed arrangement.

The idea that only certain seating arrangements are appropriate in the classroom has been instilled in generations of Americans. One has only to observe a college class enter a room and begin automatically to arrange the chairs in rows, all facing the front of the room, to realize this. The assumption is that this is the way to sit in a classroom. Of course, most teachers—at all levels—teach using this arrangement. When a teacher uses a room and arranges the chairs in some other way, even the janitor, when he sweeps, will assume the furniture is out of order and will replace it in the accustomed rows.

"Why don't you put the chairs back the right way after you use the room?" one colleague whose class met immediately after mine, asked me.

"If I must rearrange the seats when I come in because the person before me has the chairs in rows, why shouldn't you do the same thing for yourself?" I asked.

"But you're the one who changes the way they're supposed to be!" he answered indignantly.

He and the janitor agreed that there was a right way to arrange the seats—and it was not mine!

Seating and Ownership

There are other factors that interfere with the implementation of the idea that the seating arrangement should depend on the objectives of an activity. When each desk is used to store the individual's books, papers, and other supplies, it can be disturbing to him to have that desk pushed from place to place all day, and have its contents a prey to the curiosity of the person who happens to be using it at any moment. Few children or adults can tolerate with equanimity seeing someone rummaging through their belongings. If individual storage spaces are provided for the children, there will be less apprehension about moving the desks around and sitting sometimes at one and sometimes at another.

In many classrooms, too, the chairs are of different sizes and colors. It would be gratifying to believe that the differences are in response to the different sizes and tastes of the children in the class, but this is almost never the case. The fanatical clutching at *my chair* seems attributable to the fact that the chairs are easily identifiable; so, in the frustrating environment of the classroom, clutching at a personal possession becomes a substitute for more constructive self-assertion. The simple, immediate thing to do is to see to it that the chairs are all alike, so that no one can easily claim a particular one. The long-term solutions, of course, involve eliminating factors in the classroom that are unnecessarily frustrating, helping the children to cope productively with those frustrations that cannot be eliminated, and encouraging them to be assertive in obtaining satisfaction for their needs in the face of bureaucratic and/or adult unawareness or insensitivity.

A General Plan for Seating

When a significant number of children in a class are unable to respond to the expectations of settling into the routine of the classroom, it is futile to begin the ritual of calling the names of children, making demands to "sit down" and "pay attention." It is not even reasonably productive to focus on the reinforcement of acceptable behavior by identifying those who are already sitting down and do seem ready to listen to what you have to say. The noise volume alone absorbs your reinforcing words, and the Brueghel-like activity of the children interferes with any attempts of those involved who might consider breaking away. The teacher's frantic attempts to get order in the classroom inevitably escalate, becoming louder and more frantic as the noise and activity also become louder and more frantic.

It would seem that the initial responsibility of the teacher is to provide immediate opportunity for those children who are ready to work, in spite of the difficulty the others are having. (The teacher can also benefit from the sense of accomplishment she gets from seeing at least some of the children engaged in productive activity. Putting off teaching until the whole class is orderly and waiting with baited breath for the words of wisdom is often doomed to failure. The teacher who lives day after day with the sense of her own failure is destroying herself, both personally and professionally. Eventually, to save herself, she will become the agent for the destruction of the children.)

Those children who are ready to work need some specific help if they are not to give up and resign themselves to the apathy of extreme frustration, or join the revelers who act out their frustration in more obvious ways. They need appropriate physical space, a feeling of separation, and finally, tangible rewards.

Physical Space. The easiest way to provide such space is to mark off a part of the room with whatever furniture is handy. A free-standing bookcase, a table or two, even the children's desks can be used as a barrier between the workers and the not-yet workers. Whatever seating arrangements are provided behind the barrier (floor mats, desks, tables) should strengthen the barrier by having the children's backs to it. It is no drawback if the total space behind the barrier is not large. On the contrary, as the noise in the rest of the room increases, it is important for the children who are working to get very close to each other so that they may have their mutual-assistance conversations and group discussions without shouting to be heard.

The separate space should be treated as an entity apart. It should be decorated as if there were nothing else in the room.

Supplies should be readily accessible without having to leave the space. The children should be encouraged to develop the feeling that this is their classroom, and that their activities will not be disrupted by the other children.

As the not-yet workers become workers, they may be admitted to the working room. As the need for more space increases, the physical barriers may be pushed back, until the not-yet-working part of the classroom is just a small corner.

A Feeling of Separation. The feeling of separation from the rest of the room should be fostered in order to help the children find a quiet, orderly world in which to address themselves to growing. The path to their space should be clearly defined and even marked off if it is at all possible, so that they will not need, every time they come in, to batter their way physically or psychologically through the turmoil. The teacher should keep an eye on the path and interpose herself to prevent any not-yet-worker from using it. To enhance the feeling of separation, it is even useful to give the space a different room number (like 207 *AA*) or a place name (like Serious World), as long as the implied pejoratives are avoided (like calling it Good or Well Behaved).

Tangible Rewards. Children who address themselves seriously to the business of learning should not be taken for granted. To overlook their need for recognition and praise just because they are causing no trouble, is to teach them that recognition is the result of disruptive behavior. Therefore, when they need an adult to pay attention to them, they may very well join those who are running around, throwing things, talking, laughing, and fighting. These children may be comfortable with less of the teacher's time in the classroom because they are busy at their own academic pursuits. But some of that time must be used to systematically praise and encourage them; to rejoice together at successes.

Though these children may be allotted less classroom time while the teacher works directly with the children who still need more extrinsic controls, a great deal of preparation time must be spent if they are to be engaged in more than just busy work.

Children very quickly lose their enthusiasm for endlessly repetitive workbook exercises and such marking-time activities as the outlining of textbook chapters. They will not reside in Serious World for very long if they cannot seriously respect their own efforts.

A Universal Seating Error

In visiting classrooms over the years, one seating error strikes me with its universality: the children are almost invariably too far from each other and from the teacher. Contrary to the belief of many teachers that considerable distance between children is necessary to keep them from disruptive talking and "laying on of hands," I have always found that the distances tend to interfere with all those processes that operate to maintain productive and orderly interaction:

1. If your objective is to teach children to cooperate with each other, help each other, care about each other's difficulties and frustrations, then it seems logical to permit them to be close enough both to communicate difficulties as they arise and to proffer assistance as it is needed. (Of course, if your objective is to have the children work alone in silence, to speak only when they're spoken to by you, and to care nothing about a classmate who is slowly going down for the third time, then by all means maintain a sufficient physical distance between them so that they cannot easily interact with each other.)

2. If your objective is to focus on working in the classroom, then the children should be close enough together so that the occasional things they want to say to each other can be said easily and casually. If, every time a child is moved to say something to another child, he must make a production out of it because he must move so far and must speak so loudly, the focus will soon shift from working to discipline.

Casual remarks, laughter, and expressions of surprise, interest and frustration are all natural concomitants of many working situations. Rather than detracting from efficiency, they often contribute to the sense of comfort by easing the pressure of work. They add to the feeling of friendliness. They contribute to the atmosphere of "realness," reducing the artificiality inherent in learning to live while seated within the four walls of a factorylike building.

3. If your objective is to have the children pay attention to you while you teach, demonstrate a process, or give directions, having all the children sit as close to you as possible will give you more control over them. It will be easier to establish eye contact with more of them, you may be able to sit among them and lean toward them as one does in friendly communication, and they will be able to encourage each other with body language and nondisruptive murmurs to respond to you as a group. In addition, the nature of your communication may be different: it may be softer and more intimate and so more likely to be responded to by more people in friendlier ways than if you are perceived as making a speech to a monolith called "class," to whose individual responses you may appear insensitive—unless they are actively disruptive.

If the children are very far from you, and less far from other children, they will find it easier to communicate with each other when they feel the need than to continue to listen to you. Since, in a class of twenty-five or thirty, there is always someone, at every moment, who needs to say something, children will be talking. Instead of talking softly to you or to a neighbor, they will be raising their voices and/or moving out of their seats, and so shifting attention from your communication to problems of discipline.

Their distance from each other also inhibits spontaneous response; those individuals who do nevertheless manage such response are—because of the formality of the seating arrangement— perceived as disruptive. It is something like the expectation in a large auditorium; the audience is not expected to talk loudly to each other or to talk to the speaker at the lectern. Such talking comes under the heading of "protest" or "demonstration," and is viewed as deliberate disruption of the speech. However, the soft, spontaneous comments between people in adjacent seats go on throughout most speeches and are not seen as threatening, disruptive, or generally disturbing.

Crowdedness

Though too much space between people in a classroom can cause difficulties, too little space causes another kind of problem. There are many classrooms that seem almost Victorian in the way every available space is filled with a piece of furniture. Desks, tables, and chairs are packed in so tightly that changing a furniture arrangement for some purpose inevitably results in children bumping into each other, chair legs caught in other chair legs, children needing to carry furniture held over their heads with the danger inherent in this. I have seen more fights start when somebody's chair was pulled from under him in an attempt to disentangle another chair than start for any other single reason.

The noise alone in a bare-floored room crowded with furniture is awesome, unless far too much time is spent by the teacher in trying to keep movement at a minimum.

It may be wiser to consign some of the furniture in a cluttered room to a closet, from which pieces may be taken as they are needed. Or, perhaps, it is more convenient to get along with the least possible number of desks and tables, and vary the program sometimes by sitting on the floor. The general decrease in noise and mayhem may be worth the sacrifice of a few chairs, and the more open appearance of the room may help everyone feel less hemmed in and, consequently, somewhat less irritable.

Problem 2
A MATTER OF WORK CENTERS

I have asked dozens of teachers what behavior in the classroom annoys them most and seems more prevalent than other inappropriate behaviors. A very large number of responses deal with talking out of turn. When the teacher is trying to teach, the children who insist on talking—usually not to the point of the lesson—are a distraction to the other children. More importantly, however, they interfere with the coherent presentation of the lesson. The result of this is that the other children are often confused about important points in the lesson. And, because the problem behavior has used up valuable time, it is often impossible to explain further, or even to complete the lesson.

Sometimes, other children are influenced to mimic the behavior of the first child, so what starts out as one child without self-control, ends up as chaos or near-chaos in the classroom.

Nor is the teacher the only one who is interrupted. Not infrequently—perhaps more often than interrupting the teacher—children interrupt each other, so that many children do not get the chance to complete a sentence or a story.

Reprimanding the children, telling them clearly that this is inappropriate behavior, punishing them—nothing seems to help. If one child exercises self-control for a while, other children begin to demonstrate the problem behavior, so it is a constant battle to maintain order and get some teaching done.

The Modification Target

Talking and Learning

Though there are some things that can be done to change the behavior of the worst offenders,[1] the behavior will continue to manifest itself to some degree as long as the physical arrangement of the room interferes with the nature of the children's learning process. What are the factors in that process that almost inevitably precipitate talking?

First, when a child encounters a completely new field, an initial look into it provokes all kinds of questions based on interest, surprise, curiosity, or fear. These questions are spontaneous and the motivation to ask them very strong.

If the child is prevented from asking some of these questions *immediately*, at the moment when he is strongly moved to ask them, it may easily result in a drawing back from the subject matter and a dampening of the feelings that accompany active involvement in learning the new material.

---

[1] See sections on "Self-Other Perceptions" and "Skill Development."

As the child continues to work in the field, or hear about it, other reasons for talking emerge. He may recognize a fact or a circumstance that reminds him of a fact or circumstance in his own life. Both the new information and the old experience suddenly assume great importance by virtue of the connection, and he is moved to share the realization of that importance.

If we prevent him from sharing this new insight, we may also prevent him from fixing in his mind the relevance to him of the new material. Being discouraged from recognizing the connections between his past and current learnings may interfere with his understanding of the subject and his continuing interest in learning more about it. A subject that appears to be important only to the teacher and the school is rarely learned very well by the child.

Just incidentally, if we prevent the child from sharing such insights, we deprive the other children of the opportunity of learning from him and catching his enthusiasm. The subject, then, may be a dismal chore for the rest of those children who never make the connections that the "problem child" makes.

Another factor that motivates a child to talk is confusion. If he does not understand something, he is moved to ask for clarification. Sometimes, his request seems unrelated to the subject, and he is accused of not paying attention or merely being willfully disruptive. But his confusion may be so profound that he cannot even ask an appropriate question.

Preventing the child from talking will cut the teacher off from vital information. He may go blissfully on with his teaching, never knowing that learning is not proceeding at the same rate as the teaching. It may also be that there are other children in the same state of confusion, but too "well behaved" to talk out of turn.

One reason for talking out, on or off the subject, is sheer boredom. A child may be trying, rather unskillfully, to do what we adults often do somewhat more skillfully—change the subject. Or he may talk on the subject, because talking is usually more interesting than listening, especially if the subject is boring.

Again, this is important information for the teacher who, presumably, wants to make the subject interesting to the children, because he knows the relationship between interest, motivation, and achievement.

Of course, the child's talking-out behavior may not be related immediately to the subject, but may be counteraggression resulting from any one of many aggressive acts against him. (We consider this in other sections of the book.)

Arranging the Room for Talking

If, then, the total teaching-learning process depends to some considerable extent on the child's speaking out when he is motivated to do so, then it seems counterproductive to compel him to change his behavior. Rather, we need to arrange matters so that the talking-out is encouraged. We must also see to it that it happens in a setting where it does not annoy others (including the teacher) and where it does not interfere with other people's objectives.

One of the most obvious ways to arrange for this is to change the physical layout of the classroom. Of course, this inevitably implies changing teaching strategies, because the physical arrangement must be consistent with the strategies used, as well as with the educational objectives implied in the use of these strategies.[2]

Let us, then, move away from the usual physical arrangement of the traditional classroom, where the teacher teaches the class a lesson from her position at the front of the room, within convenient reach of the chalkboard, and the children sit—more or less—in rows, facing her. In such a setting, talking out of turn interrupts the teacher and the lesson. Instead of teaching the lesson, let the children learn the lesson.

The Plan. Suppose your objective for the day's lesson is to have the children in possession of instruments for finding out more about their community.

---

[2]For example, to have a class discussion with twenty-five children seated in rows, one row behind the other, is inconsistent with the objective of having everyone participate.

Step 1

After the children have left school (on the day before the lesson) prepare four parts of the room with materials that will enable six children in each part to reach the objective from a different route.

Route A. A large card is tacked up on the wall. *Written in red*, the card reads:

WHAT DO YOU WANT TO KNOW
ABOUT THE POLICE
IN YOUR NEIGHBORHOOD?

(You have an idea that the children are interested in talking about the police, who have been in the newspapers and on television for several reasons over the past few weeks.)

Hanging from the card, and easily removed as they are needed, are procedure cards. Each one, *written in red*, raises questions or gives suggestions for tasks that will carry the group toward the final objective. Route A cards read:

1. *Suggestion.* It may be helpful to write down all the things you want to know about the police, so you can keep track of everything you have to find out.

2. *Suggestion.* There are all kinds of ways to find out the things you want to know, like asking questions or reading. Can you think of any other ways you can use to find out some of the things you have listed?

3. *Suggestion.* If you need help from the teacher, ask for it.

4. *Question.* What methods have you decided to use to find out what you want to know? What preparations do you need to make for each method? (For example, do you need to write down the questions you will ask if you decide to interview someone?)

5. *Question.* What information do you still need before you can complete your preparations?

6. *Question.* How much more time do you need to complete all preparations for finding out what you want to know? (We will discuss the need for more time before we leave today.)

Route B. A large card, *written in green*, is tacked up on the wall. The card reads:

THERE IS A LARGE HOLE IN THE SIDEWALK ON M STREET,
HALFWAY BETWEEN BENDER AND POLK AVENUES.
WHAT CAN YOU DO TO GET IT REPAIRED?

(This is true. The children know that this condition really exists.)

Hanging from the card, and easily removed as they are needed, are procedure cards. Each one, *written in green*, raises questions or gives suggestions for tasks that will carry the group toward the final objective. Route B cards read:

1. *Suggestion.* It will be helpful if you are very clear about the problem, in case you need to describe it to someone in authority.

2. *Question.* How does a person find out who is responsible for dealing with different problems in the community?

3. *Suggestion.* Make a list of the things you need to know if you are to succeed in getting the sidewalk repaired.

4. *Suggestion.* List the steps in a plan for getting the sidewalk repaired. Indicate, at each step, how much time you should allow for completing it. (For example, if someone promises to call you back, how long should you wait before you go to the next step?)

5. *Suggestion.* If you need help from the teacher, ask for it.

6. *Question.* How much more time do you need to complete all preparations for getting the job done? (We will discuss the need for more time before we leave today.)

Route C. A large card, *written in blue*, is tacked up on the wall. The card reads:

WHAT DOES JIM BRACHE HAVE TO DO
NOW THAT HE IS MAYOR
FOR A WEEK?

(A local student who used to attend this school has just been appointed mayor for a week, and the children have been talking about it.)

Hanging from the card, and easily removed as they are needed, are procedure cards. Each one, *written in blue*, raises questions or gives suggestions for tasks that will carry the group toward the final objective. Route C cards read:

1. *Suggestion.* There are all kinds of ways to find out the things you want to know, like asking questions or reading. Can you think of any other ways you can use to find out some of the things a mayor does?

2. *Suggestion.* It may be helpful to make a list of all the possible sources of information about the mayor's functions. You will have to be specific about names, titles (of people and writings), repositories (like libraries), etc.

3. *Question.* What methods have you decided to use to find out what you want to know? What preparations do you need to make for each method? (For example, do you need to write down the questions if you decide to interview someone?)

4. *Suggestion.* If you need help from the teacher, ask for it.

5. *Question.* What information do you still need before you can complete your preparations?

6. *Question.* How much more time do you need to complete all preparations for getting your job done? (We will discuss the need for more time before we leave today.)

Route D. Written in purple, a large card is tacked up on the wall. The card reads:

WHAT DO YOU WANT TO KNOW ABOUT
THE DIFFERENT NATIONALITIES THAT LIVE
IN YOUR NEIGHBORHOOD?

(The school neighborhood is made up of Black and Puerto Rican families, with one or two families of Chinese American or mixed Chinese and Black American backgrounds.)

Hanging from the card, and easily removed as they are needed, are procedure cards. Each one, *written in purple*, raises questions or gives suggestions for tasks that will carry the group toward the final objective. Route D cards read:

1. *Suggestion.* It may be helpful to write down all the things you want to know about the different nationalities in your neighborhood, so you can keep track of everything you have to find out.

2. *Question.* There are all kinds of ways to find out the things you want to know, like asking questions or reading. Can you think of any other ways you can use to find out some of the things you have listed?

3. *Questions.* What methods have you decided to use to find out what you want to know? What preparations do you need to make for each method? (For example, do you need to write down the questions if you decide to interview someone?)

4. *Question.* Because of what you have already learned about prejudice and discrimination, what measures have you taken to make sure the information you finally get is accurate?

5. *Suggestion.* If you need help from the teacher, ask for it.

6. *Question.* What information do you still need before you can complete your preparations?

7. *Question.* How much more time do you need to complete all preparations for finding out what you want to know? (We will discuss the need for more time before we leave today.)

At each work center, have a brief bibliographic list of pertinent reading materials. Depending on the ease of access to a local or school library, have several or all of the listed readings right there in the center.

You may find that, occasionally, a group may decide they need to make a brief telephone call before they can proceed with the development of their plan. Just because this bit of technology did not appear until long after we decided to limit formal education to the classroom is no reason to keep the children from using it. Let them out of the room for a few minutes; there is probably a public telephone in the building.

If you are fortunate enough to have the assistance of a classroom aide, you may provide something extremely important to the successful management of this lesson. You will notice that, unless the children are specifically encouraged to move around, they may very easily believe that all the work must be done seated at the work center. This sort of constriction for children can only cause all kinds of behavior identified as disorderly. The children should be helped to realize that some of their investigating must take place away from the center, and even, perhaps, away from the school. Measuring a hole in the ground, popping into the City Hall, which is located just across the street from the school, going to the public library, or using a public telephone are all legitimate parts of the educational experience. Having an aide in the classroom provides another adult who can make these brief trips with one or two groups. If there is no adult assistance provided for the teacher, perhaps a parent can be persuaded to lend a hand occasionally.

A really caring teacher may spend a couple of hours extra after school to make some of these trips with the children, or the children may arrange to do these things on their own. However, though this solves the problem of getting the necessary opportunity for exploring and searching, it does not provide the needed physical movement during the school day. Some provision must be made for such movement, whether or not it is immediately connected to the academic objective.

Be sure, also, that each work center has a small supply of paper, pens, and pencils, so there is no problem about borrowing or arguments about who gets to write. Make yourself available to supply some easily obtainable materials that the children discover they need as they work. For example, felt pens in various colors, large sheets of paper for charts, several rulers, and pairs of scissors should be kept within easy reach. Perhaps even a Polaroid camera is not too much to expect. The children will probably understand if some of their requests for esoteric machinery and materials (like computer terminals) are not immediately filled. However, if they decide they need something like that, there is no reason why plans cannot be made for them to have an opportunity to at least try to get what they need. If they finally discover that it is not possible, they have made an important discovery, and part of their educational experience involves both that discovery and the evaluation of alternative equipment and supplies.

Step 2

With all the planning in advance, the management of the process with the children is really not at all difficult. Even with a class that has had no experience working in small groups, the teacher's calm and confidence that accompanies detailed planning is communicated to the children, who feel comfortable with the clear and simple directions. Also, the fact that the teacher is right there to give support, advice, and practical assistance carries the inexperienced along.

On the day of the lesson, tell the children that they will be working in small groups and that each group has to figure out the best ways to find out more about their neighborhood.

Each child is given a color-coded card when he enters the room and is directed to a center where everything is written in the same color. The card in his hand states, in a way he can understand, the behavioral objective of the day's (or hour's) work. The Route A card, *written in red*, says: At the end of the day (or hour) your group is supposed to have a plan for finding out everything you want to know about the police in your neighborhood.

The Route B card, *written in green*, says: At the end of the day (or hour) your group is supposed to have a plan for getting the hole in the sidewalk repaired.

The Route C card, *written in blue*, says: At the end of the day (or hour) your group is supposed to have a plan for finding out the things the mayor has to do in the course of a typical week.

The Route D card, *written in purple*, says: At the end of the day (or hour) your group is supposed to have a plan for finding out everything you want to know about the different nationalities in your neighborhood. Tell the children, "There are directions in your work place for helping you. I will also be available to help you."

The class of twenty-four will be divided into four groups of six, with each group in a separate part of the room. The first thing each group will see is the question on the large card tacked up in a conspicuous spot in the work space.

Step 3

Say to the children: "From each large question card you will see hanging a number of smaller cards. Take off one card at a time and use it as a help in getting the job done. By the time you get to the last card, you will probably have completed the plan that is described on the card in your hand. I will go from group to group and give you help if you need it. I think you will find, however, that you can accomplish a great deal without my help. All right. Go to work."

Step 4

At the end of the time allotted for this lesson, the children are asked to move away from the work centers into a whole-class group for the purpose of discussing the time factor.

Permit the children to maintain the outlines of their work groups, even though they are all facing each other. The reason for this is that the questions being discussed are of concern primarily to the work groups, not to individuals. Separating the work groups completely may encourage opinions and points of view that are divergent, and the small-group needs may be lost sight of. Also, sitting more or less in their groups will enable the children to have a quick caucus to reach consensus when a question arises that they have not discussed previously at the work center.

Thus, when the teacher asks, "Which groups need more time to finish their plans?" the show of hands will indicate whether or not there is consensus on this question. If there is a difference of opinion within a group, then the six children can quickly and quietly talk it out even while the rest of the class is going on to the next question.

The teacher may then ask each group that has not finished, "How much time do you think you need to finish?" If all the groups are within a short range of time needed, then plans can be made to work for a while sometime during the following day. If one group needs much more time than the others, then some planning must provide for them, while the rest of the class goes on to the next step in learning about their community.

In this plan, there is not much opportunity for children to talk out of turn or to interrupt the teacher's teaching. If, in the small group, a child interrupts the other children more than is generally accepted in our culture, then the chances are that the children know how to communicate their objections to this kind of behavior, and so control it. By circulating and participating first with one group and then with another, the teacher may notice that the children in a group do *not* have appropriate skills for dealing constructively with a peer who constantly interrupts the learning process. It behooves her, then, to plan for self-awareness development lessons (primarily to help the interrupter) and skill development lessons (primarily to help the others). Diagnosis of educational needs is one of the most important functions of the teacher who is acting as a resource person while the children work busily at their own education.

Problem 3
A MATTER OF WITHDRAWAL

"I feel frusterated," announces four-year-old Paulette. "I'm going to my room to lie down." She marches off to her room, closes the door behind her, and busies herself with a favorite toy.

Four-year-old Roberta also feels "frusterated." When her brother makes a funny face at her, it is the last straw. She begins to cry. She cries for so long that her mother becomes "frusterated," and whacks her bottom. Oddly enough, this just makes her cry louder. Finally, her mother shoves her into her room, dumps her on the bed, and goes out, closing the door. After a while, Roberta cries herself to sleep.

By dinner time, both children are calm and smiling, ready for dinner and pleasant conversation. But, whereas Paulette has had a reasonably comfortable day, Roberta has suffered acutely. Also, Roberta will probably have similar periods of such painful discomfort that leave her with a vague feeling of sadness and dissatisfaction. Paulette feels in control of her person.

The Modification Target

In the classroom, even very young children can learn to recognize and appreciate different emotional states in themselves and in others, and respond in ways that are constructive and helpful rather than always at the reflex or most primitive level.

Developing Awareness of Needs

In one classroom I have visited, children can choose each morning from a pegboard a picture of a face to pin on their shirts. They select a smiling face, a sad face, or an angry face to announce to the world how they are feeling that morning. They also have scheduled opportunity to talk about how they feel if they wish to do so, and what they think made them feel that way. And they are encouraged to help each other examine and test out ways to make them feel different if that is what they want. They can also change the face as their feelings change during the day.

In this classroom, it is not unusual to hear one child say to another, "You pushed me because you feel angry today; you never pushed me before." Though the first child may sometimes rationalize the pushing ("I pushed you because you pushed me first!"), more often he will confirm that he is mad at his brother or his mother, and he will apologize for pushing his friend.

In another room in the same school, pushing and retaliation are a maddening pattern of behavior, a pattern that is exacerbated by every disappointment the children experience, every frustration they must deal with.

Here is an exercise that the children may engage in for the purpose of increasing their knowledge about human behavior: causes, effects on self, effects on others.

Sitting in small groups, each child is asked to complete the sentence, "When I get mad I _____." In one such session, children told each other:

- When I get mad I holler at people.

- When I get mad I scratch people.

- When I get mad I punch people.

- When I get mad I like to get a gun and shoot up the place.

- When I get mad I act mean.

- When I get mad I break my brother's models.

- When I get mad I curse.

For a while after this, the children began to try to top each other's madness, and they—half laughing, half excited at the subtle naughtiness of it—said such things as:

- When I get mad I throw my baby down the stairs.

- When I get mad I kill everybody.

- When I get mad I kick Miss Waters (the teacher) in the foot.

"OK," said Miss Waters. "Now, let's talk about what happens when you do all those things. What do people do when you holler at them? What do they do when you punch them? What do they do when you act mean and do all those other things?"

Sam: Everybody acts mean to me when I act mean.

James: Not me! When I act mean, you better be afraid of me!

Susan: I'm not afraid of you! But I won't play with you if you act mean.

James: Who cares if you play with me! I don't play with girls!

Ellen: Once I acted mean to my mother and she wouldn't make me a birthday party. And she broke her promise.

Sam: What did you do—cry?

Ellen: No. I just felt mean. I was mean to everybody.

Susan: Did I come to your party?

Ellen: I told you! I didn't have a party, stupid!

James: Why are you acting mean now?

Ellen: I wished my mother had the party for me.

Susan: It's not my fault you were mean to your mother!

Ellen: I know.

It is this kind of exchange that encourages children to think about what they do, why they do it, and how their behavior triggers behaviors in other people. Of course, they do not always arrive at this level of awareness as quickly as the children above did. And reaching that level does not insure that they never again will displace their negative feelings onto innocent victims. But it is in this kind of interaction that the level of consciousness of self and others grows, and the children are increasingly able to deal constructively with their feelings instead of being buffeted mindlessly by them.

Providing a Safety Valve

Miss Waters' children at one point decided that there were times when they needed to get away from other people and be alone until they felt better able to work and play together. They recognized that if they were too unhappy, they could not enjoy a game; or if they were too angry, they would not feel like learning math. One child said she wanted to shut herself in the closet when she felt that way. Miss Waters asked how they would feel if she got an easy chair for the big supply closet, and a person could go in there and sit in the chair until he or she felt better, felt ready to be with the others.

The children were excited about the idea, and several of them offered easy chairs from their living rooms at home to furnish the closet. Miss Waters said she had one she didn't need that they could use and that she would have it brought to the school. They spent some time discussing how long a person could use the chair, what would happen if more than one person wanted to use it at the same time, and did they have to just sit in the chair doing nothing (like being sent to your room for punishment) or could they read or play a quiet game.

The children themselves made decisions about each one of these questions. They decided a person must use it for as long as he needed it, and that they would be glad to wait their turn. They said that sometimes, if someone needed it very badly, he could send someone to tell that person, but no one would force the one in the chair to give it up. They all agreed that needing to be alone was no reason for punishment, so the individual could read, doze, or do whatever helped him to feel better. The chair in the closet became a safety valve that contributed significantly to the comfort of the children and their teachers and helped sustain the goodwill they all felt toward each other.

As time went on, the children found that it was not necessary to sit in the closet if alone time was needed. They could go to one of the centers around the room, or sit in the back of the room; all they had to do was put up a sign that said, "I need to be alone for a while," and no one would bother them. Two such signs were always kept available for anyone who should need them.

In more and more classrooms, even where the children are not systematically learning to identify cause and effect relationships in their behaviors, they are being provided with "quiet corners" to which they may repair when they feel the need. Out of a momentary need for catharsis, a child may behave in a way that the teacher perceives as inappropriate. The ensuing reprimand or punishment focuses attention on something that, left to itself, would be of no importance. As it is, it may result in antagonism in both teacher and child, fear in the child, the child's dislike of school and reluctance to come to class the following day. It may embarrass the child, make him feel guilty, or make him wish for some kind of revenge. It will interrupt academic teaching and learning not only for the child misbehaving, but for the other children in the room.

And all for what? Because Johnny left his seat without permission? Because he threw his pencil against the wall? Because he slammed down his desk top—not once, but a *second time*?

Better to encourage the child to recognize when it is time to withdraw than to engage in continuous confrontation, first with one child, then with another.

Caveat

There is, of course, a caveat that both teacher and children must consider in this matter of withdrawal. To leave a situation because a child feels he cannot handle it effectively, to put off doing his work because he feels momentarily incapable of tackling it, to avoid people so that he may be alone while he gets his feelings sorted out are all appropriate responses to life's recurring difficulties. However, when a child—or an adult—avoids people all the time in order to be alone, or when he often cannot work because his feelings are overwhelming him; when he is forever escaping from the realities of everyday interaction to soothe himself in solitude with a book, a game, or a daydream, then we must question the appropriateness of the withdrawal. The child may need special help in developing satisfying relationships; he may need special consideration at home for one reason or another; or he may need more time to talk about what is disturbing him and driving him away from his peers.

Nor must we overlook ourselves while we struggle to make classroom life satisfying. Teachers, too, have needs for withdrawal, and children—the people with whom teachers do so much of their living—must learn to consider and respect those needs as much as they do their own and their peers'. For the teacher, too, the caveat applies.

Problem 4
A MATTER OF DECORATION

One of the most unpleasant arguments I ever had with a principal while I was teaching children concerned bulletin boards. It was my second year of teaching, and I was responsible for seeing to it that the sixth graders in my class learned literature, grammar, mathematics, science, social studies, health, and some Spanish. I was spending eight hours in school and almost that many hours outside of school planning and gathering materials that would complement the textbooks. And I did not want to decorate bulletin boards in addition to everything else I had to do.

The principal of the school encouraged parents to visit the school, though he stopped short of permitting them into the classrooms to observe what was going on. Occasionally, if a parent insisted that this was what he wanted to do, he was allowed to sit for a while, but mostly the principal conducted parents on guided tours of the plant, proudly pointing out the physical advantages and the obvious fact that the children walked quietly and in an orderly fashion through the corridors. He also stopped at each bulletin board to explain the legend and to give the parent an opportunity to exclaim at this concrete evidence that good things were going on in the school.

To this principal, the bulletin boards constituted the major public relations thrust into the community, the almost Madison Avenue approach to convincing parents and school board that the school was doing a magnificent job, and he insisted that the teachers devote considerable time and energy to composing these commercials. And they did. Some of the presentations were elaborate works of art; others had only tangential relevance to the work the children were engaged in.

Significantly, much of the contention that characterized the relationships in the school revolved around the bulletin boards. Though some of the teachers enjoyed an occasional opportunity to express their esthetic inclinations, most of them resented having to expend so much time and energy on a nonteaching function, and their behavior with the principal was often colored by this resentment. So the matter of the bulletin boards affected teachers' receptivity to the principal's ideas and suggestions, imbued their responses with negativism, made them passive in the face of his enthusiasms, and caused them to give as little of themselves as possible to the governance of the school.

The great bulletin-board war really came into its own in the relationships between the teachers and the children. The bulletin boards on the doors of the classrooms were in the path of dirty hands, careless shoulders, and coat sleeves. The bulletin boards on the walls were just low enough for resting heads and backs. The ones on freestanding easels were—disaster is the only word that comes to mind.

> *Teacher*: Johnny, you're tearing the poster! Be careful! Don't move! It's caught on your sleeve!
>
> *Johnny*:   [Jerking away and causing even more damage.] Aw, it wasn't my fault!
>
> *Teacher*: It certainly was your fault! Why can't you be more careful?

Johnny: [Mutters something as he moves away.]

Teacher: What did you say? Come back here this instant!

Johnny: [Returning with great reluctance.] I didn't say anything!

Teacher: Don't lie to me, young man!

And so it goes.

The Modification Target

Decorating and Learning

Admittedly, the great bulletin-board war represents a somewhat extreme case, in which the decoration of the school actually precipitated management problems—for the teachers and the principal, too. But the whole idea of bulletin boards and other displays can actually be used to foster all the factors that make for effective classroom management. Enthusiastic working can be reinforced when children are encouraged to display the products of their work. Their creativity can be given reign when they plan and design displays of various kinds. Their learnings can be put into practice as they devise illustrations of various themes in social studies or literature. Their self-concepts are enhanced by the appreciation and admiration of everyone who sees what they have done.

The point is that it is the children who become involved in making the bulletin boards, and the decorating of the school becomes, not just another teacher chore, but an extension of the teaching-learning process. When it is the children who are responsible for all of this, and who expend their creativity and energy to make it attractive and meaningful, then the children are likely to be more careful not to spoil the effect by carelessness or malice. Even if something is torn or broken, the tired, overworked teachers who are dealing with their own egos when they decorate have no such great emotional investment that they need to confront every instance as if it were a major crime.

It is probably true that the results of the children's efforts will look less like Madison Avenue and more like Jimmy Smith and Suzie, but we must ask ourselves the question, "Exactly what was that principal trying to sell the community, anyhow?"

Decorating and Living

I have seen many classrooms carefully decorated by the teachers that are as sterile and comfortless as railroad waiting rooms. The traditional letter charts, the lists of do's and don'ts, the calendars, and a stereotypical picture commemorating the current holiday are all rarely noticed by the children. Though it would be difficult to attribute the children's lack of enthusiasm for school even partly to the dullness of the walls, we can certainly say they add nothing to the atmosphere that would encourage the children to feel good about the school or about themselves. Who knows that fidgeting, boredom, irritability, and even absenteeism might not be somewhat alleviated by a cheerful, attractive classroom? (How would you feel about coming home at night to a house decorated the way some of these classrooms are?)

I have also seen drab, institution-colored walls and meshed windows completely devoid of any decoration. This is particularly characteristic of secondary school classrooms, whose teachers seem so often to have picked up so much that is bad about the teaching they have experienced in their university classes. (That is not to say they then also do not use many of the good things they learned about teaching during their professional education!) We sometimes forget that we *live* in these rooms for a large part of our lives, we teachers and our students, and we owe it to ourselves to avoid spending our days surrounded by cream-colored or light green painted walls, starkly lighted by fluorescent tubes. Not to decorate is to deny that we really are living there, that significant things really are happening to us in those classrooms.

Decorating and Intergroup Relations

Another word about decoration may illustrate even more directly the relationship between children's self-concepts and their academic success. Have you ever walked into a room where all the children were Black, and the pictures on the walls were all of white people? Have you been in rooms with Latino children and not one Spanish-surnamed famous person was pictured in the decorations? Of course, you have been in classrooms where all the children are Caucasian, and all the people in the pictures around the room are also Caucasian!

The connection between all this and classroom management is very easy to make. Children working in a classroom that suggests to them either that their own group is not important or that their own group is most important of all are being mis-educated in the areas of self-concept development and intergroup relations.

Of immediate relevance to classroom management are the behavioral results of prejudice and self-concept damage. Children being taught by teachers whose behavior implies that they do not think much of their racial or ethnic group are not likely to invest their confidence or trust in those teachers. Because of this lack of trust, they may view with doubt and suspicion the teacher's requests, assignments, and stated objectives. They may refuse to cooperate, they may disrupt in retaliation for what they think is the teacher's opinion of them, they may displace their distrust onto their peers and seriously affect the harmony among the children.

These children who see themselves discriminated against and downgraded may respond also with self-doubt; they may find it impossible to achieve academically because they take on their teacher's evaluation of themselves. (The connections between underachievement and behavioral problems are made throughout the book.)

Children whose teachers imply that their group is most important of all also may contribute to management problems, though these may not become apparent immediately. If white children think that by virtue of their whiteness they are superior, they may be less motivated to achieve in school, believing that they will inevitably get what they believe they are entitled to. Thrown into association with children of other groups—and, later in life, with adults of other groups—they may be dismayed and irreversibly discouraged when they realize that their whiteness does not insure success.

In addition, their belief in their own superiority to other groups may cause them to insult others, attack others, and avoid association with others—all behaviors that can and have caused serious problems in schools where children of different groups come together. Desegregation does not cause the management problems we hear about; the miseducation of the children is the cause of those problems, and sooner or later that miseducation will result in disorders in their lives.

Thus, what may seem like so minor a decision when we consider all we must decide about in our teaching, how to decorate the walls may have very serious implications for classroom management and for life in general.

Problem 5
A MATTER OF LIGHTING

Teacher: Now what's the matter with you today? Why can't you get through one whole day without some kind of disturbance?

Pupil 1:   I'm not doing anything.

Teacher: Never mind that! Just sit still and stop shuffling your feet!

Pupil 2:   When I look outside and then I look inside I have purple spots in my eyes.

Teacher: Don't look outside! You have no business looking outside when we're doing social studies.

Pupil 3:   I get spots when I look inside.

Teacher: Stop being silly and let's get on with what we were doing!

Pupil 3:   I can't see what I'm writing!

Pupil 4:   I don't see purple spots, I see red spots!

Pupil 5:   I see yellow spots!

Pupil 6:   I see all colors! Rainbow spots!

Teacher: Do you want to do all this for homework? You will if we have to stop now!

Class: [Groans and protests.]

All winter the classroom has been dull and dreary, the incandescent lighting barely adequate for reading, much less for providing a bright and cheery ambience. Now it is spring, and the sun shines through the streaked and cloudy windows with a brilliance that the dirt seems to magnify. There are no curtains or shades on the chain link-guarded, ceiling-high windows, and in the early afternoons (during the time allotted to social studies), the sun's rays are pleasantly warming and disconcertingly blinding. The teacher appreciates the pleasant warmth, and she—almost unconsciously—is repeatedly drawn to stand in it as she teaches. The children who must look at her must gaze also at the brilliant light that falls across her body.

The Modification Target

It seems almost silly to believe that a teacher would be so unaware of what is happening to the children, so lacking in empathy for what they are experiencing, so deaf to what they are saying, that she would permit the class to disintegrate into chaos just because the sun is shining. But we adults seem to get into the habit of thinking that children are irresponsible, that they need to be forced to work, that they will employ any ruse to disrupt a lesson. So we convince ourselves to get on with our teaching in the face of every symptom of resistance. Sometimes the resistance is justified.

Writing in the Dark

Not so long ago, I came to the door of a classroom because I had an appointment to observe one of my students teaching. I was a few minutes early, but I did not expect to see through the glass pane nothing but a dark room. When I opened the door, I realized that the children were sitting in the dark looking at slides. I was surprised to see that each of them had his notebook open and was writing, presumably notes on the comments the teacher was making about each slide.

The children were quiet enough while this was going on. All the little noses were within an inch of the desks, there were occasional murmurings of discomfort, but they all seemed absorbed in what they were doing—what they *had* been doing, I later learned, for almost half an hour. It was not until my student tried to work with them that the feelings generated by the discomfort and frustration of not seeing clearly exploded. If I had not been there early, I would have searched for all kinds of explanations for the crazy behavior I witnessed: they would not sit still and listen for a minute; when we got one child seated, two others got up; one little boy sat and rubbed his eyes until they teared and his face was beet red; all the children responded to each other and to us with irritability and impatience. The student and I together could get nowhere with the planned lesson.

Lighting and Individual Needs

Have you ever noticed the lighting in the various offices of a single building that houses a school or a business? I use as an example a building I am currently familiar with: the office wing of a college of education. Though each office is equipped with a fluorescent lighting fixture in the ceiling, each occupant has made adjustments in the illumination to suit his own needs. One person has the ceiling light on, yet insists that she cannot work without the added incandescent glow from a desk lamp. One man never turns on the ceiling light, but works only with a fluorescent desk lamp. He says the ceiling light hurts his eyes. Another person uses no artificial light at all, preferring to tie his draperies back as far as he can to let in the daylight. On cloudy days I have been startled to see him working in what seemed like darkness to me, but he maintains that he is quite comfortable with as much natural light as he can get. Some people prefer softer light sometimes and brighter light other times. Some people sit in the dark to think; others need extreme brightness to stay awake. The point I am trying to make is that, left with our freedom to make ourselves as comfortable as possible, we adjust the lighting to suit ourselves.

We do not accord such freedom to our children, and they are compelled to work in what may be acute discomfort—yet be orderly, compliant, and motivated.

Admittedly, it is not as easy to satisfy individual needs when there are thirty individuals housed within four walls. However, we need not start with the assumption that no adjustments can be made. There can be table lamps in working corners. There can be curtains, draperies, or shades on windows, and there can be freedom to move about so that the most comfortable light is attained.

We know that children have differences in visual acuity, and we generally try to make accommodation for the differences—by putting nearsighted children closer to the chalkboards, for example. But we need to be less simplistic about this and help children utilize and adjust light to make their lives comfortable. This objective becomes even more complicated in the achieving as we get children in our classrooms who might other times have been relegated to schools for the visually handicapped. No child should be compelled to work in too much light, too little light, light coming from the wrong direction or concentrated so as to cause discomfort. This is one kind of accommodation to the group that may result in discipline problems.

Problem 6
A MATTER OF SOUND

Before the advent of the open classroom and open-space schools, the noisy classroom was the problem of the classroom teacher—and of her neighbors along the corridor every time the door to her room was opened. And classroom teachers dealt with noise in a variety of ways, each dependent on the level of her awareness of children's needs, her teaching strategies, and her philosophy of human interaction.

Needs. Sometimes we forget that children need to move about very often. Making them sit—even if they are supposed to be busy working—for long periods of time, will cause them (1) to make shuffling noises in their attempts to exercise their muscles; (2) to use the furniture as percussion instruments in a similar attempt to exercise or in an attempt to communicate their discomfort nonverbally; (3) to talk to the other children, poke and fuss with them, even get into arguments and fights because they are uncomfortable, and they are displacing their anger and annoyance on to their peers and indirectly getting back at the real perpetrator of their discomfort; and (4) to find all kinds of reasons why they should have permission to get out of their seats. The result of all of this activity is a noise level that is not comfortable, perhaps not so much because of the noise itself, but because it is not "good" noise.

Often, the teacher's discomfort results in punishments and arguments that do little but increase the noise level.

Strategies. Some teachers direct the major part of their efforts to maintaining a quiet classroom. They believe, as did the principal who complained about the noise in a young teacher's room and was told that it was good noise, that "there is no such thing as good noise!" In a silent class, the strategies are all silent strategies, or at least so limited in sound as to be remarkable. Children do an awful lot of sitting at their desks completing workbooks and outlining chapters. There is no manipulation of materials or experiential activity because these things inevitably require movement and talking. To control the sound, communication is initiated only by the teacher, and responses to her questions are made by a few pupils. The duration of these responses is strictly limited by the teacher, and students quickly learn that they may not respond to each other's responses. The essence of the teaching strategy is control—especially control of sound.

Philosophy. Some people believe that quiet is necessary in a classroom because any noise interferes with the learning process; that children cannot use leeway in self-control and that, permitted some noise, they will inevitably get very loud and even boisterous; that noise in the classroom indicates that the teacher has lost control over the situation.

The Modification Target

Since experiencing, responding to experiences, and communication are essential components of learning, there must inevitably be some noise if learning is to go on. Since judgment and self-control are legitimate pedagogical objectives, to the extent that children do not demonstrate these qualities, they are undereducated; keeping them quiet will not teach them judgment and self-control. Noise cannot be evaluated only on the basis of volume; quality of noise must always be a significant factor as is demonstrable in comparing the cheering at a ball game and the shouting during a riot.

Open Space and Noise

Today, in schools built with open space, the noise problem is no longer a function of one person's teaching, but has become, rather, a symptom of a gross failure in teacher education.

As a profession, we have permitted and continue to permit the building of schools designed for a way of teaching we have no intention of using. I have been in new school after new school, representing millions of dollars in investment of public money. Principals point with pride to the open space, the pods that surround fully equipped laboratories, the colorful walls, the innovations in lighting. And in the pods, in the open spaces, children sit in rows, the classes separated by invisible walls, the teachers forever fighting a losing battle to keep the sound of the teaching and learning down so that the other classes will not be disturbed. Nor is this arrangement generally a temporary one, providing for a gradual changeover to open education. The teachers tell me that open education "doesn't work" for them, or for "these children," or with this principal, this community, this school board. If there was never any intention of changing the way of teaching, then why was the school built that way? Well, apparently someone had the intention, but the people doing the job were not adequately involved.

How does it happen that a profession permits itself to be excluded from the essential professional decision-making processes? I think it is largely because our teacher education institutions do not consider it a part of professional education to develop skills in the governance of the profession. If teachers remain aloof from their school communities, their professional organizations, and their unions; if they think that being a teacher means just teaching the children assigned to them, then they will never have optimal conditions for practicing their profession.

We forget a cardinal rule of effective teaching—that the physical arrangement must be consistent with the immediate educational objectives. If we do not want children to talk to each other, then we cannot seat them too close to each other or facing each other. If we want quiet, we can't have 120 children within one open space. If we want 30 children all paying attention to one person talking, we had better not have two or three other people, each talking to a group of 30 children, in the same room at the same time.

If teacher education programs really did the job, teachers compelled to work in an open-space setting would proceed to teach in ways appropriate to that setting; there would be no question of trying to maintain a traditional classroom organization when it is so obviously inappropriate.

Though everything in teacher education implies that it is important that the seating arrangement in the classroom facilitate rather than interfere with teaching goals, we do not practice, in our teacher education courses, analyzing goals in terms of physical arrangement. It is not unusual, for example, for an education student to submit lesson plans in a methods course, and make no mention in those plans of how the children will be deployed for the lesson. If the omission merely implies—as it usually does—that the children will be seated in the traditional arrangement of straight rows facing the front of the room, it is the rare education instructor who raises the question, "What is the relationship between your seating arrangement and your teaching strategy and objectives?"

Seating and Noise

A curious kind of aberration has recently crept into the matter of seating, that compounds the problem of inappropriate classroom noise. With the great interest in encounter groups, T-groups, and small-group dynamics, many teachers—at all levels, right through the university—insist that students sit in a circle rather than in rows. Interestingly enough, the teacher's method does not always change to fit the seating arrangement, and he continues his lecture method of disseminating information. However, because the students are seated in such a way as to suggest informality and because they are inevitably drawn to make eye contact with each other, they talk a lot with each other, interrupting the teaching and creating noise and what the teacher perceives as disruption.

Professional Interaction and Noise

We do not know how to interact effectively with our peers for professional purposes. It seems to me that the change to team teaching, to interdisciplinary teaching, even the change to more frequent utilization of resources other than the teacher, are all hindered by the fact that professionals have not learned some vital skills: we do not know how to teach *together*. Most of our so-called team teaching is actually "in-turn" teaching. We just take turns teaching the students what we know about our own areas of expertise. We do not sit down with our peers and work out a mutual understanding of how our various areas of knowledge relate to each other, to the children, and to the problems we set the children to solve. Therefore, we never communicate these relationships in our teaching.

Besides not interacting effectively for teaching purposes, we do not interact effectively on matters less immediately concerned with the day-to-day teaching but which inevitably affect our daily work. We gripe about problem children, problem classes, problem parents, problem principals, even problem maintenance people, but we rarely plan concerted action to solve the problems. The old teacher saw, "When you close your door, you're on your own," still pretty much holds true. Even for those teachers who "share" open classrooms, the responsibility for one's class generally remains one's own. And the teacher who has a noisy class remains, anachronistically, the teacher who "has no control."

chapter 2

Solutions Based on Management of Time

Problem 1
A MATTER OF COOPERATIVE PLANNING

It would appear to be efficient for the teacher to come to class all prepared with the day's lessons, what is to be taught, how she will teach, what objectives she expects to achieve. Then all the little baby birds, sitting there, ready, with their mouths open, will take the nourishment she gives them, chirping only when they want more, or want to be fed faster.

Actually, however, the baby birds often do not like what we feed them, sometimes do not even know that they must open their mouths if they are to get any nourishment, and, not infrequently, beat at us or at each other in their frustration with the whole feeding process. And, in the end, much of the time spent in the process is wasted.

Perhaps we should not start out to be efficient. Perhaps we should not prepare our lessons, following faithfully the form we learned as student teachers. Perhaps the planning—at least at the outset—should focus on a process for helping the pupils plan for their own learning. It would be a somewhat cumbersome process, seeming to waste valuable time that should be spent on history, science, and math. But in the end, the students would have less reason for resisting learning, more reason for becoming actively involved in educating themselves.

In one school, where the youngsters circulated from teacher to teacher for forty-five-minute periods in the different subjects, the teachers were forever in confrontation with the pupils in what were sometimes called discipline problems and other times called academic problems:

1. The hallways during class-change time were incredibly chaotic and noisy, and the chaos was increased by the teachers on hall duty who pounced on this or that student for dawdling, pushing, shouting, or any one of a hundred other behaviors that can be observed in such a situation.

2. Pupils were almost always five or six minutes late to class. Because it happened so often with so many of them, it was virtually impossible to enforce the rules about lateness. These required that each late student go to the vice-principal's office and report himself, upon which he was issued a tardy pass, which he presented to the teacher for admission to the class. If this rule were enforced, classes would have had to commence with five or six pupils, and be interrupted throughout the period as the rest trickled back with their passes.

3. Assignments were almost never handed in on time, so the teachers never felt confident in going on with the planned curriculum. Threats, reduced grades, and just scolding and nagging did nothing to change the behavior. Valuable time was lost—not only with the nagging and scolding—but with collecting papers, checking to see which ones were still due, and returning them to face arguments about the "unfair" way they were graded. Teachers could not plan their own time because they were always reading assignments that should have been in at different times in the past, as well as those that were due now.

4. The daily homework was a hit-and-miss affair, with the students openly copying each other's work, when they bothered

to do it at all. This meant that time was wasted by the students as they scrambled to "get the homework" when they should have been doing classwork. Also, the teacher had to waste class time repeating much of the material because he had no evidence of what the students had learned.

The Modification Target

One of the teachers in the school finally tired of wasting his time and the students' with all the arguing, threatening, and punishing and little or no learning, and decided to scrap the whole process for a new approach to these children. He decided to focus on changing his way of managing time and to help them manage their time differently, too.

He realized that he could not impose a new plan with any more hope of success than he and the other teachers had ever had with the old plan. So he started from scratch and caught the interest of enough pupils in his classes to get them involved from scratch, too.

One Friday, he announced, "There will be no homework. Forget about all assignments. Don't bother bringing your textbook. Just come in on Monday. We're going to do something completely different."

"You don't want us to bring our books?"

"Not if you don't want to."

"No homework for Monday?"

"No."

"No more assignments?"

"Not from me."

"What's the catch?"

"No catch."

"What are we gonna do?"

"It will be up to you."

"Whatever we want?"

"You'll make the decisions."

"Yeah!" [With derision.]

[The teacher smiles.]

On Monday, it seemed as if ninety percent of the pupils were on time to his classes. They had not completely lost the curiosity they had had in the first grade!

The Focusing Questions

In each section, the teacher started with the statement: "In eighth-grade social studies, we are supposed to learn about:

- How the different people in North and South America see themselves.

- How the different forms of government of the countries of North and South America affect the daily lives of the people in the different countries.

- What the people in the different countries of North and South America think is important and not important.

- Predicting the future for life in the countries of North and South America.

(He pointed to each topic that he had written on the board.)

Now, is there any other topic you think we ought to add to the list? Remember, this is social studies."

(You will notice that he wrote the broad themes that were in the mandated curriculum, not the names of wars or countries. This would give students with varying specific interests opportunity to contribute to the broad theme from a variety of points of view and subject areas.)

Each class added one or two more topics, some of which were repeated in several sections. The complete list included:

- What products they produce.

- Do they study about us?

- Do they have TV?

- What the schools are like.

- The different foods they eat.

- How do they feel about us?

However, he added to his own list in each section only those topics mentioned in that class.

Then he asked, "Which topic would you like to start with?"

Each class, after some discussion, came up with another answer to the question. One wanted to start with the schools. Another with predicting the future. Three of the six sections wanted to work on all of them at once because "staying with the same thing for a long time got so boring" that they didn't even feel like coming to class!

The teacher had no idea how to start the management of a semester where every topic in the curriculum—and two or three additional topics—were being studied in a class at the same time. But he was committed to it, so he decided to go along and see what happened. He concentrated on thinking up some cogent questions to help the pupils focus on the management process.

The Management Questions

As they talked about how to start, who should investigate each topic, how much time should be spent in research, in discussion, in presentation of findings, and even what the teacher's role should be, the teacher asked the following questions at appropriate times (only the questions that concern the management of time are discussed here):

(1) Are you going to work in groups or individually?

(2) How will you decide what topic you want to work on?

(3) Now that you have selected your areas of study, what is the next thing you must decide?

The children in one section wanted to go immediately to the school library to find books on their chosen topics. The teacher had a moment of speechlessness at the vision of thirty students leaving the room and descending on the librarian with more than a dozen requests for material to be produced immediately. That teacher was not quite ready to field the barbs that this would precipitate, and he tried to communicate his anxiety to the students. Then he raised this question: (4) "What are you planning to do during the regular class time from now on?" Their immediate response was that there was really nothing for them to do in class, since all the information sources must be in libraries and other places. They saw no point in coming to class only to read the social studies textbook.

As they continued the discussion, the teacher asked:

(5) If you were to go to the library now, what would you do after you got the books you wanted?

(6) If the books don't tell you everything you want to know, where will you go to compose the written questions you need to ask and to decide whom you will question?

(7) When you discover everything you want to know, will you keep it all to yourself? Where will you make plans for what you will do with the information?

Gradually a plan emerged for the use of class time that seemed workable and satisfactory to all the people who were involved in using the time. They decided to meet during the regularly scheduled time each day until some cogent reason arose for changing this decision. All those who felt the need to report progress, get feedback, test out ideas, or share something particularly interesting could use part of this class time. The largest part of the time would be used to plan the next steps in the inquiry: people working on different topics could devise questions for further study, consolidate materials collected by individuals, cooperate on writing preliminary reports, and get whatever help they needed from the teacher. The teacher would also use this time to listen to discussions and deliberations and make suggestions concerning omissions and apparent errors. The final note of the plan was the decision to leave it open for revision should any unpredicted problem present itself.

(8)   What about homework? What will you do for homework?

With amazing maturity, the children discussed the question of homework and concluded (a) that there was nothing intrinsically important about homework; (b) that the important thing was to find the answers to their questions wherever they needed to find them; (c) that if they didn't always have time enough in school to complete what they planned to do, they would use time after school to do so; and (d) that it was not necessary to have a policy about homework.

The Results

As the class worked during the semester, it became apparent that they were spending more time on social studies than the traditional schedule called for. They no longer came late to class. They were too busy to waste their time dawdling in the hallways, and they were usually in a hurry to put last-minute preparations on a presentation or to talk with their own groups before they had to listen to someone else's problem. So, though the hallways were still noisy and the other students still came late to their classes, this class no longer added to the problem.

Since they planned how to use their own time, they were able to make decisions about when they would share and report. If they found that they had underestimated the time they needed, there was no problem about planning for another date. Usually, when they had miscalculated on the time needed to complete something, they were encouraged to talk about the reasons for the miscalculation: Had they been mistaken about the availability of materials? Had they been put off by people they wanted to interview? Had they neglected to give other people enough time to meet with them or find information for them? Were they having trouble understanding the written material? Discussions of such questions helped to educate the other children to avoid the pitfalls of use of time.

Ultimately, it was certainly clear, as final examinations indicated, that all the students had learned more than what was generally expected of students at that level. And this was without that anger and those petty frustrations that added nothing positive to the learning experience. There was no question about the interest and involvement of the pupils, and some reasonable expectation that they would remember more of what they had learned about social studies than most of us do from our own school days.

Problem 2
A MATTER OF FLEXIBLE WORK TIME

"All right, clean up your tables and let's go on to social studies."

Nobody moves. Everyone is busily involved in sorting the buttons that come out of the science kits.

"Put the buttons and other science materials away! It's time for social studies!"

Several children respond to the impatience in the teacher's voice and begin to gather up the buttons. They do so slowly and apparently with great reluctance, hating to break up the piles they have separated of large ones, small ones, green ones, pearl ones, etc.

"Harry, did you hear me?" Harry is the one who never "hears," so Harry gets singled out for one-on-one instruction.

Harry sweeps his hand across his table and brushes all the buttons onto the floor. They scatter and roll in all directions.

"Harry, pick up every one of those buttons, then get over here to me! That behavior will be dealt with! You're not ready to learn science!" (The children love science; they are fascinated with the variety of materials provided that they can feel, smell, and touch.)

Harry gets down on all fours, presumably to gather up the buttons. But five minutes later he is sitting under his desk, his chin resting on his knees, and his angry face a signal of trouble to come.

Also, Jane has been reprimanded for not following directions; Al has been yelled at for being so slow; James has dropped a couple of dozen buttons and been rewarded with an angry glare; and nobody seems very happy about social studies.

The Modification Target

One of the annoyances that children always seem to be faced with is the necessity for responding to an adult's command to stop whatever they are doing and to do something different. Though this kind of abrupt shift from activity to activity is probably necessary many times (given our society's preoccupation with time), it is not the optimum situation for effective, satisfying learning.

The Fragmentation of Knowledge

I knew a woman who started college in middle age. After two years of struggling to learn within the system, she threw up her hands and quit, announcing that the structure actually mitigated against every effort to learn. Just when she was getting involved in an idea being explored in a class, the fifty minutes were up and she had to run to another class, another subject, another idea. No one ever seemed concerned with the relationship between subjects or the connections among ideas. For each course, a single textbook or two or three paperbacks constituted the curriculum, and no time was permitted to explore any subject in depth. The term papers represented a smattering of scattered readings and inadequately developed ideas, and the prevailing lore had it that the graduate assistants who taught the courses never even read them.

But the younger students seemed to accept all this matter-of-factly, and came away from the university each day sublimely ignorant and as sublimely unaware of their ignorance.

Though the woman had managed, over many years, to throw off the effects of her early school experiences, most of the other students had not. They were products of a fragmented elementary, junior and senior high school education, and they really knew no more effective alternatives to learning—even if the university system had allowed for them.

In the high school, English Literature was synonymous with sixth period, and it was sometimes difficult to learn from them exactly what was involved in English Literature *besides* sixth period. World History was fourth period with Schlackman—ech! And the relationship between English Literature and World History? What relationship *could* there be? One was English Literature, sixth period, and the other was World History, fourth period, Schlackman—ech!

Integrating Learning

The elementary school system appears to have more immediate potential for breaking down these arbitrary divisions of knowledge and, in the process, preventing some of the management problems that seem to be caused by an inflexible work schedule. There are some ideas involved in avoiding such problems, and it might be useful to discuss them here.

If the children are involved in planning each day's schedule of work and activities, it is more likely that in the process, they will have made some decisions about those things that are more important and those that are less important—to them and in the scheme of things generally. If they have agreed that it is important to do something at a certain time, it is more likely that, at the appropriate time, they will leave what they are doing without a hassle.

If the approach to learning is an integrated one, it is rarely necessary to drop abruptly one activity or subject for another. Rather, activities and topics are a function of the problem under consideration, and students become involved in one or another as it is needed for the understanding and solution of the problem.

Thus, in a study of the Colonial Period in American history, students may be working on the question: "How do the educational concerns of the colonists for their children compare with the educational concerns of people today for their children?" If they wonder about the content of education, they must study history and economics. As they become aware of the costs of education, they must study economics and mathematics, and probably religious institutions. Mathematics is a tool for studying populations—school populations as well as the geographical distribution of general populations. Comparative psychology is necessary for understanding adult-child relationships, and science and technology for examining educational strategies.

In utilizing the knowledge in all disciplines to understand the subject under study, children do not need to have their school days broken up into forty- or fifty-minute time blocks, into which are inserted so much mathematics (and no more!) and so much social studies (but no more!). The children's own interest and progress will dictate which subject they will be studying at any particular time, and the problem of making them leave one subject and go to another expeditiously and in an orderly fashion never presents itself.

Flexibility and Motivation

Though it is true that most children respond positively to a certain order and routine in their lives, the desirability of order and consistency in the classroom does not rule out the need for flexibility at appropriate times. If all the children are caught up with fascination in observing and recording the eating habits of the hamster, why should we insist that it is of greater importance—*at that same moment*—to switch to a phonics lesson? We are not suggesting that phonics is unimportant or less important than science. It just seems too bad to pull the children away from an exciting learning situation and begin from scratch to make a different situation just as exciting. In the inevitable competition, phonics will lose—mostly because of the resistance-set that the children will start with.

One can always try to utilize the interest and excitement in the current activity to switch to the other topic. Are there sounds and words associated with hamsters that can be introduced even as the children are crowded around the cages? Are there scientific generalizations that may be put into language that illustrate phonic generalizations? Can the information, opinions, feelings, and conclusions involved in the science lesson all become raw material for the study of phonics? If we can do these things, then the break between hamsters and phonics becomes obscured, and the resistance in going from one to the other is eliminated.

Flexibility and Individual Needs

There seems to be a belief in many schools that reading and mathematics should be taught in the morning and everything else should be left to the afternoon. The underlying rationale for this belief is that children are fresher and more wide awake in the morning, their thinking is sharper, and they should attack the more difficult and more important subjects when they are in tip-top condition, thereby maximizing the probability of successful learning.

However, the facts do not square so absolutely with the prevalent belief. For one thing, though there are children who *are* fresher and more wide-awake in the morning, there are also many children who do not come to their optimum level of functioning until later in the day. How logical is it for them to be subjected to the same schedule as the "morning people" are?

For some children, mathematics and reading are much less difficult to understand and learn than are the concepts and skills included in social studies. Interacting effectively with their peers, examining the problems of prejudice and discrimination, applying mathematics to an understanding of economic concepts like supply and demand are important parts of the curriculum and of their lives; but the best they can do is read words (with adequate literal comprehension) and do math problems without ever connecting them to real life. Should they be left to tackle these difficult subjects during the time of day when they are not at their best?

There are children who spend their whole school lives constantly embattled because they are "not motivated," or they are "underachievers," or they are "discipline problems." They rarely change their behavior and just as rarely succeed in school. Would it be too much for teachers to just drop the whole battle with such children and leave them free to pick up one subject or another as the spirit moves them?

I really do know all the arguments against this sort of thing. He must have some order in his life, or he will never work through to any conclusion of a task; he will never get anything done in his life if he doesn't learn now. Most jobs in life require that one maintain a regular schedule; if he doesn't learn to do this as a child, he will inevitably fail as an adult. We can't run a classroom where everyone does what he wants to do, when he wants to do it; the result would only be a chaotic situation, with no learning going on. Children left to their own devices will pick up only those tasks that are easy and otherwise congenial to them; they will avoid—and remain ignorant of—whole areas of knowledge that are vital to their growth and development.

I also have some arguments in favor of this extreme flexibility in the case of a particular pupil. If, after a reasonable time of trying to motivate him without success, is it better to keep on and on at him, or to give up and settle for his motivation to do the things he wants to do? So he reads in a corner when others are doing arithmetic. If you force him to read during the reading period and to do arithmetic during the arithmetic period, he will neither read nor do arithmetic, and then what will be gained?

Perhaps, if he is praised for his reading, he will be encouraged to try for praise in other things, and so begin to change his pattern of behavior. Over a period of time, if you keep track of his activities, you may find that he works in every subject area, though he does it in a different order from the other children. If the primary object is his academic education, you may find that it is being achieved, so why strain for conformity in this case? He evidently has an order in his life that provides for reasonable accomplishments, so why the need to impose your order on him?

Since most of the other children are quite satisfied to work according to the established schedule, there is little danger that they will all copy his behavior and create chaos in the classroom. At any rate, a part of their education should be to learn that individual needs vary and that sometimes a person needs help in finding his own way to satisfactory achievement. (A reasonable flexibility provided for them, too, can help them to accept the other child's needs.)

Such flexibility for individual children can be provided in the classroom no matter what the organization is. In the open classroom, the teacher is constantly on the alert to encourage and guide children into neglected areas of learning. Generally, however, he is reluctant to use an authoritarian approach to forcing a child to study what he is systematically avoiding. Rather, the attempt is to raise interesting questions with him, provide attractive activities for him, and even enlist the aid of his friends in enticing him into territory he knows little or nothing about.

As an example, Johnny is fascinated with the listening center. He will, if permitted to do so, spend all day every day comfortably encased in the monster earphones listening, head to one side, to the sounds on the tapes. He will, if he is asked nicely, point to the various pictures in the center that represent the sounds he is hearing. All kinds of animals, machines, and people are pictured in the sounds of the city and the sounds of the country. He will not use the reading or mathematics tapes, or go to any of the other centers. He will not even make tapes of his own. No coaxing or blandishments from the teacher or his peers over a period of a month have worked to move him.

Finally, his teacher decides to take what he likes and uses and gently expand it to give him some other experiences. She makes copies of the two sound tapes he has been listening to, but, instead of copying them exactly, she stops them at periodic intervals and inserts different things. For instance, when the police officer blows his whistle, she inserts the question, "Johnny, did you know that Grace's father is a police officer?" After the first startled reaction, Johnny smiles and nods his head. "Her brother is also a police officer," the tape goes on. "How many police officers does Grace have in her family?" Johnny holds up two fingers, and then the familiar sounds on the tape resume. At the end of the tape, Johnny is reminded, "Do you remember how many police officers Grace has in her family? Go and tell her what you know.

She'll be surprised." And Johnny finally removes the earphones to take a trip across the room to surprise Grace. One giant step for Johnny, and, once in the center with Grace, he may see something there that interests him—even if, at first, it is only for a little while.

Little by little, using the listening center that apparently fulfills some very strong needs and provides some great satisfactions, Johnny's teacher weans Johnny away from that center and provides him the opportunity to expand his horizons. Though it may still be a long time before Johnny goes systematically from one center to another completing the required work, the teacher's flexibility provides the time that he needs.

In the more traditional classroom, the child who makes unusual demands on the teacher for flexibility may be harder to provide for, not because it is more difficult to provide what he needs to learn, but because the teacher who prefers the traditional organization is probably less comfortable about having a pupil who does not "fit in." However, making the few provisions necessary for him is far less trouble than interrupting the teaching to scold him five or six times a day, punishing him in a variety of ways with all the resulting fears and animosities on both sides, creating an unpleasant atmosphere in the classroom and a despairing sense of failure in both the teacher and the child.

All that is necessary is a small work center in one corner of the room to which Johnny can repair to work on something when he doesn't want to do what the rest of the class is doing. If the center is adequately provided with materials, not only Johnny can profit from it, but so can any other child who occasionally feels that he wants to get away from what the whole class is doing.

And, while the rest of the children are working in workbooks or on other follow-up activities after the formal lesson, the teacher can spend a little time with Johnny, showing him how to put together the electrical circuit he is tinkering with or asking him an inference question or two about the story he is reading. No scolding, no punishing, and no interfering with the other children's learning.

Problem 3
A MATTER OF ROUTINE

We know that if we help children to establish daily routines of work, rest, and play—or even if we set the routines for them—they learn quickly what is expected of them in school and feel reasonably safe and comfortable as they go about their business.

The alternative is demanding that the children do this or that according to the whim of the moment, or according to a schedule in the teacher's mind that she never reveals to her class. In this kind of situation, much time is lost in making the transition from one activity to another because each time the children need explanations or coercion to relinquish what they are doing and go on to the next thing. If they are finished with one thing, they must wait for the teacher to tell them what to do next, and while they wait there are opportunities for behavior that may be termed disruptive.

However, Emerson's "foolish consistency" sometimes comes to mind in situations such as this classic one. It is the third week in September, and after several Indian summer days, suddenly it is snowing; large white flakes fall lazily to the ground, screening the world from itself, and soon the schoolyard is covered, pure white and unmarked.

Bobby: [In the midst of the reading lesson.] Look! It's snowing!

Jimmy: [Runs to the window.] Snow! Snow! Look!

The other children jump up, interested and delighted, prepared to run to the windows for a closer look. But their teacher says, "We will study about snow in January. Stay in your seats, please, and let's go on with our reading." And for the rest of the morning she struggles to keep the children in their routine, blaming the inclement weather for her inevitable failure.

If children's lives are orderly, if they can see sense in what is happening to them and what is expected of them, they can lend themselves to surprises, sudden changes in routine, even sudden losses—of teacher, of classmates—with a measure of equanimity. It is those children who see no sense in their lives at all, who are immersed in a confusing morass of demands, rules, requests, information, and supplies that have little connection with each other or with them—it is these children who go to pieces when a substitute appears in the morning, or a fire bell sounds, or a stranger comes into the classroom.

The Modification Target

In one class, each day's schedule is posted in a conspicuous place and no child can justifiably ask what he is supposed to be doing at any particular time of the day. This is not to say that he must be doing the same thing that all the other children are doing at any one time. There are alternatives from which he may choose throughout the day; there are individual projects and interests he may take up; and there are times when he must check to be sure that he is not falling too far behind in any one area of study.

In another class there is also a posted schedule, but the teacher takes all the children through the schedule each day as a group.

The children in both classes seem contented with the plans and go about their work with a minimum of resistance. There is order to their day and they seem to feel safe in that they know where they are going. Though I personally prefer the way the first class is managed, the second one is better than the kind of bedlam I see in the following classroom situation.

A Case Study in Bedlam

It is Monday morning and the teacher is ten minutes late. When she rushes in, breathless, some of the children have already been there for half an hour, having wandered into the building in spite of the rule against coming in early. (Their parents go off to work and so they must send the children to school before they go no matter what time it is. And the temperature outside is below freezing, much too cold to stay in the schoolyard for any length of time.)

The children are not sure how the teacher will start the day: sometimes she begins with arithmetic; sometimes by asking them to copy their homework from the board; sometimes, when she seems to remember suddenly, she asks them to salute the flag and sing "My Country Tisofee". Last Wednesday the teacher read them a story first thing, and yesterday morning they learned how to do well in the standardized tests. So they are just waiting around for the teacher to come and tell them what to do today.

When she comes in, she throws off her hat and coat, orders the children into their seats, becomes impatient when they do not move quickly enough, and tells them to take out their reading books. (Anything else will require some checking of pages, and she wants to get them started doing something immediately.) For half an hour, while the teacher gets herself organized, the children are supposed to be doing something with their reading books, but it is clear that each one of them has a different idea of what this something is. The teacher's attempts to organize her own day are somewhat retarded since she must stop repeatedly to reprimand children for talking, arguing, punching each other, and dropping their books.

This teacher is a charming, creative woman who truly likes working with children. Her own life is characterized by a lack of organization: she is often late to appointments and always rushing to make up for time she spent doing something of more immediate interest to her. Her friends see her artistic confusion as a large part of her charm, and secretly she agrees with them. Her pupils like her; she is pretty and warm in her relationships with them.

But none of her charm touches their confusion about their life in school. She is systematically making them feel helpless, not in control of their environment and their lives, and vaguely anxious at their inability to find a pattern to school. Inevitably, their problems with adults and with each other grow and intensify, and before the year is out other teachers are seeing them as a problem class.

It never occurs to their teacher to question her right to visit her style of life on thirty other people, without involving them in making choices for themselves. If she really were caring, she could help them organize their lives into some meaningful order without changing her own style very much. She need only help them plan a schedule and then provide materials for them to use systematically. Every time she comes down to earth, she could step into what they are doing and give the procedural help they seem to need, ask the pertinent questions, and suggest additional resources. She could thus continue her charming insouciance, and the children could have their comfortable and comforting routines.

Problem 4
A MATTER OF SELF-PACING

Very often I see administrative insistence, abetted by faculty concurrence, that certain subjects be taught at certain times of the day. The rationale for the scheduling is based on conventional wisdom. As conventional wisdom so often is just plain wrong, and more often overlooks substantiated data, the rigid scheduling of subjects may lead to learning problems.

For example, as we noted in the section on flexible work time, mathematics is to be taught first thing in the morning, presumably because everybody is clearheaded and fresh, not worn out from so much cerebration, and ready to tackle the more difficult subject with reasonable expectation of success.

Similarly, reading is generally a morning subject. Because it is so important for the children to learn to read well, it also must be taught when they are fresh. (By this same reasoning, science also should be taught in the morning because it is a difficult subject for so many people, and social studies because it is so important for effective living. But the reasoning breaks down here. Science and social studies—if they are taught at all to elementary school children—are relegated to the afternoon, and to only two or three days a week. But this is another aspect of the problem, not immediately involved with the matter of pacing.)

Janie has never been able to do well in math. She is in the fifth grade, and it seems to her that she has forever been struggling with math when she is too tired to concentrate. She loves social studies! Her older sister, who is studying to be a teacher, tells her that it is not unusual for people who are not very good at math and science to be very good at social studies. (Since nobody ever teaches Janie science, she is unable to check on the validity of the total proposition, but she is certainly growing up thinking that she just cannot do math.) Sometimes she feels like crying during math. Her teacher wrote on her report card under "Personality" that she sulks when she does her work incorrectly.

Johnny has trouble with reading. His eyelids refuse to stay up as soon as he sits down in the morning and opens his reading book. It is not that he is not interested in the stories; it is just that he cannot keep his eyes open. He's fine while he's running around in the schoolyard before school starts, but as soon as he sits down, he feels as if he'd like to stretch out and close his eyes. He never feels that way after lunch, when a lot of his friends can't keep their eyes open. Yesterday his teacher said he was lazy and would never amount to anything if he did not apply himself to his work.

The Modification Target

Differential Biorhythms

How many years has it taken each of us to realize that we are day people or night people, morning people or afternoon people? How much have we been able to control the demands made on us, so that we can utilize our self-knowledge to make our lives more productive? I do most of my work between eight in the morning and noon. Every piece of work I must do after dinner takes three times as long as it would if I did it in the morning. It also takes so much more effort that I am exhausted at the end of it as I never am at the end of a morning's concentrated work. Nor is it because I am more tired in the evening after having worked all day. I respond in the same way to evening work when I have done nothing all day.

I know people who work nights because they feel more alive, even happier, at night. I've known students who did all their studying from two until six in the morning—wide-awake and sharp of mind.

How often have you heard someone say, "I never even get started until eleven o'clock," or "I wish I could come to work after lunch." Sometimes, of course, it is because they haven't had enough sleep the night before. But very often it is part of a pattern in their lives, a biological response that is out of sync with the conventional nine-to-five pattern in our culture.

Is it possible that, if we were to teach mathematics at noon, both the morning people and the afternoon people would have a more equal chance of succeeding? And, if we were to be brave, could we have the morning people learning math in the morning and the afternoon people learning math in the afternoon? Perhaps, then, we would also reduce the incidence of behavior problems in the morning by afternoon people, and problems in the afternoon by morning people who are experiencing frustration and failure when they try to function at an optimal level when their bodies need to function at a lower level of activity. (Of course, there is always the assumption to reconsider that mathematics is a difficult subject. This belief may very well be a function of the failure in math so many of us experienced because *our* teachers believed math was a difficult subject, and so on back to antiquity.)

Learning or Preparation for Life

The matter of self-pacing is also a factor in similarly idiosyncratic situations that schools cannot seem to accept. The child who wakes one morning with a slight headache, the child who just feels out of sorts one day, the child who cannot keep to the routine one day for reasons he cannot explain—these children are still compelled to continue with the classroom schedule and produce the allotted amount of work. One may argue—and many do—that in adulthood, the wage earner will have to show up at work and produce at the expected level even if he has a headache or spring fever, that the world will not support him if he gives in to every internal nudge to idle. Here we must enter upon an argument that is partly philosophical and partly logical.

Children are not adults who must earn money on an assembly line nor is childhood merely preparation for life on the assembly line; it is a time for nurturing; it is a time for learning to understand one's self and to determine the ways in which one can be his most and best. A child needs time and opportunity to get a feeling for his unique body rhythms, his unique responses to external factors. He must try out alternative responses and examine the consequences of each, so that he can make his own decisions about how he will live his life. Coercing him to fit into the standard machinery is an affront to his humanness.

We talk so much today about people who hate their jobs, work inefficiently, and don't care about maintaining standards of operation. I think the people who can be described in these ways are manifesting a lack of knowledge about themselves, a lack of knowledge of viable alternatives in life, and a lack of experience in examining the consequences of those alternatives. They are products of faulty education; the chances are they are also products of school systems and classrooms where the fight went on to make them conform to patterns that they neither understood nor accepted, and they became adept, not at living effectively, but at resisting.

Individualizing Instruction

The usual concerns with self-pacing revolve around the child's rate of learning. It is obvious to most of us teachers that a child cannot learn something new if it is based on something else he has not yet learned. It is obvious, also, that children learn different things at different rates of speed, and that children generally have individual rates of learning. These are three facts that should establish, once and for all, the futility of teaching the curriculum to a whole class at the same time and at the same rate. Many of us, however, continue to do it anyhow. That is why some of us are able to maintain the fiction that a certain percentage of children in a class must inevitably fail and that most of the children will achieve at an average (read mediocre) level.

The attempts to provide for self-pacing through individualized instruction have usually been hindered by the indiscriminate use of mass-produced materials that very soon become boring to the children. Even more objectionable in the use of these materials is the tendency they foster to keep the children in isolation from each other, discouraging the development of necessary interaction skills and sensitivities to each other's needs. There is ample experiential evidence that all of us can present to make the connection between boredom and behavior problems, and inadequate socialization and behavior problems.

The Teacher's Pace

There is another thought about pacing that has often occurred to me that I never considered for most of the time I was directly involved in teaching children. That is, that the children's pace in the classroom almost always is regulated by the teacher's idiosyncratic pace. When the teacher slows down, the children are forced to slow down. When the teacher is on the *qui vive*, full of energy, the children are herded along at his pace. The management problems that result from children being forced out of their own pace are not often amenable to scolding or exhortation.

chapter 3

Solutions Based on Pupil-Teacher Communication

Problem 1
A MATTER OF RESPECT

A class of eighteen four-year-olds have grown from infants to self-assertive young people in four months. Their teacher had systematically brought them to the point where they made decisions about their school day and assumed responsibility for those decisions; they had developed significant skills in cooperating with each other, and they did not hesitate to question adults who made demands on them.

Each day began with a moment or two to exchange good mornings and a comment or two about the weather or an occurrence on the way to school. Some individuals, forced to leave unfinished an interesting bit of work from the day before, just waved a general good morning and went right to the place where the unfinished project had been left, before the day's formal planning began. Although there was no time to continue the project now (unless they had managed to come in half an hour before the official opening of school), it was as if they wanted to reassure themselves that the threads were where they had dropped them, ready to be picked up and drawn together. Mrs. Forman was part of all this, also saying her good mornings, sharing an occasional pleasantry, or fingering some work she had left the day before.

At exactly half-past eight, the children gathered in a cozy group at the front of the room, prepared to review the plan for the day's activities. It had not been easy to get them to this point of apparent comfort with the beginning of the day. They had become accustomed to coming in at eight-thirty—the official opening of the school day—and waiting around until nine to start work, because children straggled in at different times. Those who came before nine were supposed to become involved in educational games. In most of the classrooms, there weren't enough games for all the children, and those that were there often had pieces missing or had long since been rejected as old or boring.

Because the children who arrived on time had nothing much to do except to wait for the teacher to begin the day's work, they not infrequently began to do things that might easily be viewed as destructive or disorderly. They began to jostle each other and engage in other noisier forms of horseplay. They played games with the furniture in the room, pushing it around noisily, lifting it over their heads dangerously, or even throwing it—"all in fun." By the time the teacher was ready to start, they had already been reprimanded and threatened several times, some were already angry at the reprimands, and one or two were ready to go back to bed to recoup their used-up energies. Certainly, the sharp enthusiasm for a new day at productive work had been somewhat blunted for both teacher and pupils.

Mrs. Forman had slowly helped the children to change this pattern, and she did it largely by involving them in a serious consideration of what was happening to them. *They* were the ones who told *her* that they were angry at having nothing to do when they came early—even though, in the same breath, they admitted that they enjoyed just "hanging out." They realized, however, that they often did not even bother to come into the classroom on time, because there was something more interesting to do outside.

Of course, there were some children who came in on the school bus, and they were often late because the bus was late. All of them decided to solve this problem by planning the next day's schedule at the end of the day, so the children who came late could participate in the planning. The schedule displayed in pictures and materials was then posted on the board, so whoever came late could review it whenever he came in, even though the rest of the class had already begun the day's work.

When the children got involved in learning something or making something that was so absorbing they didn't want to leave it, there was no compulsion to go to recess because "it was time." Even lunch could be postponed, because Mrs. Forman arranged to have lunch with the children in the classroom. If some children wanted to stop while others did not, Ginny, the student teacher, stayed with one group and Mrs. Forman with the other, the two adults in the room providing a fortunate flexibility that the teacher alone could not. So lunch and recess became less a reason for school than the job at hand. (Remember, over the years, all the half-facetious interviews with children who were asked what they liked best about school? Have you ever heard one of them say anything but "recess"?)

Even with these four-year-olds, there was systematic learning going on. Some were reading, others were developing skills in dealing with aggressive behavior, still others were learning to cope with their feelings in nondisruptive ways. To a stranger visiting the class for several days, they were a fantastically interesting group of four-year-olds—articulate, serious, caring. This is not to say there was never pushing, shoving, running around the room, or throwing things. It was just that the isolated incident rarely sparked universal chaos, and a push did not usually provoke a reciprocal push. There was an easiness, a lack of tension in the room that was like a sigh of relief.

One day Mrs. Forman was unexpectedly absent; only disabling illness would have kept her from work, and the children knew it. They were dismayed but not destroyed when the principal brought them a personal message from her. She was not well, but she was sure that her recovery would be swift, and she hoped that they would continue with their work with the help of Ginny and the substitute teacher. She especially wanted Jimmy to help Lucille with her numbers; and she hoped that William and Barbara had found a way to work together even though they were often interested in different things.

Until the substitute arrived, Ginny was in charge of the class. The children were quite satisfied with this. Ginny was an integral part of their lives, and her presence helped reassure them that this change was not unmanageable.

The substitute was Myra Clark, a woman with fifteen years of teaching experience who now preferred to work only two days a week. As a regular teacher, she had taught fifth and sixth graders, but she was a competent, mature individual who had no trouble picking up the threads and maintaining the continuity in any classroom where the teacher was temporarily absent. Administrators and other teachers were always pleased to see her come into the school, because her presence meant that they would be burdened with no extra work because of the absence of a colleague.

Mrs. Clark opened the door of the classroom and closed it behind her. For a moment she stood and watched what was going on; slowly her lips tightened and a small frown appeared on her forehead. The scene was not to her liking. Small figures moved from place to place in what she thought was mindless abandon. Others worked at tables and on the floor in outrageous contortions—on their hands and knees, prone, huddled in a corner. One small boy sat cross-legged on a table, apparently directing two others who sat at the same table bent over a drawing. She shook her head in brisk disapproval, removed her coat, and prepared to do something about this atrocious state of affairs.

She rapped on the desk for silence and attention, announced that she was Mrs. Clark, and said that it was time for recess. Everyone was to dress and leave immediately, and stay in the schoolyard until she came to get them. One or two of the children started to say something, but she shushed them kindly but firmly and told them they were to do as she had requested. They moved reluctantly to the coat closet. The one child who remained on the floor, apparently absorbed in going through a pile of pictures, she lifted bodily and set on his feet, and turned him also toward the closet. During all this, she said nothing to Ginny. Now she smiled a little grimly at her and said, "Would you mind taking them out? I'll have to do something with this room before they get back."

"You know . . . ," Ginny began.

"Would you mind going now?" Mrs. Clark smiled. "We'll have a chance to talk when we're a little more organized." And she turned away, taking it for granted that Ginny, too, would do as she was told.

When the children returned after recess, they were ushered by a breathless but smiling Mrs. Clark into the seats that she had arranged in neat rows facing the front of the room. Tables, bookcases, and other furniture had been hurriedly pushed to the room's perimeter. One child let out a howl of anguish when he realized that his project had been pushed together with miscellaneous sheets of colored paper, crayons, and other paraphernalia into a heap under one of the tables. (A look from Mrs. Clark silenced him in mid-howl.)

"Can't we finish our stories?" asked Angelina.

"Raise your hand if you want to speak," admonished Mrs. Clark.

"Why are we sitting like this?" asked James.

"Quiet, please." said Mrs. Clark.

Mary began to cry softly. Her friend, Bobby, started to put his hand out to her, but he stopped when he caught Mrs. Clark's eye on him. The other children were very, very quiet.

For the rest of the week Mrs. Clark kept the class in quiet, orderly submission. She taught reading readiness, she taught numbers, and each day at exactly ten-thirty and two o'clock all the children lined up and went out to recess. The children were always very quiet.

At lunch one day, Ginny finally had the opportunity to

spend a few minutes speaking with Mrs. Clark. She had participated with growing dismay in each day's activities and could
hardly restrain herself now as she tried to convey to Mrs. Clark her
very strong feelings about what was happening to the children.

"Mrs. Forman's goal was to help the children become
independent individuals," she said.

"They can be independent when they know what to be
independent about," was Mrs. Clark's philosophy. "Children don't
know what they want; they must be guided in the right direction
until they are old enough to make their own decisions."

"Guided, yes," Ginny argued. "But not pushed. These children were participating in all kinds of decision making—about
rules, about schedules. And they were really taking hold! They
were managing very well!"

"My dear," Mrs. Clark said kindly, "You have been sadly
misled. You don't do children any good when you permit them to
exist each day in a state of confusion and chaos. Please leave it to
me. You can see how quickly I've got them working quietly at
their seats. When they've learned some discipline, then we can
begin to see about giving them a little more freedom."

Ginny retreated—not gracefully. She felt absolutely sullen
about what was happening.

On Monday, Mrs. Forman was still out, but, happily, on
the way to complete recovery. Ginny gritted her teeth on the way
to school and told herself she could last a few more days, and the
children would probably not be irreparably damaged.

Until ten o'clock, the eighteen four-year-olds obediently
sat at their desks, learning to raise their hands, speaking only when
called on, and stiffening their spines when they were reminded to
stop fidgeting. But at ten o'clock, James got to his feet and announced he had to go to the toilet.

"The word, James, is lavatory. And you will go when it is
time—during recess."

"But I have to go now," insisted James.

Mrs. Clark frowned. "Sit down, James."

James continued to walk toward the door.

Mrs. Clark raised her voice. "James, I said, 'sit down,' or you will feel the consequences."

James hesitated for a breath, then continued to the door, opened it, and went out.

Mrs. Clark strode forcefully after him. Behind her Angelina stood up at her seat. Robert reached across the aisle and picked up the extra pencil on Angelina's desk. Angelina turned and hit him on the head with her open hand. Peter ran quickly to sharpen his pencil, turning and turning the handle while the pencil visibly diminished. Susan and Cathy began to talk to each other. John slammed a book on the desk top.

When Mrs. Clark came back practically dragging a reluctant James by the arm, the room was in turmoil. She gave Ginny, sitting at the back, a scathing look, forced James into a seat near her desk, and took up her position in front of the room.

But her demands for silence and order went unheeded. The higher her voice went, the louder the children became. When she got one of them to sit down, two others got up. They paid no attention to her attempts to give directions for resuming work. They were completely out of control. Finally, in desperation, she sent them out to recess ten minutes before the scheduled time. Ginny wandered out after them, carefully keeping her face free of any expression.

After recess, two or three of the children came into the room and sat down, prepared to take whatever instructions Mrs. Clark had in store for them. The others tumbled in with Ginny bringing up the rear. The rest of the day was spent trying to get them quiet. Mrs. Clark tried everything from calm firmness to corporal punishment, but the response was hardly worth the effort. At two o'clock, with a sigh of relief, she chased them out to recess, and for almost half an hour, she sat at her desk with her head in her hands. Never in her teaching career had she encountered anything like it, not even with the older pupils she usually taught. She was exhausted, but not yet discouraged. She would just have to firm up her discipline, perhaps make a really painful example of one of them. That should get them all in line.

After recess, she saw the children beginning to bunch up at the door, with the ones in front standing on the threshold and creating a bottleneck. She quickly stood up to move them into the room with a hand on each back, but they flinched away from her outstretched hand. One of them looked up at her and said, "I want to go home."

Before she knew what was happening, almost all the children were marching around the room chanting, "We want to go home! We want to go home!" They had even joined hands, so the resemblance to an organized protest demonstration was almost frightening.

Somehow she managed to detach them from each other, but when she tried to get them back into their seats, they evaded her, and one by one they retreated to their individual storage cubicles set around the perimeter of the room. And there they crouched, looking like ferocious little bear cubs, prepared to struggle and scratch if anyone attempted to get them out.

Mrs. Clark launched into a long lecture about respect, obedience, and "you are here to learn," but she knew that no one was hearing her.

"Very well," she said, "I will speak to your parents, and I will see to it that every one of you is severely punished!" Then she sat down to wait until she could dismiss them.

The Modification Target
The Other as Object

The part of the total situation here that needs some changing if conditions are to be alleviated is the nature of the communication between pupils and teacher. Just as Mrs. Forman interacted with the children as if they were sentient human beings, Mrs. Clark dealt with them as if they were objects. She acted as if they would not respond with frustration if their need satisfaction were thwarted, as if they would not become angry if they were thus frustrated. She implied that they had nothing important to say that was not a response to her direct question, that they had no driving impulses or desires, that they could indefinitely respond obediently to her commands, without questions or feelings of their own.

In response to her treatment of them as objects, they began to see her as an object, also an insensate obstacle to their satisfaction. She was not a loving woman, like their mothers. She was not a person who had learned how to teach children because she cared about children. She was not a human being who was nervous in a new job, afraid of failure, or sometimes not feeling well. She gave no indication that there were things she needed to know or wanted to learn, no indication that she wanted to learn anything about *them*. They were not real people to her, and so she became a nonperson to them.

A nonperson has no need for the sensitivity, the empathy, or the sympathy of others. A nonperson is merely to be acted against. Since these children had a strong sense of their own personhood, they responded to Mrs. Clark's attempt to make them nonpersons by denying her right to function in her way. They did not consider the consequences for her—how it would make her feel if they refused to work, what might happen to her job, or even what she might cause to happen to them. They only knew that they were being denied their right to *be*, and they resisted.

The Substitute Teacher

It is likely that Mrs. Clark had some things of value that she could have taught the children, but they would not learn from her because it was clear that she neither knew nor cared about what they already knew, what they had already learned.

There are some key questions that a new teacher may ask children when she comes in to work with them in the middle of a term. The questions are designed (1) to help the children maintain the continuity of their lives in school; (2) to establish at the outset the fact that this adult has a feeling of respect for the children; and (3) to make clear the expectation that this respect will be mutual.

Teachers are fond of telling stories about how children test new teachers, how they torment substitute teachers, how they can be so "cruel" not only to each other, but also to adults. It has always seemed to me that the tacit assumption by a new teacher that the children did not exist before she appeared to them is at least partly responsible for the apparently hostile response of a whole class. If children are respected as individuals and left free to grow, they will test only themselves and their developing skills; they will have no need to batter themselves against the arbitrary restraints of adults.

The demands that "You will now be seated this way," "You will begin to do this piece of work," "You will respond in this manner rather than that manner," are predicated on the expectation that the children have no current commitment to any unfinished piece or work, that they have established no feelings of comfort in particular physical settings, or that they have not examined the nature of their manner of responding and agreed on acceptable forms. Why should they change their whole lives because a stranger arbitrarily demands that they do so? Reasonable human beings make no such demands on each other!

So, the teacher who assumes that some of the people in the class have some unfinished work they would like to get back to will be appreciated by those who cannot wait to pick up a book they put aside the day before, finish an essay they started at home, or check on some growing plants. "Who would like to get back to some work she started?" is a welcome question. Perhaps only three or four children are so involved—depending on the kind of classroom situation they are in—but those three or four children, off doing their own things, may make the difference between a friendly and an impatient atmosphere with the substitute teacher. It also reduces the number of children who will require more direct teacher supervision, and so makes the physical situation more manageable.

The fortunate substitute teacher has been in touch with the regular teacher, knows the school, and is known by the children. Unfortunately, it is too often the case that the substitute is completely a stranger and has no information about the school or the class culture. She might overcome the disadvantage somewhat by coming early and studying the absent teacher's plans. However, even if it were always easy to work from someone else's plans, the chances are that she was called to work at the last minute, and the children are already waiting when she arrives.

The best first choice in working with a class of small strangers is to let them go on with what they were doing, especially if they have obviously developed self-management skills. If they have not, then some instruments are needed to discover where they are in their work, what they need, and what they are able to do. A duplicated story with comprehension questions can be used to test reading skills. A mathematics game can catch interest and check math skills. A bag of buttons or a box of variously textured materials can get children involved in elementary science. Because these materials belong to the teacher and she is familiar with the problems and questions that arise with their use, she will feel more comfortable in the unfamiliar setting and probably communicate that comfort to the children. Teachers who are acting as substitutes should have traveling cases of such basic materials that can be used for a variety of revealed needs and across age lines. At a moment's notice, the teacher can be prepared to work with any group of children without frustration and hostility on either side.

"I see from some of your faces that you feel unhappy this morning. Would you like to share your feelings with the rest of us?"

This kind of question indicates that the adult appreciates that these young people may be having some feelings of disappointment, anxiety, fear, or sadness at finding their teacher absent from her accustomed place. A callous disrespect for such feelings results in the substitute's attempt to pick up—so very efficiently— the teaching job and go on as if nothing more important had just happened. Because she has no such feelings about the teacher's absence, she seems not to know or not to care that the others may have them.

Respect and Good Manners

Sometimes respect is confused with good manners, adherence to a set of behavioral rules that involve ritual responses, like saying "please" and "thank you." It often is interpreted to mean obedience to the commands and demands of people in authority. For example, a child's disagreeing with the teacher's opinion may be seen as lack of respect for the teacher, rather than a basis for further communication.

Respect and Education for Maturity

Actually, respect or lack of it relates in profound ways to a person's belief about the nature of human beings and the consequent value he places on them. If you agree with the teacher who says that children don't know what they want; you must tell them what to do; children need to be firmly controlled or they will run wild; children are cruel; and children will test you to see how much they can get away with, then your view of children is quite clear: you think they are not much as people. If you value them, it is only insofar as you expect that, when they are adults, they may be worthy of respect—if, that is, you are able to make of them the kind of adults you think *are* worthy of respect.

If you agree with the teacher who says that children have rights; children need to feel free; and children often are the best judges of what they need, then your view of children is equally clear: you think they are real, whole people who are entitled to a significant amount of control over their own lives—a control that is quickly enlarged as their education involves them in a growing variety of experiences.

Both teachers will provide the kind of education that is consistent with their perceptions, and that education will actually serve to confirm and reinforce their respective perceptions. That is, the first teacher will make the children's decisions for them, will tell them what to do and when to do it, will set down rules for them to obey, and will protect them from each other. And, because the children will be unable to make sensible choices when they are given the opportunity, because they will lose all self-control with a substitute teacher, because they will be forever trying the patience of adults, she will be even more sure than before that her perception of children is accurate.

The second teacher will plan each day with the children, saying in effect that they have ideas and desires that are valuable and that they have a right to participate in the planning of their own lives. There will be times when the children are free to make spontaneous choices from a variety of alternatives, and they will have opportunity for examining and evaluating their choices and the consequences. The children will be encouraged to express how they feel and develop empathy for each other's sensitivities and needs. This teacher, also, will have her perception of children confirmed, for her children will take the initiative, make decisions, manage themselves for productive ends, and generally respect themselves and others.

The power that lies in the teacher's hands is truly awe inspiring!

"We are strangers to each other. I would like to know you all better, and I would like for you to know me, too. Can you tell me something about yourselves that you'd like me to know?" And the teacher, will, of course, do the same.

What seems to be communicated here is that the substitute is not afraid of the children, since she is obviously willing to reveal something of herself to them instead of maintaining a distant and stern façade. It also seems to indicate that, in the exchange of personal items, the atmosphere of the exchange will be one of acceptance: you tell what you want and so do I, and the mutual expectation is that you will respect what I offer as I will respect your offering. The groundwork is laid for seeing the teacher as a human being, worthy of respect, just as she sees the children as human beings, equally worthy of respect.

There is an end to the story of Mrs. Clark and the self-assertive four-year-olds. When Mrs. Clark was replaced (word of the problems she was having got back to a competent principal), the children cheered. They didn't care that she had lost a job, experienced failure, or was saddened. Her treatment of them had blunted the sensitivity that they had worked so diligently to develop. Mrs. Clark's failure was, ultimately, theirs, too.

Problem 2
A MATTER OF SELECTIVE PERCEPTION

I have a friend who insists there is no such thing as a fourth grader: there are only children assigned to a fourth-grade class; some can decode and others are trying to learn each word as a new configuration; some have a reading vocabulary of five hundred words and others have a vocabulary of two thousand words.

Similarly, there is no such thing as an urban or inner-city child: there are only children who live in the city. Some of them live in overcrowded run-down neighborhoods, while others live in stable, well-kept neighborhoods; some have broken homes, and others have the full complement if parents; some are low achievers, some do well in school, and some rarely show up in school. You find them all in both kinds of neighborhoods, of all races and nationalities, of both sexes.

The point is that the same education books that deplore the destructive results of poverty and discrimination in our culture imply strongly in their titles that only Black children are "discipline problems," that only inner-city children are streetwise, that urban children need some special formula applied to them in the classroom if they are to benefit at all from educational opportunities.

In reality, if we look a little more closely at our classifications and definitions, we find that we are doing the very things—stereotyping and overgeneralizing—that we explicitly warn against.

Though we learn that pinning a label on a child can have a devastating effect on his development, we carelessly make an exception of this kind of label, which implies a host of misconceptions rooted in racial and socioeconomic prejudice. The fact is that like causes result in like behaviors, and it is not necessary to postulate broad social-psychological phenomena to account for school behaviors of children. Children who are made to feel inadequate will respond with reluctance to learn, bullying of peers, and annoyingly inappropriate behaviors to get recognition and acceptance. Whether the child is a Black child from a central city, a Chicano child from the Southwest, a white Anglo child from an ethnic city neighborhood, or a wealthy child from a main line residence near Philadelphia, feelings of inadequacy result in similar behaviors. The assumption that the behavioral consequences of feelings of inadequacy need some more esoteric approach in Harlem than they do in Beverly Hills is unwarranted. The belief that dealing with the problem behavior is less likely to succeed in Little Italy than it is on Central Park South is what paralyzes many teachers of city children and prevents them from using what they know to change the behaviors.

What contributes to many teachers' distorted perception of the problem behavior is not the nature of the behavior—which is the same among children everywhere—but the *incidence* of the behavior. In one setting, you may have two children in a class whose behavior is disruptive; in another setting you may have ten children who engage in such behavior. So dismaying can this large number of problem children be to the teacher, that he further distorts the picture and actually imagines that all—or all but one or two—of the children in the class are presenting serious problems.

Instead of providing opportunities for learning for the majority of the children in such a class, and systematically working to change the behavior of the rest of them so they, too, can begin to function adequately, the teacher may succumb to the combined strength of prejudice, anxiety, fear, and fatigue, and consign 80 or 90 percent of the class to psychological evaluation and classes for the emotionally disturbed and/or mentally retarded.

Of course, the consignment is generally a fantasy one, for few children ever get to a psychologist, much less a psychiatrist, and most of them are not taken out of the regular classrooms. But, for all practical purposes, they may as well be in the limbo of the special class, because teaching and learning are suspended for them.

"What's the use of teaching them if they can't learn?" "How can I teach the other children when these are creating chaos in the classroom?" "It's not my fault; too many of the children need psychological help, and no one seems to care to do anything about it." These are the rationalizations that help many teachers maintain their self-respect while they abrogate their responsibilities. And generation after generation of children are lost to the full life.

The Modification Target
The Urban Teacher

The target for change in the urban classroom must often be the classroom teacher. He must systematically divest himself of the cultural misconceptions about city children and begin to teach them as if he really believes that they can learn. Even if the teacher is himself a product of a city school, he cannot be complacent about his freedom from misconceptions. Actually, he may be so anxious about his own narrow escape from urban poverty that his prejudices are almost indistinguishable from those held by the rest of the population.

I have on numerous occasions encouraged such teachers to take a walk around the area of the school they teach in and try to identify the feelings they experience as they encounter the various facets of the community; an abandoned house, a broken street, a row of gaily painted window boxes, a scrubbed front stoop, an old man, a group of youths. Almost invariably, those who were reared in similar neighborhoods are most reluctant to take the walk. "I don't have to walk around here; I know exactly what it's like," they protest. And they clearly imply that there is little of value to be observed there.

It is those teachers who come from suburban areas who are often struck by the ease with which they make contact with people they thought were so different from themselves. They are touched by the apparent struggle of the very poor to do the best for their children. They see evidences of love where they thought to find only harshness and even brutality. And they are almost incredulous at seeing middle- and upper-class families living where they thought only the poorest people lived.

Urban Parents

Parents in the city who become convinced that their children's teacher is really committed to their children's welfare will help the teacher see clearly that the causes of classroom mis-behavior are universal. Not all poor children use dirty words to communicate with each other. (Nor are all wealthier children ignorant of those words; they probably have just learned to restrict their use to those times when there are no disapproving adults within earshot.) Not all city children must be bullied into staying in school, and most city parents do want an education for their children. City children more often spray paint the walls of buildings, perhaps because none of the property that surrounds them is their own. In city areas where there is a high proportion of home-owners, there is considerably less writing on walls. (In exurban areas—not quite the suburbs, but not the inner city, either—the writing is done on school toilet walls—less vulnerable to adult disapproving notice.) How is one motivated to develop a respect for other people's property, when there is no empathy arising out of the perceived possibility that one may some day also be an owner of property?

There are teachers who actually believe that poor parents love their children less than more affluent parents love theirs! The corollary to this belief is that poor parents do not care if their children do not do well in school. And if parents do not care, what influence can the teacher muster to motivate the children to learn! The most reasonably obvious conclusion is that the teacher is not accountable if the children do not learn in school. And it is amazing how easy it is to become the unwitting agent for the children's failure; one does not use all his professional resources to succeed if the end result is inevitable failure!

Urban Children

In the preceding chapter, those four-year-olds were system-atically taught to resist the impositions that one day might make them into incorrigible, unteachable, "inner-city" kids. They would not need to lash out at teachers and peers, they would not need to reject opportunities for learning just because hurting things that they could not control were happening to them. If, at the age of four, they were already in command of the situation, one can feel confident that, with the continuation of the kind of education they were getting, they would still be in control at the age of fourteen; they would be able to identify the factors in their lives that needed changing, and organize systematically to make those changes.

Learning to Live with Change

Though the teacher cannot, by himself, change the fact that inner-city children have substitute teachers many times more than suburban children do, he can understand the effects of this fact and he can do something to minimize—if not eliminate—those effects.

We know that children often react to sudden change with disorderly behavior. Suburban children give substitute teachers a hard time the one or two days a year that they have one. City children give them the same hard time, for the same reasons, for fifty or sixty days a year. We must conclude, not that city children are more disorderly than suburban children, but that both urban and suburban children are not competent to deal with changes in their routine.

How can we, as professionals, be content merely with recognizing what happens to children when they are subjected to sudden, unexpected change? Surely this should be perceived as a problem of education and move us to devise strategies for helping children live with change! But most of us see no connection between the chaos confronting the substitute teacher and Toffler's description of "future shock." The interesting thing is that I see people—including children—accepting without trauma fantastic changes and going to pieces at relatively minor changes that affect their daily lives and routines. Here is where the teacher can define a job for herself.

Specifically, when preparing children to work cooperatively with substitute teachers, we must raise their level of consciousness about the nature of their behavior and its effects. And we must help them recognize the connection between their feelings and their behaviors.

Before there is any immediate expectation of change, the question might be raised with the children: "How did you feel the last time you had a substitute?" This question is raised, not with the whole class, but with a group of not more than eight children, so that each one is sure to have the chance to express his feelings if he wants to and feels comfortable enough to do so.

You will discover that the children not only express their feelings, but begin to describe some of their behaviors, and even with relish picture the discomfiture of the hapless substitute. Here is an opportunity to define the situation a little more clearly and then have the children enact it.

First, make the situation into a story, slightly changed so that the children are not quite so committed to defending their past behavior as it is presented in the story:

> Here is a story about what happened in a classroom one day. The regular teacher was absent, and a young woman named Miss Smith was called up and asked if she would like to be the substitute for a day. She was delighted to do this for several reasons: (1) She had studied in college for a long time how to be a teacher, but she had not been able to get a permanent job because there were no openings. She was eager for the chance to practice what she had learned. (2) She really needed the money. Without a job, it was very difficult for her to get along, even though she lived at home with her parents. (3) She really liked children very much, which is why she became a teacher in the first place, and she welcomed the chance to be with children again, even if it was only for a day.

You will note that the substitute teacher is rather completely and carefully described. It is important to make her three-dimensional, clearly a sentient human being who is vulnerable to attack and hurts when she is hit.

> Now, suppose, Virginia, you be Miss Smith, the substitute. And the rest of you be the class. Miss Smith, you have just walked into the room, and all the children are standing or sitting around and talking. Act out what happens.

The children present a fairly clear picture of what happens in *their* classroom when a substitute comes in. When the scene is over—either because the children have nothing more to say or they start going over the same ground again and you stop the scene—you start the discussion by asking a "pupil" how she felt. You accept what she says without comment of your own and permit the discussion to proceed. Only when there is a lull, can you ask a child who has not yet spoken how *he* felt during the scene.

The children will talk a great deal about the "substitute teacher," how she felt, what she did, whether or not her behavior really demonstrated that she liked children. At some point in the discussion, it might be appropriate to ask the children how they might have gotten the substitute to respond differently to them. After a suggestion or two, get them to replay the scene using the suggested behaviors. When the scene is over, they again discuss feelings and behaviors, and pinpoint the immediate causes of some of the behaviors they demonstrated.

The last part of the discussion should be some general statements *from the children* about causes of behavior, feelings of substitutes, or feelings of pupils. The teacher can encourage such statements by asking a question like: "What did you learn from all of this that you didn't know before?" or, with older children, "What conclusions can you draw from this experience?"

What the children have done in this exercise is to heighten their awareness of why they respond the way they do, and to become more sensitive to the humanness of someone that they may have perceived only as a stereotype. This kind of experience, taken together with the variety of other experiences all designed to help them become more caring human beings, may not only make life for substitutes more bearable, but will also help make the children more able to live with the interruption of their life routines by other strangers.

Developing a Positive Self-concept

Because urban children have so much more experience at being disorderly (partly because the change of teachers occurs so much more frequently for them), they also are more often scolded, punished, and clearly informed that they are not "good." All of this is material for encouraging an image of themselves as undesirable, inferior to other children, and generally not worthy of love.

Add to this such things as the substandard physical surroundings that are so often a fact of their lives; the evidences of government neglect that informs them that the wider community cares little for their health or comfort; the inescapable evidence of their senses that the people important to them are—compared to others—less successful, less important to the world; and the assault on their concept of themselves is overpoweringly destructive.

There are other factors that contribute to the continued perception they have of themselves as inferior. If they are Black, Chicano, or Native American, the presentation of their groups in the textbooks—if they are presented at all—is often filled with error and implications of group inferiority. Though some school systems have made attempts to supply basic texts that treat all groups fairly, too often children must learn their basic skills from printed matter that acts as a barrier to effective learning. If you are hurt or angry at a book that purports to teach you mathematics, you will hardly be motivated to study that book. If the teacher insists that the book is worthwhile and important, then the hurt and anger may be—quite properly—visited on her. Again the motivation to learn from this person who condones an insult to your race will not be high.

Children need substantial evidence that the prejudice and discrimination that still exist in our culture are not given tacit acceptance by teachers, administrators, and schools. Such evidence can be defined:

1. If books that omit and/or distort information about minority groups cannot be discarded as inappropriate for use in school, they should be used constructively. That is, they should be read with skepticism and analytically; they should be supplemented by and compared with other materials, and omissions and errors should be clearly documented. Children might also be encouraged to communicate with publishers and authors, as well as with admin-

istrators who buy books, and inform them of the results of their studies.

2. Teachers should be very clear about the criteria they use for evaluation and grading. These criteria should be made equally clear to the children so there can be no lingering doubt that group membership constitutes a criterion for success in school. If children do not know what the criteria are so they are able to check their own work and substantiate the fairness of a grade, then they may easily conclude that the cultural prejudice they have grown up with is also a part of the school culture.

3. Children should be encouraged to express their feelings and beliefs about prejudice and discrimination, so that plans can be made by the teacher to clarify the base of these feelings and beliefs. If the children's perceptions are, in fact, accurate, and they are being discriminated against, they should be helped to gather information and develop skills to resist such treatment, and so gain some sense of control over the factors that infringe on their lives.

The surprising thing is not that there are children whose self-concept is severely damaged and whose behavior is consequently destructive to themselves and to others. The really surprising thing is that most children thus victimized are still able to see themselves as valuable, worthy of respect and consideration, worth educating, and likely to make a satisfying success of their lives. This is the fact that many teachers overlook when they face a frighteningly chaotic classroom.

Prejudice, Discrimination, and Hostility

If there is prejudice and discrimination in our culture, then we teachers have been tainted by it in some way. It is not unreasonable to assume that, just as there are business managers who believe that Black people do not make good workers, there are teachers who believe the same thing. Just as there are police officers who suspect that all Chicanos are violent, there are teachers who suspect the same thing. Just as there are bankers who expect that Native Americans cannot be trusted to repay loans, so there are teachers who believe that Native American children are not trustworthy.

People who believe these things about others are not likely to be open, friendly, and accepting about those others. They are much more likely to be fearful and hostile in the presence of Black people, Chicano people, and Native American people. Children who sense the fear and hostility of teachers may very well be moved to reactive fear and hostility, and respond with behaviors that teachers see as wanton lack of discipline.

Are there instruments teachers can use to keep a continuous check on their own behaviors, so the archaic attitudes inculcated in us before we could reason are not reflected in our behavior? There are some simple devices that serve the purpose of raising consciousness about prejudice and discrimination, though there is no substitute for a systematic, long-term approach to dealing with this problem.[1]

Here is a checklist to help you identify the behaviors that may easily be seen as discriminatory, especially by people who have already been victimized by prejudice and discrimination and/ or by those who are sensitive to the widespread evidence of prejudice and discrimination in our culture:

1. Are the behavior problems you identify always, or almost always, attributed to one group? Is it always boys who are most troublesome, Black children, girls, or Chicano children?

2. Are your children divided in their seating, with the girls all on one side and the boys all on the other? Or the Black children all on one side and the white all on the other? Or the "low achievers" separated from the others?

---

[1] Some teacher education institutions offer courses to teachers to help them develop knowledge, skills, and sensitivity in dealing with problems of prejudice and discrimination in the teaching of children. See my book, *Affective Subjects in the Classroom: Exploring Race, Sex and Drugs* (Intext, 1972), is an example of a textbook used in such a course.

3. Do you spend more time with one group than another? That is, do you stand and teach on the side of the room where one group sits? Do you direct your comments to and make pleasant eye contact with one group more than the other? Do you actually work more often with one group rather than the other? (Not counting the ones that may actually need more of your help in order to achieve.)

4. Have you indignantly dismissed, without serious consideration of the possibility that it may be true, an accusation by a child that you are prejudiced against a particular group?

5. Are your friends among the faculty of only one group?

If you are in a school situation that is not desegregated, and both the pupil population and the staff are all of one group, it is more difficult to detect evidences of prejudice in oneself. And, of course, the opportunities for discrimination do not exist. However, there are some cues that can be spotted, if you care to do so. The following questions may be helpful to you if you are in a majority-group situation, but they also are relevant for those in multigroup or minority-group schools:

6. Do you systematically avoid serious movies and television films with all Black casts? That is, do you find that these films are not interesting, probably because you cannot identify with the characters?

7. When the discussion does arise, do you deny that the minority-group people in your town are systematically discriminated against?

8. Do you teach literature to the children without including the works of minority writers?

9. Do you teach history from the adopted textbook without making corrections and filling in omissions about minority groups?

10. Do you use, without commenting about this to the children, reading books that do not include stories with minority-group characters?

11. If you are a teacher of minority children, do you teach them different things than you would teach majority children? Do you set standards of work for them that are different from those you would set if your class were made up of majority-group children?

Not only may minority-group children respond with disruptive behavior when they are victimized by discrimination, but very poor children experiencing victimization in the school setting may react the same way. One has only to see the look of distaste on a teacher's face as she approaches a child who has apparently not been bathed for weeks to know that she rejects this child because he is dirty. Even if the child is not sensitive enough to get the teacher's message, it is probably conveyed to the other children, who often read it to mean that they, too, are justified in rejecting the child.

It is not surprising that someone turns up his nose at a bad-smelling body. But the teacher must assume responsibility for learning; viable alternatives must be explored, consequences of choosing one alternative or the other must be examined, behavioral norms and reasons for not living by them must be identified. Merely rejecting the child out of hand is not justified in an educational setting.

If there is any doubt of the teacher's contempt and rejection, one has only to hear her in the faculty lounge: "Really, water is free, and soap is not so expensive. The least they can do is keep themselves clean. Why, we were very poor when I was a child, but the one thing my mother always insisted on was that we be clean! We had old clothes, but they were *clean*!"

If there is no water for bathing, or the family has run out of soap and must wait for the next month's relief check to replenish the supply, the child is rejected without being helped to change the situation. And the other children are helped to reject him without really understanding the bind he is in. The victimized child and the other children may easily behave in ways that are defined as discipline problems—the victim by lashing out in frustration; the others by scapegoating and retaliating when the victim turns on them.

Generally, what we need to do is teach all children to be knowledgeable about themselves and their own lives, independent, and skillful in making what they want of their environment. All children need this kind of education. To the extent that they are deprived of self-knowledge and sense of control, to that extent they are withdrawn or disorderly, submissive or hostilely aggressive. All these responses are "disciplinary" problems that not only interfere with immediate educational objectives but also with broader life goals.

Instead of excoriating urban children because more of them demonstrate "disciplinary" behavior, we ought to deal educationally with the factors that make them act that way. And the same observation might be applied to more and more suburban children who are making life in school so difficult for those around them. The teacher's accurate perception of the children and their behavior becomes a sound basis for open pupil-teacher communication and effective teaching and learning.

Problem 3
A MATTER OF LISTENING

Very often, control in the classroom is perceived as a problem of listening to the teacher. The children do not listen to instructions, do not listen to reminders to behave, do not listen to exhortations to shape up. Consequently, the room is disorderly, and teaching and learning are constantly interrupted.

> *Teacher*: I thought I told you not to speak until I called on you!
>
> *Sally*: But I wanted to answer what Trudy said. She's wrong!

Teacher: Just wait your turn! James, do you have something to add to this discussion?

James: I didn't hear what Sally said.

Teacher: Never mind what Sally said! What do you have to say?

Sophia: Trudy is right. My father said the same thing.

Teacher: Does your father do that kind of work, Sophia?

Sally: You let Sophia talk without being called on!

Teacher: Be quiet, Sally! You're interrupting the discussion.

Sally: Why do I always have to sit in the back of the room?

John: Yeah! Me, too! I never get to talk!

Teacher: Just raise your hand and wait your turn!

John: My hand *is* raised!

Teacher: Be quiet!

Evan: Ow!!

Teacher: Evan, leave this room immediately!

John: Can I leave, too?

Teacher: *You* will go to the principal's office!

John: That's not fair!

Teacher: Out! All right, class, let's go on with the discussion.

This same class, two days later. The children come charging into the room after lunch. They scatter—some to the closet, some to their seats, others to resume altercations that had earlier beginnings.

Teacher: Sit down, all of you! I said, sit down! You know the rule! If you are not seated in two minutes, you will go to the principal! John, Sally, Trude, go at once! I said leave this room!! Get out!!!

The bedlam continues while the teacher, apparently giving up the fight, retreats to her desk in a corner of the room with two of the "well-behaved" children and engages them in lengthy conversation.

The Modification Target

We may well focus on the need for improved pupil-teacher communication in a disorderly classroom. However, when our efforts result in apparent order, we must not assume that improvement has indeed occurred. As long as the communication continues to go only one way, from teacher to pupils, the communication is essentially defective. In any plan for maintaining control, the best kind of control implies that *everyone* involved is a part of the communication system. All the people in the class talk to each other freely and openly in their attempts to get and keep an orderly, optimally functioning situation.

Control in the Classroom

On page 97 is a schema that pictures alternative approaches to classroom control. Though, initially, it would appear that a teacher-dominated classroom is light years away from a chaotic classroom, in actual practice they seem to be two sides of the same coin. If a new teacher takes over (temporarily or permanently), if something occurs to change the total situation somewhat (like the necessity for moving to another room, or just preparing to go to an unscheduled assembly), the teacher-dominated class may easily explode into chaos. And, faced with chaos, an authoritarian teacher will rapidly and forcefully herd the children back into silence and rigid order. Even the time of day can cause rapid shifts from quiet to noise, from compliance to overt resistance. A build-up of frustration can cause a sudden break in the veneer of control late

CONTROL IN THE CLASSROOM

Teacher-Dominated Control	Situationally Determined Control	Chaos
Teacher-made schedule	Activities planned by teacher and children	Teacher-made schedule
Physical arrangement generally fixed often inappropriate	Physical arrangements appropriate to activities	Physical arrangement generally fixed often inappropriate
Teacher-made rules generally enforced sometimes ignored	The children understand: objectives sequence of activities teacher's expectations their own and others' needs	Teacher-made rules generally enforced sometimes ignored
The maintenance process is quick and time-efficient	Rules arising out of felt needs	The maintenance process is quick and time-efficient
Efforts to enforce increase in intensity	Very few rules interaction productive because of broad-based understanding	Efforts to enforce increase in intensity

The same class shifts from one to the other as

the teacher changes
the situation changes
the time of day changes

The process is part of the curriculum

in the afternoon. Or the children can start the day completely out of control, especially if the authority figure is not right there the moment they come together.

It is also quite obvious, and it has been noted in the education literature repeatedly, that children controlled in an authoritarian setting will probably act without the normal constraints as soon as they are released from that setting. Thus, it is not the teacher who is "too easy" who is responsible for the chaotic behavior of a group of children. Rather it is the authoritarian teacher they have just come from who is causing the problem.

Effects of Different Control Styles

If we are to make sound choices of control styles, we must consider the possible effects on the children's development.

1. Children reared in a dictatorship may learn that dictatorship is an appropriate organizational style and may reject out of hand alternative organizational styles. They may forever respond to authority with submission and, alternatively, seek to impose their own will on others.

The immediate classroom management problem presented by the class bully is an easily recognized one; the problem of the apathetic majority is not so easily or quickly recognized.

Probably the most conventionally based reason for not limiting children's experience to functioning in a dictatorship is the traditional mandate of the schools to perpetuate our heritage. There can be no doubt that, in precept at least, our heritage is a democratic one. We cannot perpetuate a democratic heritage in an autocratic learning setting.

2. Children reared in a dictatorship may respond to perceived injustice with apathy, hardly appropriate response for a citizen of a democracy. Or, lacking structure and opportunity for effecting change in an orderly fashion, they may rebel violently, causing damage and destruction to themselves and to others.

The school rebels are numerous enough to present problems everywhere. They may not, however, always be recognized as rebels against perceived injustice. They may be seen as gangs engaged in destructive activities, individual students who disrupt classes, graffiti artists, stubborn and uncooperative children, absentees, and dropouts.

3. The effects of chaos may be great anxiety for children unable to make sense out of the part of their lives they spend in school, they may suffer from all kinds of vague fears that interfere with comfortable living and continued development. Such anxiety may be turned into destructive aggression—out of frustration and out of attempts to communicate these feelings in inappropriate ways.

In a continuously chaotic situation, children cannot learn to expect reasonable behavior from the people they live among, nor can they expect to be treated by others as if others expected reasonable behavior from them. In such a society, we cannot trust each other, and we hit first because we expect imminent attack.

4. If the control in our classroom is situationally determined, we can expect the children to grow in independence (they are able to identify resources within themselves); in self-direction (they participate in the planning for their own lives); in skill in effective social/political interaction (they make their own rules, they learn to care about each other's needs); in intellectual functioning (they identify real problems and become skillful in solving them).

Situationally determined control means a maintenance of balance in control and implies that everyone listens to everyone.

Problem 4
A MATTER OF CLARITY

Teacher: Start your art projects now.
[Children begin to crash their desk tops up, rummaging for supplies. Others make a dash for the supply shelves. The level of noise in the room goes up appreciably.]

Teacher: [Shouting above the noise.] Those who haven't finished their math cannot work on the projects. You must finish your math first.

[One or two children seem to hesitate for a moment, and then resume their scrambling for paper, crayons, and scissors.]

Teacher: [Speaking loudly.] Allen, have you finished your math?
[No response.]

Teacher: [Speaking louder still.] Allen, I asked you if you have finished your math.
[Allen makes eye contact with the teacher and finds it impossible to look away.]

Teacher: Sit down and finish your math, Allen.

Allen: [Throws his handful of crayons on the floor, and throws himself into his seat.]

Teacher: Allen, pick up those crayons before someone falls and gets hurt!

Allen: [Kicks out at a crayon and scatters them even more.]

Teacher: Allen, come here to me! There will be no project work for you today—or any other day this week.

Cynthia: [She has come up to the teacher, and stands there for a few minutes. Now she insists on being heard.] Can I do my project, Miss Banyon?

Teacher: Yes, of course, Cynthia. Go and get your supplies.

Allen: [With a sudden anguished wail] Waw!! She didn't finish her math! How come she can do the project and I can't?

Teacher: Haven't you finished your math, Cynthia?

Cynthia: [Reluctantly.] N-n-o-o.

Teacher: Then you can't do your project.

Cynthia: [Also wailing.] But you said I could do it!

Teacher: I said you could do it when you've finished your math!

Cynthia: You said I could do the project!

Allen: I want to do the project!
[The noise in the room is growing steadily louder.]

Teacher: Class, quiet down! You're getting too loud!

Cynthia: You said I could!

Allen: Why can't I do the project?

Teacher: Allen! Cynthia! Please leave the room! Leave the room at once!

[The noise grows louder.]

The Modification Target

There is no doubt that many management problems are caused by directions and regulations that are not understood by the children. They do the disruptive, the inappropriate thing sincerely believing that they are following the instructions that have been given them. They may be misunderstanding the meanings of words being used by the teacher, as when she says, "Show some restraint when you get up to select your colors; impulsive behavior will get you into trouble." Or they may be misinterpreting the teacher's intent, as when she says, "Move your chairs out of the way," and they begin to move chairs haphazardly in all directions. Often, the teacher is giving more than one direction at the same time, and the result is the children's confusion about which one to follow first. For example, a teacher might say, "The first row form a circle right here, and we'll have a discussion." Then, "No, don't start talking yet. Let me finish giving directions to the rest of the class!" All of these errors are easy to spot and can be quickly remedied.

Child's Sense of Control

However, the problem of clarity is often a much more profound one and not quite so easily remedied. It lies in deep-seated errors of perception that act as unconscious impediments to clear communication. For example, the problem with Allen and Cynthia lies not in a lack of understanding of words, or even in a misconception about the teacher's purpose in giving her directions. The problem lies in the children's sense of control over their own lives.

It is likely that both Allen and Cynthia knew very well that the rule in Miss Banyon's class was that math workbooks and reading assignments were to be completed before such things as free time, art projects, and board games could be started. The fact that she neglected to remind them of this rule before announcing that it was time for projects did not affect their memories; it merely gave them an opening for trying to establish some control of their own.

Allen has a history of failure in mathematics; that is why Miss Banyon singled him out to check. Allen has a great deal of difficulty learning math and, somehow, the pages and pages of workbook examples he struggles with every day offer him neither enlightenment nor skill. It is probable that no one has yet been able to hit on the combination of activities and explanations that can help Allen *think* math. It is all an inexplicable mystery to him.

Added to his dismay at watching his peers work comfortably at solving math problems while he has so much trouble is the frustration of the constant exhortation from the significant adults in his life to "do better" in math. As if he would not do better if he knew how!

His whole life seems to be colored by his failure in math, and he feels inadequate and somehow guilty because he cannot do better. There is an awful feeling of helplessness, of being powerless to change the forces that are controlling him. His attempt this time to abandon the math for something that provided a sense of success and satisfaction was an attempt to exercise some control over his life—perhaps a test to see if he was really at the mercy of forces he could not hope to resist.

Cynthia, too, wants to control her own life, though her situation is different from Allen's. She is a high achiever, does her work expeditiously and well, follows directions, and is in most ways a "model" pupil. Every once in a while, however, Cynthia digs her heels in and says, "I won't," in the face of all reason and expectations. Generally, everyone is so surprised at her uncharacteristic response to a direction or a demand that she is permitted to prevail by default. She gets her way, even if she must (figuratively) kick and scream for a little while, because she is always so good that there must be a reason for her behavior. Whatever the reason is, she is usually permitted this occasional lapse from the straight and narrow.

I would hazard a guess that Cynthia needs to reassure herself occasionally that she is in control. Generally, she does feel that she can be or do anything she wants to. (Her constant success in school contributes to that feeling of power and control.) However, because she is a bright child, knowledgeable about adult expectations of children and perceptive in her assessment of other people's sensitivity to her, she is compelled, sometimes, to demonstrate to the teacher that she is her own person, with needs and motives that the teacher knows nothing about.

Child's Ability to Communicate

In the situation just described, there would seem to be some lapse on the teacher's part in communicating her expectations clearly—a simple matter of timing, perhaps, or an assumption that the children have learned what they actually have not; the lack of clarity, however, is much more profound than that. Not only is the teacher not clear in her directions and the way she voices her expectations, but the children are not clear in the way they are communicating what they need. And the remedy for this lack of clarity lies in the nature of the teacher's approach to classroom management.

Still another example of apparent lack of clarity in pupil-teacher communication is illustrated in the story about the child who began to cry when the teacher told her to get the colored paper for her project. When she was finally able to answer the bewildered teacher's questions, she sobbed that she wanted the same paper all the other children were using. This Black child was not just making a small error in perception; she was victim of a much larger social problem and her perception in this instance was a function of that problem.

Clarity, then, for the teacher is more than just a problem of giving directions in words that the children know. It is, not infrequently, a problem of understanding much about the world of the child, his perception of his place in that world, and his idea of what the teacher feels about him.

A Simple Strategy

There is one rather simple strategy—though profound in its implications and effects—that can assist pupils and teachers to communicate clearly with each other. It is the teacher taking the time fairly frequently to ask the question: "How do you feel about it?" and then listening carefully to the answers, accepting them without argument or evaluation. The effects of this strategy are varied:

1. Children whose free expression of feelings is accepted become more comfortable about having such feelings and are able to be more accepting of themselves. They do not—as is so often the case—need to feel guilty because of their own anger or hostility, or embarrassed about having good feelings for reasons that are unusual.

2. With practice, the children learn to identify more accurately the real causes of their feelings and reduce the incidence of displaced hostility and aggression on to innocent people or unprovocative situations.

3. A legitimate educational objective is to help the children grow to independence, and the opportunity to express feelings freely encourages children to take the next step by asking, "If my feelings are justified, what can I do to change the disturbing situation?"

4. The sharing of feelings freely among peers becomes a link in the relatedness among children. To see each other as having feelings, and even of having in common many of the same emotional reactions to similar situations, becomes a basis for communicating understanding and acceptance.

5. Over a period of time, the responses to "How do you feel about it?" will give the teacher bases for changing teaching strategies, providing activities more appropriate for some children, altering classroom management factors, and expanding the curriculum.

Effects of the Strategy

Let me illustrate each one of these effects, with special reference to management factors, by drawing on the experience of the teachers in one urban school. Though the example comes from an urban setting, I do not think that suburban and rural teachers will find it too far from their own experience.

Accepting One's Own Feelings. For the first time since the elementary school was opened, eighth graders are retained instead of being sent on to junior high school. A serious consequence of this change is that eighth graders, who expected to be doing all the things junior high school students did are now terribly disappointed. They are forced to continue the practice of walking in straight lines while changing classes instead of just walking along the corridors with their friends. They must remain in the building for lunch, when they were looking forward to walking down to the hoagie shop near the junior high school. They continue to sit at "baby desks" instead of using desk-arm chairs as they do in junior and senior high school.

Though their teachers have told them the reasons for having to remain in the elementary school building for another year, the only overt recognition of their feelings has been the statement, made several times by different people, "I know you must be disappointed." It was almost invariably followed by, "But it won't be for long—just one more year." The "discussion" was then at an end, and the class was expected to resume the scheduled work.

It was only three weeks into the semester when it became clear to the faculty and administration that something was amiss: the children in the school were suddenly at each other's throats— literally. A casual touch in the hallway could cause a knock-down, drag-out fight. Children were shouting at each other, calling each other names at the slightest difference of opinion. Children who were usually cooperative and serene resisted the mildest requests from teachers and seemed always to be angry or on the verge of tears.

Though the very youngest of them did not appear to be affected by the turmoil, it had already reached the third graders. However, the worst offenders were quite clearly the eighth grad- ers. The behavior was spreading from them throughout the school.

The four eighth-grade teachers decided to deal directly with the behavior, not by continuing to punish or exhort, but by helping the children understand what was happening to them. They started by asking the question, "How do you feel about not going to junior high school this year?" In each eighth-grade sec- tion, the instant flood of feeling was almost shocking in its inten- sity. The children shouted their hatred of the school, the teachers, the principal. They made speeches about the unfairness of it all and observed that it just went to show that nobody cared about them or what they wanted. They committed themselves volubly to resisting all attempts to make them work: they didn't have to if people were going to treat them like babies. Some children even cried with the strength of their feeling, reduced to helplessness by the overwhelming injustice of it all.

Though some of the teachers tried to interrupt the tirade to introduce a calming note of reason, they could not be heard, and there were moments when they were sorry they had raised the question. However, one of the teachers just listened, and was her- self almost moved to tears at the children's anguish.

When the crest had passed, and the voices had thinned out somewhat and reduced in volume, the teacher said quietly, "I hear what you're saying: you're disappointed and angry. And you don't want to be treated like elementary school children."

"That's right. That's right." For a moment the flood threatened to start again, but they had shouted and talked themselves out for the moment. The bell rang and they were all relieved to be getting away.

Identifying the Cause of One's Feelings. The next day, the teacher said to her class, "Yesterday you talked about how angry you were, how unfair it was to have to do things that eighth graders don't usually have to do. You sounded mad, you really yelled about how mad you were. [Laughter and some muttered agreement.] What other things have you been doing lately to show how mad you are?"

[Some rueful smiles, and a few giggles.]

"I pushed a kid."

"What do you mean, kid?! You pushed me!"

"I didn't mean you!"

"I didn't even do anything! You just shoved me—hard!"

"Well, you shoved me back!"

"Everybody's yelling."

"Why is everybody yelling?"

"John just walked past my desk and threw everything off."

"I didn't mean it!"

"Yes, you did! I saw you throw his things down on purpose!"

"OK. So I did! So what!"

"What did I do to you?"

"I was just mad!"

"But I didn't do anything to you!"

"I was just so mad!"

"You were just so mad," clarified the teacher, "that you took it out on the first person you passed."

"Yeah."

"He sure did."

Developing Independence. On the third day, the teacher said to her class, "Look, you're all stuck here for the rest of the year. [Mutterings of agreement.] Let's talk about what can be done to make you feel a little better about the whole thing. First, what are some of the things you have to do that you think you're too old for?"

Very quickly, the children identified the following things, which they listed on the board:

- walking in lines

- staying in for lunch

- going to assembly with the babies

- not having shop

- not having a foreign language

"All right, now," said the teacher, "Let's see about these things. 'Walking in lines.' Is there something we can do about that?"

"We shouldn't have to walk in line."

"Yeah. Let the babies walk in lines."

"They can just stay out of our way!"

"They might get hurt if we go running down the hall."

"We don't have to run."

"We can watch that *they* stand in line."

"Yeah. We can watch them!"

"We can make them behave."

"Yeah! They'll have to listen to us!"

"You don't have to act that way!"

"Yeah. You don't like it when people act that way to you."

"Are you saying," asked the teacher, "that you would like to help with getting the younger children from one place to another in an orderly way? [Clear agreement responses.] Well, how do we arrange for that?"

It was clear sailing after that. Each point of contention was examined. Suggestions were made for defining the parameters within which some change might be effected. Plans were made to get to the decision-maker with the suggestions. Compromises and alternatives were considered, refined, accepted, or rejected.

In as long a period of time as it had taken for the children to work themselves up into a frenzy of displaced anger, they regained some control over the situation and over their own behavior. Further, the blow to their self-concept was neutralized, and they felt even better about themselves than they ever had before as they recognized in themselves the capacity for and ability to function independently.

Developing Understanding and Acceptance. As the children worked with each other, trying to develop a new role and new behaviors for themselves in their old school, they often expressed feelings of frustration at failures, elation at successes, anger at and even hatred of individuals and situations that acted to interfere with their objectives. They learned to recognize in each of the others something of themselves. In that final year as elementary pupils, old cliques were broken up, new friendships formed, and even the customary racial and sex separation virtually disappeared.

Changing the Curriculum. The teacher of this eighth-grade class gained a new respect for the children. She saw them as capable of learning in areas that she had thought at first they could never manage. Subjects like drug use, relationships between the sexes, old age and death, and race relations no longer seemed too sophisticated, too likely to cause disruption.

She also felt more confident in loosening up her management and strategies so that the children could assume more initiative for their own education.

This teacher had listened to the children, and they had come through clearly to her. The result was that she could begin to communicate to them her revised perception of them as people. "How do you feel about that?" became a signal between them that it was time to stop and listen to each other.

Problem 5
A MATTER OF THE USE OF TIME

Teachers often complain that they are at a disadvantage in trying to teach children the more affective subjects because they have relatively little time to overcome the negative effects of the home and the street. Hours of watching television, they say, will nullify attempts to contemplate the blandishments of the media analytically and with a healthy skepticism. Vehemently anti-Black parents will easily override the influence of intergroup education in the classroom. The antischool values of street-corner society are not weakened by the example of the teacher or the experiences in the classroom. There simply isn't enough time—during the few hours spent in school each day—to change the whole direction of a child's life.

I do not accept this pessimistic view. We so rarely change the direction of a child's life for the reasons that we do not believe it is changeable, and we do not use the time we have to advantage.

There is ample evidence that school experiences largely serve to keep children at the socioeconomic level of their parents. There is additional evidence that, despite all our talk about a generation gap, many values from generation to generation remain remarkably similar. All of this says something about what we teach and how we teach.

But let us, for the moment, deal only with the single factor of the use of time and examine the relationship of such use to the behavior of the children in the classroom. The broader implications touched on above may be left for another time.

An average school day may be scheduled for five hours. However, if we look closely at that day, we see very quickly that only a fraction of that five hours is systematically allotted to teaching and learning (though the incidental learning can be enormous—and enormously significant in the life of the child). On those days that the children are actually in school—when there is not a holiday, a teacher's meeting, a broken water pipe, a shortage of coal, heavy rain, or a snowstorm—they usually are not even permitted to come into the building for fifteen or twenty minutes after the scheduled starting time. If they do come in, they wander about waiting for everyone to assemble, and sometimes start off their day with a reprimand for getting into something they should not have gotten into.

A significant amount of classroom confrontation and confusion are a function of other use-of-time factors. While the teacher is trying to straighten out the bookkeeping concerning milk-money or lunch-money collections, Jimmy gets into a loud argument with Johnny, Della begins to cry, half a dozen children begin to wander about the room, and the level of noise is enough to drown out the teacher's plaintive pleas for additional information.

A great many instances of "problem behavior" arise during the school day at juncture points. That is, when the time approaches for switching from one activity to another, more children seem to "act out" or act up. Generally, the teacher seems to attribute such behavior to something called "lack of self-control," which is a commonly used catch-all phrase to ascribe causality to behavior that bothers the teacher.

Problem behavior somewhat more subtly attributable to time management involves the actual teaching situation. Here, the length of the lesson, the content, and even the process of presentation may have significant time factors that are directly related to the problem behavior.

The Modification Target

It may, at first, seem far-fetched to suggest that what needs to be changed here is the nature of the communication between teacher and pupil. Though there are undoubtedly other appropriate modification targets that might alleviate these problem situations, much can be done by improving the quality of teacher-pupil understanding.

Importance of Time

What teachers and children often fail to communicate to each other is the fact that they are all real people with a vested interest in the time they spend together. The teacher and the child both want to spend that time in a way that has some meaning for them, and, generally, each will resist pressures to engage in activities they consider a waste of their time.

Unfortunately, neither teacher nor children are tuned into the other's perception of meaninglessness; too often, each believes that what he thinks is important or meaningful must inevitably be important and meaningful to everyone. Further, the belief persists that anyone who does not see eye to eye with "me" on this must—one way or another—be brought into agreement with me.

Thus, children who wander about before the opening of school are unable to communicate to the school's adults that they come to school early so that they may have time for the informal give-and-take that there is so little time for during the school day. They enjoy a brief time for shouting and laughing in the schoolyard. They look foward to the possibility of a few casual words with a teacher about a subject never touched on in the classroom. When they are told not to shout; when they are herded into lines or organized clusters in the yard; when the teachers they want to talk to never appear, the children are deprived of a chunk of their time, time that is important to them and that is now filled with annoyances and disappointments. When they try to communicate their thoughts and feelings about this, they inevitably do so badly. Thus, the protests become impertinences, the explanations become whining, and children are punished for their lack of skill in

communication. Ultimately, they get back at their punishers for
depriving them: they destroy or deface school property (which is
important to the punishers); they come late to class; somewhere
between home and school they lose their way for the day; and
once in class, they carry with them the unpleasant memory of
their day's start.

I firmly believe that money collections should not be made
by the teacher. This would eliminate many of the behavior problems that become apparent because the children's time is being
wasted. However, if the teachers in a school cannot devise some
more efficient method of making the necessary collections, each
classroom's occupants can discuss the matter with an eye to understanding each other's point of view. It may finally occur to the
teacher that it makes no sense for the children to spend their time
sitting and doing nothing while the teacher struggles with archaic
bookkeeping. And the children may realize that the teacher feels
her time is being wasted too and that the longer it takes her to get
the job done, the more of her time she is wasting.

Planning for Efficient Use of Time

Out of such discussion and awareness may come the commitment to help each other cut down on time wasting, and all
together they may plan for:

1. interesting work for the children to do during the col-
    lection time.

2. more efficient ways to do the collecting.

One idea that came out of such a discussion was the organization of a bank—with real money. Six "tellers" were chosen by
the class for their skill in arithmetic. A bank "manager" was appointed for his ability to answer questions and resolve problems as
they arose. Each week, people deposited money in the bank for
lunches, for milk, for special trips and other supplies, and each had
his deposit recorded in a book that was issued him. (A check was
placed next to his name on the lists the tellers kept to indicate

payment.) Lunches and other things were paid for by writing a check, which each child deducted from the total in his book. The question of earning interest arose, and the children examined the differences between savings and checking accounts, and the whole business of financial transactions was studied on a higher level of sophistication than is usually the case in the third grade.

In relation to the problems of classroom management precipitated by money collecting, both children and teacher were no longer bickering with each other about unnecessary noise, rudeness, and lack of consideration. Nobody felt his time was being wasted.

Communicating About Time

Why do children manifest shuffling and fidgeting, talking out of turn, getting out of their seats, and gossiping with each other when the teacher is teaching a lesson? And why does the teacher become annoyed when these things happen? Is it far-fetched to suggest that both of them may—at least partly—be responding to the feeling that their time is being wasted?

Children sit through a lesson and are unable to say: This doesn't interest me. I don't understand any of this. There is something else of vital concern to me that I must deal with now. We have been at this for long enough; I need to go on to something else. Since I am not able to learn this now, my time sitting here is being wasted.

Teachers present a lesson from beginning to end and are unable to say: I never was interested in this subject. I've taught this for four years, and I'm bored with doing it again. I don't really think this is important for you to learn, but it's in the mandated curriculum. I'm just tired. I'm wasting my time at this when I would prefer to be doing other things that interest me, give me pleasure, make me feel worthwhile.

They never say these things, but they think them, and the thoughts hang like an opaque curtain between teacher and children, cutting off all productive communication—including the learning of the material being taught.

Probably the most effective way to deal with problems that arise for the reasons the children and the teacher aren't saying out loud is to abandon the practice of teaching a mandated curriculum, at the same time, in the same way, to a whole class of children. This brings us to the matters of cooperative planning and self-pacing (see chapter 2).

But short of such large changes for the teacher who prefers the more traditional organization and strategies, the answer may generally be in less talking by the teacher and more active involvement of the children. In this way, the teacher's lack of commitment to and interest in the subject need not be so much of a burden on her, and she may concentrate more on the children's involvement in the *process* of learning and spend her time helping them refine their skills. For the children, active involvement often generates its own interest, and they may be carried through the learning process less painfully.

Juncture Points

The inappropriate use of time at juncture points throughout the school day often causes management problems that might be reduced somewhat if pupil-teacher communication were more effective. We have all known teachers who regularly kept us in their classes beyond the scheduled leaving time, cutting in on our between-class socializing, our lunch, or even our next class. Even in the university, students have trouble telling a professor that she is behaving inappropriately; the professor, in turn, is annoyed by the shuffling of feet, the closing of notebooks, and the putting on of coats, "problem behavior" that she has precipitated.

It might be worthwhile, too, to consider the impatience with and resistance to the introduction of a new topic by the teacher three or four minutes before the end of a class—or the end of a day. It is the rare teacher who stops at either of these last two situations and asks the pupils, "Why are you shuffling and closing books?" or "Why are you making those angry sounds?"

If the question is really asked like a question and not like a reprimand, the teacher may actually profit from the responses. In one class the pupils told their teacher honestly that they felt they had worked hard during the period and had come to a natural ending point, even though the period was not yet over. And, to the teacher's great satisfaction, they took the occasion to tell her that they were enjoying the course, were really interested in the subject, and appreciated her as a teacher. All in all, a bit of pupil-teacher communication that intensified the feeling of all the participants that they were using their time to advantage.

Time and Individual Help

The teaching process used by many teachers may not always be the most efficacious way of encouraging learning because it actually reduces the amount of direct pupil-teacher communication. Probably the most widely used mode of teaching a new lesson is for the teacher to present it orally (with some visual aids) to the whole class. Many teachers find that they spend most of their time doing this because there is so much subject matter to cover and they want to get through it all before the end of the school term. They teach (by talking), answer an occasional question from a student, assign homework, and give tests.

As a result of this process, most students pass out of a course or a subject with grades ranging from low to high, with most of them falling in the average group. A few are obviously failing, in spite of exhortations to do better and threats of disaster if they don't. And teachers continually bemoan the fact that they do not have the time to give individual help to pupils who could thereby avoid failure or very low grades.

Teachers know that individual help (the one-to-one communication between teacher and pupil that goes on day after day apart from the whole-class, lock-step process of teaching and learning) can help a child not only to do better academically but to see himself generally in a more positive light. Taking the time to do this after school hours or during lunch blurs the effect, for staying after school or missing lunch with the other kids may easily be perceived as punishment.

However, if the organization of the classroom and the

strategy of teaching were changed to allow for more small-group work, pairing for specific tasks, and even working alone to accomplish something, the teacher could spend less time with those who were more skillful in achieving educational objectives with minimal teacher direction, and more time in one-to-one communication with those pupils who need it. An interesting outcome of such communication goes far beyond the matter of academic tutoring. A teacher who might have perceived a poor student as "lazy," "unmotivated," even "stupid," may, as he gets to know the student better, see him as motivated but confused, and bright but unlearned, and not lazy at all, when one considers all the activities he is engaged in after school. Whereas the first set of judgments tends to see the student as unteachable, the second set sees him as quite able to learn.

Asking Questions

The use of time in ways that prevent or minimize management problems are many. Some of the most discussed and, at the same time, unused are the ways in which teachers ask questions and wait for answers. Since the question is probably the basis of pupil-teacher communication, let us look at *how* many of us ask them:

> 1. Ask a question. Before anyone can answer, reword the question. Before anyone can answer, ask another question.

Asking questions is the essence of effective teaching (remember Socrates?). But if the pupils are confused about what you are asking them, there can be little basis for further communication. Of course, if pupils could say to the teacher, "What, exactly, do you want us to respond to?" communication could go on. But generally students just make a start at what they think is wanted and too often they are rebuffed for their efforts. The remedy is to ask *one question* and *wait* for the answers.

> 2. Ask questions and permit the same two or three people who respond at once to answer them every time.

When teachers talk about "class discussions," they are generally talking about two-way communication between three or four pupils and the teacher. They rarely wait long enough for the other children to take part in the discussion.

3. Ask a question and call on someone who has no answer.

Coupled with the widespread reluctance on the part of teachers to wait for answers to a question, is the compounding of the error by calling on someone who has not volunteered to answer. Here, a little empathy is called for to experience what the child must be feeling caught without words in front of his peers.

4. Ask a question and wait one second for the volunteer to answer. Then call on another volunteer and give him ten or more seconds to come up with the answer.

We have evidence that so-called "bright" students are given more time to answer questions than are slower students. Are we so sure that it is a waste of time to wait for the slower student's answer? (But isn't he the one who probably needs more time to answer?) Are we, perhaps, setting that slower student up for continuing failure when we arrange the time so that there is little or no pupil-teacher communication?

Finally, the amount of time spent in the classroom on matters that are not important to children can be significantly reduced by more effective pupil-teacher communication. To ask the question, "What interests you?" or "What moves you?" or "What do you want to know about?" and then listening to the answer, is the kind of communication that can lead to so productive a use of school time that there will never again need to be a mention of "back to basics" or literacy tests for high school seniors!

chapter 4
Solutions Based on Pupil-Pupil Communication

Problem 1
A MATTER OF SELF-CONCEPT

Mr. Jones was teaching science to his sixth-grade class. Because the school had never had enough money to equip a proper science laboratory, he was doing an experiment while the boys and girls watched. Those in the back of the room had left their seats and had doubled up with those down front, so they could follow the process going on in the assortment of beakers and test tubes on the teacher's desk. No one could complain that the class was not interested in the lesson.

Every once in a while, one of the watchers would wail in something like agony, "Oh, Gee, Mr. Jones. Let me! Let me!" and the teacher would relinquish a retort or hand over a test tube clasped in forceps, with instructions on how to hold it or what to do next. He never accepted the offer of help from one of the girls, no matter how eager she might be to participate. Always it was a boy whose pleas were answered.

Slowly, as the experiment went on and the teacher began to encourage the asking of questions and the discussion of observations, the girls in the class imperceptibly moved (or were nudged) farther and farther back. If anyone had cared, by the end of the period he might have noticed that the girls were all behind the boys—some still looking on over the heads in front of them, others having drifted back to their desks, still others obviously engaged in other things.

A closer look would have revealed one girl standing at the forefront of the observers, her nose a dangerous inch from the Bunsen burner on the desk. Her absorption in the experiment was total. Once, half mesmerized, she put out her hand to touch a piece of equipment held out by the teacher, who jerked it back and said testily, "No, no. You'll ruin the experiment!" And he handed the equipment to the boy standing next to her. A slight frown creased her forehead, but it disappeared in her absorption as the experiment proceeded.

When the discussion was over, Mr. Jones said, "All right, everybody. Back to your seats now. The bell will be ringing shortly." Then he looked pointedly and somewhat quizzically at the girls, most of whom were already in their seats. "Don't worry about it, girls," he said, "We won't let science keep you off the honor roll." And he smiled benignly at them.

Some of the children laughed, but several of the girls looked annoyed. One boy teased the girl who had watched so avidly, "You want to be a physicist, Gail? You can be a physicist if you want to, Gail! Maybe you'll be the only woman physicist on the Mars shot!" And he laughed at the absurdity of it. Some of the others—boys and girls, too—laughed with him.

This was not the first time he had teased her about her interest in science. Usually, Gail just looked at him without comment and turned away, refusing to be baited. This time she surprised herself and everyone else by swinging her arm back and letting him have a punch in the face. Stunned silence in the room as everyone watched him pick himself off the floor. Then one of the girls laughed, another applauded surreptitiously. Before Mr. Jones could intervene, the bell rang and everyone left for lunch.

In the social studies class that afternoon, Miss Merton was

having a discipline problem with that same class. When she instructed them to get into their project groups, some of them began to complain that they didn't like working in those groups. One girl lashed out furiously at another over what seemed like a minor matter, and every time a boy said something, one of the girls reduced what he said to some kind of irrelevant absurdity or called him stupid. There seemed to be an oppressive overlay of hostility in the group, and she could not get them started on the work she had planned for that day.

Miss Merton was inclined to attribute the problem to the usual thing—twelve-year-old boys and girls being unable to cope with the dawning awareness of their sexuality. A natural sexual attraction became perverted into irritability and antagonism because they were self-conscious and uncomfortable with each other. It was just a developmental thing, she thought. She would keep them separated for a while and it would pass—until it cropped up again in a few days. This sort of behavior was perfectly natural; they would grow out of it. There was nothing she needed to be concerned about.

"That will do, Helen," Miss Merton admonished one of the girls when she surreptitiously flicked Peter's book off his table. "We won't have that here, if you don't mind."

Helen betrayed not a bit of remorse as she flounced away.

What a nuisance, Miss Merton thought to herself. Just when I thought I had this class organized to work productively. Now she would have to rearrange the work groups and mount guard to see that they didn't get too close to each other. Always some fool thing to make life difficult, she thought wryly. Whoever said teaching would be easy?

It was to be even more difficult as the days went on. She was never able to control the obvious hostility between the boys and the girls—and even among some of the girls. She thought she had never encountered such a bad situation between boys and girls. It was true that she had often seen second- and third-grade boys and girls refuse to play with each other or even sit near each other. But the tension between sixth-grade boys and girls was usually different: the behavior was more teasing than angry and hostile. She shook her head in despair and worked harder at keeping them apart. She gave out more reprimands, more banishments from the room, more threats to reduce grades and inform parents.

The behavior persisted and the work suffered.

The Modification Target

Though Mr. Jones's behavior was the precipitating factor in the pupils' problem behavior, the foundation of the problem had been laid much earlier. Miss Merton observed it—though she did not recognize it—in the second-grade children, but it had started even earlier than that. The women's revolution exacerbated it, though both Mr. Jones and Miss Merton would have vehemently rejected this idea. Yet the chances were that, before all the talk and activity about the equality and liberation of women, such total disruption of a sixth-grade class would probably not have occurred. One girl and her best friend might have confided their resentment to each other, but it would have remained an individual, personal resentment. The effect on this class was more like a social phenomenon, and though Miss Merton never became aware of it, it grew to much more significant proportions and was translated into action that had surprisingly far-reaching results.

Ambition

In high school, Gail majored in science and did very well—whenever her teacher was a woman. She became nervous and inarticulate with a male instructor. Since almost all the science instructors were men, she eventually decided she didn't want to be a scientist after all. As the other girls grew more vocal about women's rights and ran for high school offices on women's rights platforms, she became more and more like the traditional version of the housebound wife. At one point, in their senior year, their consciousness raised to a level of sophistication Miss Merton would have been amazed at, the girls discussed what had happened to Gail and decided to attack the problem head on.

But Gail was not only lost to the women's movement; her talents were lost to the world. She simply did not know what her friends were talking about. She insisted that she was doing exactly what she wanted to do—go to college and then get married. A career was just not for her; she wanted another kind of life. She laughed a little when they reminded her of her fascination with science. Kid stuff! She'd grown out of that a long time ago.

Teaching to Self-concept

But what about those sixth graders who gave Miss Merton discipline nightmares? Was there a solution to the problem they presented?

Whether Miss Merton believed the problem was developmental or situational, a number of teaching strategies might have been employed to ameliorate the situation. In addition, she could have attempted systematically to modify the children's behavior in their relationships with each other. Following are some suggestions that may prove helpful to teachers experiencing similar problems.

1. Since cognitive, academic experiences are usually so much easier to provide, the teacher may begin by helping the children add to their store of information about the accomplishments of women. Without being so obvious as devoting a unit to the contributions of women to the fields of science, literature, political leadership, etc., such contributions may be examined and compared to similar contributions by men.

With this kind of knowledge, the girls can begin to identify with women who have broken out of the stereotypic mold. They can begin to see themselves as shakers and movers, side by side with the men. It may help them to be more assertive in the face of discrimination and less likely to accept a low evaluation of themselves.

2. If the question arises—and it probably will—of why so few women appear in the list of historical and literary greats, the study can move into the area of obstacles to achievement: role expectations, social attitudes, educational and employment discrimination.

3. It is likely that, at this point, some of the children's feelings will begin to surface, and provision can be made for them

to say how they feel, not only about the problems that women in the past have encountered, but also about what is happening to women—and to sixth-grade girls—today.

Such expression of feelings facilitates learning that goes far beyond the mere acquisition of facts. The free pouring out of anger and resentment in a safe situation helps children realize that they are not alone in the way they feel.[1] They may go on to realize that cooperative efforts to effect change are probably more likely to succeed than the crying out of a lone voice.

It may also be revealed to them that it is not only girls who feel that women—and girls—are being treated unfairly. They may find that there are boys, too, who have developed empathy for the victims of sexism in our society. Here we have a breach in the wall separating boys and girls, an avenue for improving communication between the sexes and, likely, reducing the hostility that is translated into classroom disruption.

In the course of such a discussion of feelings, it may become clear to the teacher that there are certain gaps in knowledge that should be filled in by future lessons. For example, girls may not be able to maintain a firm stand on equality because they do not know the connection between motivation and the expectations of parents and teachers. Boys may not see the relationship between self-doubts about developing masculinity and the tendency to assert their superiority over girls. Some cognitive exploration of these psychological factors may make both girls and boys more aware of the factors that influence their relationships with each other.

4. Now might be a time for providing opportunity for the children to identify alternative modes of relating to each other, and practicing the skills necessary in such relating. Role-playing situations, in which they practice various ways of dealing with realistic problems involving relationships between the sexes, help

---

[1] Affective discussion is more productive in a small group, where nobody takes notes, and the teacher does not participate. The function of the teacher here is, primarily, diagnosis of educational needs. (See my book, *Affective Subjects in the Classroom: Exploring Race, Sex and Drugs*, (Intext, 1972).

them examine the consequences of different ways of behaving, give them time to practice certain behaviors, and also help them develop sensitivity to the feelings and needs of the other sex.

While all this is going on, there will probably be attempts by individuals to change their own behavior vis-à-vis the other sex. These tentative changes may be reinforced by recognizing them and giving authoritative approval of them. Care must be taken not to greet these behaviors too effusively, or the experimenters may be embarrassed and retreat to the safety of separation. An approving smile, assistance in getting space and materials for working together, may encourage the firm establishment of such productive interaction.

Providing a model for such behavior and making clear that such behavior is expected also help to reinforce it. For example, a teacher once gave an example of behavior as an analogy for something the class was talking about. She said, "Have you ever had the lady of the house snatch an ashtray from under someone's cigarette and clean it after they've flicked an ash into it?"

One of the boys interrupted to ask her, "Why do you say 'the lady' of the house. Couldn't a man do that, too?"

The teacher stopped for an instant, momentarily nonplussed. Then she recovered. "Thank you." she said. "You're quite right to call me on that. Do you see how much a part of us our prejudices are? Even if, intellectually, I reject such ideas as false, I still slip sometimes and express them as if they were true. But if you keep reminding me, I'll get that error out of my system."

In that class, the children also reminded each other—without sarcasm or hurtfulness—when they betrayed prejudice in their language and behavior.

In all her teaching, that teacher arranged the class so that boys and girls—in a variety of combinations—could have experience working and playing together. There was never any question of competition between the two groups. Neither group was ever held up to the other as a model of behavior. No one ever said to them, "Be gentlemen and let the girls leave first." No one ever expected that the boys would naturally be better at science and mathematics or the girls at homemaking.

When they were ready to make their life career choices, these children were more likely to make them on bases other than sex-related social expectations. They saw themselves as whole people first, with interests, skills, and potentialities that went beyond the bounds of their sex.

Problem 2
A MATTER OF SELF-OTHER PERCEPTIONS

Ms. Childs has a gang problem in one of her eighth-grade social studies sections. Eight or nine pupils, with Joe Hainis as the apparent leader, seem deliberately to behave in ways that cause disruption in the classroom, interfere with the activities of the other children outside the classroom, and generally call attention to themselves. They seem always to be engaged in some behavior that is deviant from the accepted norm of appropriate behavior in the school.

Each day, as the other children come in for their forty-five minutes of social studies, these eight or nine children can be seen through the window throwing a ball around in the schoolyard or just "fooling around" out there, noisy enough to announce to the world that they are not doing what they should be doing.

On days when it is raining, their behavior is even more disruptive: they stand in the corridor near the door of the classroom, deliberately blocking the other students' way, provoking first one and then another to angry words, a push or even a punch—which often explodes into a knock-down fight.

There is talk—an overheard word here and there, a half-voiced implication—that the gang is harassing students in other ways, too. Children are being forced to give up their pocket money; some are afraid to walk home after school; some of the girls have been mildly molested sexually. When asked directly about any of this the children are usually vague and evasive, and appear extremely uncomfortable and fearful.

Ms. Childs has raised the matter with other teachers who have the same children for other subjects. They have noticed similar behaviors, but they don't seem to be as disturbed as Ms. Childs is about them. It is true, however, that she has not expressed her real feelings, her fear that the gang is terrorizing the children and may, eventually, begin to intimidate the teachers. She has not described in detail the kinds of things they are already doing in her room: they are always laughing and talking among themselves and point-blank refuse either to be quiet or to have their seats changed so they are not sitting near each other. When other children respond to her questions about the lesson, they denigrate the responses, mimic the child answering, and even sometimes make fun of the question or the way the teacher asks it. On examinations, they obviously cheat, and it is clear that they don't care who knows it.

These children seem so sure of themselves, so confident that no one would dare to stand up to them, that Ms. Childs has been completely unable to use the usual remedies against disruptive behavior. Her remonstrations have stuck in her throat in the face of their arrogant demeanor, and she has been literally afraid to threaten to send them to the principal in the face of their resistance even to a request that they move to another part of the room. Any idea she might have had about reinforcing their appropriate behavior with an eye to changing them, she has rejected out of hand, so sure is she that nothing will work with these kids except outright violence. Actually, she is so afraid of them that she cannot even make an attempt to understand what might be causing the behavior. She will not even go to the principal and ask him to do something about them, because she is afraid that if his treatment is ineffectual, she will have even more trouble with them.

In Ms. Childs's eleven o'clock social studies class, it is tacitly understood that nobody talks about Joe Hainis and his gang. Everyone suffers in silence.

The Modification Target

Dissonance Between Home and School

When there is such a difference between the home and the school that the child can find no effective way to function in school, he may take a stand outside of school norms and so maintain some continuity between his home life and his school life. His essential difficulty in maintaining that continuity within the bounds of accepted school behavior is often one of communication. Because his home values are so different from school values, he cannot understand or accept as important the goals and aspirations that are taken for granted by the other children. Because his language at home serves his communication needs, he is first bewildered and then hostile when his attempts at communication are rejected because of his language. Because what is expected of him at home is so different from the expectations of his teachers and of his peers, he feels like an outsider in the school culture.

Often, the teacher is unable to establish communication with the child because of her own commitment to values and concepts that affect her perception of him in adverse ways. In addition, even her teaching style may be conflicting with his style, a style he has developed in the milieu of a background totally different from hers. The key to changing the deviant behavior of the child may lie, therefore, in the establishment of effective pupil-pupil communication. Perhaps, if the child can find wider peer acceptance, if the other children are able to communicate to him that their perception of his differences do not include the label "bad" or "inferior," if he can communicate awareness of their differences also without denigration of them, then the outsider may find himself in the group, and no longer need to maintain membership in a deviant group.

Teaching Pupil-Pupil Communication

Children can be taught to communicate effectively with each other. They can be taught to listen actively to each other, asking for clarification, building on what the other person says, indicating by eye contact, body movement, and verbal responses that they are interested in what the other person is saying and not just waiting for the opportunity to say what is on their own minds.

They can be taught to speak candidly, expressing their feelings and beliefs without fear of censure, taking stands on controversial and unpopular issues, while they accurately assess the risks involved in taking such public positions, lending themselves openly to constant evaluation of their opinions and beliefs.

They can be taught to respond to the doubts, fears, and enthusiasms of their peers, being supportive when support is needed, expressing a healthy skepticism when the available knowledge calls for skepticism, and becoming actively involved in the group's discovery, verification, testing, and generalizing processes that provide for cognitive and affective development.

Following are some classroom activities that can promote effective pupil-pupil communication:

Exercise 1: In groups of seven or eight, have the children discuss a subject they are surely interested in. Give them a choice from a list containing such topics as "That Great TV Show I Saw Last Night," "What Happened to me on the Way Home Yesterday," "Who's Going To Win the Pennant This Year?" "What I'd Like To Spend All My Time Doing". The idea is to have a topic that is not so emotional that the children will be unable to deal objectively with *the process* of discussion. They must be able, at some point, to end the discussion and begin to look at some of their behaviors and feelings associated with such things as being permitted to speak as much as they wanted to, having what they said accepted by the others, being listened to, being understood. (The gang that is giving Ms. Childs so much trouble could, at the outset, constitute one such group. As the days—and the learning— go on, one test of success in achieving the learning objectives could be that the members of this group are willing to break up and join other groups, just as the rest of the class does.)

At the end of twenty minutes of discussing, they could complete the following form. Assure them in advance that the form is for their own use, and they need not reveal anything they write on it unless they choose to do so.

How did you feel about the discussion?

I enjoyed it a lot.   _____

It was boring.   _____

It made me mad.   _____

It was all right.   _____

I'm glad it's over.   _____

Did you get the chance to say what you wanted to?

Almost every time I started to say some-
thing, I was interrupted.   _____

There were some things I could have said,
but everyone would have jumped on me.   _____

I talked as much as I wanted to.   _____

I said everything I had to say.   _____

Often the others didn't understand what
I meant to say, but they didn't give me a
chance to make it clear.   _____

There's no use talking when people don't
listen.   _____

After everyone has checked the appropriate responses, and
again reminding them that they need not talk about anything they
do not want to, tell them to let the group know how they felt
about the discussion, and why they felt that way. (You will find
that the pupils generally use their responses as a basis for the
discussion, and, after fifteen or twenty minutes they have all managed to express their frustrations about the whole discussion
process.)

After this, tell the discussants to arrive at a list of things
they would like to do the next time they are in a discussion group.
Provide the following form as a guide if you think they need it:

How would you improve the discussion?

I would tell some people not to talk so much.   _____

I would not talk so much.   _____

I would try to get everybody to say something.   _____

I would ask the teacher to stay here and keep order.   _____

I wouldn't let people interrupt.   _____

I wouldn't jump on anyone just because I didn't agree with him.   _____

Before I disagreed with someone, I would make sure I understood what he said.   _____

I would look at the person who was talking, so he would know I was listening.   _____

In this exercise, the children begin to talk about some of the factors that make for a satisfying or unsatisfactory experience. They have opportunity to hear that others share their perception of what is satisfying. And they can decide to do some things to make the experience more satisfying. Those who always feel very comfortable in a group discussion may learn that their comfort is often achieved at the expense of others. Some children may take another step in learning to control their environment instead of feeling helpless and discouraged; other children may assume some responsibility for providing satisfaction for their peers; all the children may get to know a little more about each other and recognize common needs that they share as well as unique needs that each of them has.

It is useful to repeat this exercise regularly so that the children may check and see that what they have learned is, indeed, improving the quality of their interaction with each other.

Exercise 2: Have the children pair off, encouraging them to do so with a member of their discussion group. Have them tell each other what they have always wished someone would do for them when they have been involved in group discussions. Let each person say what other people in the group can do to indicate that they are glad to have him in the group and are interested in what he has to say. Have the pair make a list of these things. Perhaps they will want two lists, if they discover that each of them looks for different indications that he is being accepted. If you think they need it, let them use the form below:

What would you like a person to say?

    I agree with you.   _____

    I'd like to know more about that.   _____

    I'm not sure I understand; how did that
    happen?   _____

    Say yes, no, sure, or things like that to
    show they're listening.   _____

    Say, "Let him finish what he's saying,"
    when someone interrupts.   _____

    Ask me, "What do you think about
    that?" or "You once had an experience
    like that, didn't you?"   _____

What would you like a person to do?

    Smile at you.   _____

    Look at you when you're talking.   _____

    Laugh when you say something funny.   _____

    Shake hands when they really agree with
    you.   _____

    Nod or shake their heads to show they're
    listening.   _____

Wait a while after you finish speaking
before they start to speak.   _____

At the end of fifteen or twenty minutes, ask them if they will make a commitment to say and do as many of those things as seem appropriate for one other person in the group. The next time you provide opportunity for small-group discussion, remind them of their commitment to one person in the group.

Exercise 3. Cover a large wall space at eye level with plain brown wrapping paper. Ask a group of seven or eight pupils to complete, on a sheet of paper at their seats, the statement: "If I favored busing for integrating the schools, I would never let anyone know because _____ ." Then have them combine all their reasons into one list, without duplications, and copy the completed list onto the left side of the wrapping paper. From each item on the list, draw a line all the way to the right side of the paper. You may end up with a chart something like this:

People would say I was crazy _____

My friends don't believe in integration _____

My parents don't believe in integration   _____

It would just start trouble _____

It doesn't matter what I believe;
   I have no say in it _____

Now, ask the pupils to look at each reason for keeping their opinions to themselves and decide how strongly they agree that it is a good reason. Encourage each person to take the felt pen and put his initials anywhere along the line he wises, from all the way at the left (meaning strongly agree) to all the way on the right (meaning strongly disagree), or anywhere in between (meaning more or less convinced that it is a good or bad reason).

When everyone who wants to do so has initialed each line, ask the pupils if they have any general observations about the chart. They may have similar observations to those listed below:

"I've thought some of those things. Not about busing, but other things."

"It matters what other people think."

"Nobody wants to be without friends."

"You can't always be what other people want you to be."

Then have each child complete the statement: "If I favored busing for school integration, I would say so because _____ ."

Set up the wrapping paper list in the same way. It may look something like this:

I'm not afraid to say what I think _____

Everybody doesn't have to agree on everything _____

I don't mind going to school with Black people _____

I don't mind going to school with white people _____

Some of my friends might agree with me _____

Again, ask the pupils to look at each reason for stating their opinions freely, decide how strongly they agree that it is a good reason, and then initial their places on the continuum that pinpoint the intensity of their agreement. When they have finished, they may make some general observations, similar to the ones below:

"It's hard if you think no one agrees with you."

"Sometimes you never know who agrees with you until you say what you think."

"I'd never be the first one to say it."

"You can always find some people who agree with you."

"Why can't you convince other people to change their minds?"

To sum up, you might ask the group if they have ever had similar experiences involving taking a stand on a touchy subject. You may discover that they speak more freely about experiencing such a quandary than they ever have before. In the process, they continue to learn from each other how often they have the same doubts and fears, and the same bursts of courage in the face of those fears. Equally vulnerable, they may be more careful not to be hurtful in their relationships with each other.

Exercise 4. Tell the pupils: "You spend five or six hours a week in this classroom. That's about one hundred hours for the whole term. Can you name one thing you want to accomplish in that time—one thing that's really important to you?"

The group can compile the goals into two lists, one made up of goals that all of them share, the other made up of goals that only one or two people have. Subsequent cooperative planning for the achievement of these goals can involve the whole group and subgroups in combinations that they have never tried before.

I remember one pupil, very much like Joe Hainis whose exploits opened this chapter. In identifying goals, he let slip that he, too, in common with all the others in the class, had as an objective getting a good grade in social studies. The first impulse of some of the pupils when they heard this was to laugh in derision. They could not believe that someone who seemed to do everything to insure his own failure really cared anything about getting good grades.

"Why shouldn't I want a good grade?" he yelled at the rest of the class. "Do you think my father doesn't care what grade I get? He cares!"

I would like to be able to report that the others never laughed at him again; and that, with the awareness of shared goals, he became a full-fledged member of the class. However, the most that happened was that, though he began to succeed academically, he continued to make it clear that most of his values were not the same as the others', and there could never be an accommodation between them.

The objective of this exercise is to help the pupils identify goals that they may have in common, as well as goals that are unique to different individuals. The awareness of shared goals helps the children find identification with the group, extension of themselves in each other. With the strength they find in being part of the group, they can feel comfortable in accepting the uniquenesses in themselves and in each other.

It is the groups to which a person belongs that help him define his identity, that help him find a basis for functioning adequately. If the classroom groups only make it clear that the individual has no place in the society, that the worth he sees in himself is not seen by the others, or that the ways he has of communicating are not understood by his peers, then that person must find his identity and his sense of worth elsewhere. That "elsewhere" may present a management problem for the teacher. It is in the teacher's, as well as in the child's interest, to encourage an atmosphere in the classroom in which common goals are identified, freedom of expression is encouraged, and differences are perceived as intrinsically neither good nor bad.

Problem 3
A MATTER OF MUTUAL ASSISTANCE

"Everyone who finishes this assignment in fifteen minutes will go out to recess. The rest of you will stay in until you are finished."

All the children in Ms. Smith's fifth-grade class bend eagerly to their papers, and for all of three minutes not a sound can be heard except an occasional rustle of paper and some heavy breathing. Then Ms. Smith looks up from her book and sees Michael shake his head at James and whisper something.

"Michael," she calls across the room, "what are you doing?"

"Nothing, Ms. Smith. I'm not doing anything."

If there is one thing that angers Ms. Smith it is the stupid denial of an obvious fact. "Don't tell me you're doing nothing, Michael. I *saw* you talking to James."

"He just asked me a question, Ms. Smith. Not the answers."

"Don't help him, Michael. Let James do his own work."

"Yes, Ms. Smith." And Michael lowers his head over his paper, happy to have escaped so lightly from the consequences of his horrendous crime—providing assistance to a fellow human being.

The Modification Target

"Don't help him."

"Do your own work."

"Attend to your own business."

"You cheated."

We probably all are aware of the story of the young woman who was beaten and murdered while people sat and listened behind their drawn blinds and did nothing to help her. Since that incident, it has become almost fashionable for behavioral scientists to experiment with our responses to people's calls for help, and the data proliferate on our lack of concern for our fellow human beings.

The question we must ask ourselves as professional teachers is: What are we contributing to this state of affairs? Oh, I am not suggesting that we are solely responsible for making people reluctant to help each other, fearful of getting involved with the crises of other people, or—as some researchers suggest—actually willing to inflict pain on others if we are told to do so by authorities.

However, since we have assumed responsibility for teaching the young, and since adult behavior reveals this serious educational gap, are we not implicitly accountable for some part of it? At least, we must look to what we do—or neglect to do—in our classrooms, and determine if there is any connection between the asocial behavior of adults and the standards of behavior we impose on children.

Cheating

There is no doubt that, in the minds of classroom teachers, cheating is a serious breach of discipline, and much energy is expended in directing the management of the classroom to discourage and prevent cheating.

At the same time, we expend even more energy in exhorting children to be nicer to each other. We don't want them to fight; we want them to be protective of their smaller peers; we don't want them to tease each other and make the vulnerable cry; and we excoriate bullies. We lecture them on good manners: don't interrupt when someone else is speaking; don't push ahead in line; wait your turn for everything; be considerate of others. All this, even while we are insisting: "Don't help each other!"

We may protest that there is an appropriate time for helping, and an appropriate time for refusing to help. But I wonder if the children ever learn this fine distinction. Can they really differentiate the degrees of appropriateness?

Let us, for a moment, try to perceive the problem from the child's point of view. Getting approval in school is usually very important to him. Recognition for academic achievement is the highest level of approval, and good grades are as important to him as survival on the job is to most adults. When he realizes that there is real danger that he will not make it, he may feel himself in crisis, desperate in his need to survive.

The chances are that he will not be able to just do what he should have done in the first place—his homework, his class assignments, and all the other things that he has been urged to do if he is to get good grades. His mental and/or physical resources may not be adequate, or the physical surroundings may be interfering. So, though he is probably motivated to, at least, get approval in the classroom, he is not able to do so through the usual routes to academic achievement.

Though his behavior may be clearly messaging that he needs and wants help, there is often no one receiving the message. When he stares out the window to escape to pleasanter thoughts than the arithmetic he doesn't understand, he is told to stop daydreaming. When he hits the child next to him to relieve some of his frustration, he is punished for fighting. When he stays out of school, he may be suspended. When he keeps fidgeting and getting out of his seat to work off some of his anxiety, he is seen as disruptive. And when he verbally expresses his anger with the teacher, he is kicked out of the room, and maybe even beaten for impertinence.

His peers, who should be sensitive to his dilemma because they are also potentially vulnerable, seem to be oblivious to his suffering. Or, if they are aware of it, the pressures to mind their own business are great enough to keep them from offering assistance.

Though some children protect themselves and survive by denying that they want approval for academic achievement, most others find available routes to only apparent achievement. (Apparent achievement very often gets the same approval as real achievement does.) They ask a peer directly for help, but by then it is usually the kind of help that is only superficially helpful. They want an answer immediately in order to reach an instant goal of approval—or at least avoidance of disapproval. And they often ask for that direct help from a friend and thereby precipitate an agonizing dilemma for the child who is asked for assistance. Is he to help a desperate friend and threaten to bring down on his own head the wrath of the adults in his life, or is he to abide by the rules and leave a friend to perish outside his window? If there are other alternatives, he simply is not aware of them. And it is at this point that the teacher's accountability may be identified.

Mainstreaming

There are even broader implications for teaching children the skills they need for helping each other. One of these involves the move toward *mainstreaming*, that is, integrating children with different disabilities with other children and teaching all of them in the same classrooms. For many children, it will be the first time they come into close contact with children who wear braces and use crutches, with children who cannot hear and/or cannot speak clearly, children who have extraordinary difficulty learning, or whose muscles and nerves do their bidding only spasmodically.

Most of us know that, as a society, we have never come to terms with having disabled people in our midst. Our public institutions are a testament to the fact that what we really want to do is forget that there are such things as disabilities. Our curbs make the wheelchair-bound also housebound. Our public transportation mocks those of us who are *not* disabled; for the disabled it is a nightmare of endless stairs, yard-high bus steps, and crowds, crowds, crowds. Buildings are rarely without an ornamental few steps in front; hand-rails are nonexistent; public toilets are simply not usable for many people.

But, a part of all of this that most of us are not so ready to admit are the feelings that we have when we see and/or meet disabled people. Can we admit to repugnance, even fear? Probably the best we can do is admit to a feeling of pity, which is often only sentimental and rarely helpful.

Children are afraid of people with braces. They feel anxiety in the presence of people whose bodies seem less than perfectly controlled. As they get older, if they follow adult models and remonstrances, they are "kind to those poor people," when, that is, they aren't avoiding them. Or, not following the overt adult model, they deal with their discomfort by teasing, mocking, and even physically hurting disabled children. This is the period in children's lives when adults—thinking they have hit on some novel profundity—are heard to say, "Children can be so cruel!" Can they not! Almost as cruel as adults are!

If we are to have in our classrooms children with more obvious disabilities than the ones so-called normal children have, then we must include in our curriculum some real knowledge of the meaning of human interdependence.

Teaching Interdependence

In *People in Neighborhoods*[2], Benito, Eddie, and Lito found a purse with lots of money in the street. "Right away Benito said, 'Let's go to the store and . . .'

" 'No!' said Lito. 'That's Mrs. Garcia's purse. . . . Come on, we'll take it to her.'

" 'O.K. Lito. We'll go with you.'

"They walked down Grand Avenue. They whistled. They shrugged their shoulders. They wanted to look like the Young Lords, those big strong boys."

In the teacher's guide for the book, there are questions to ask the children to aid in their "affective development." For example:

"How do you think Mrs. Garcia felt when she got her purse back?" (p. T60)

"How do we affect our school neighborhood?" (p. T62)

"What can we do to help make people like to live in the neighborhood?" (p. T62)

Though these questions, by implication, open up the idea of interdependence, much more can be done to help the children understand the pervasiveness of human interdependence—in the story and in their own lives.

We might, for example, raise the question of who else was affected when Lito said no. How do you think Benito felt? How do you think Eddie felt? How do you think Lito's no changed Benito's behavior? Eddie's behavior? How do you think Lito's no might have changed Benito's life? What did Benito do for Lito when he said, "Let's go to the store. . ."? (e.g., he gave him a chance to take a public stand on one of his values.)

---

[2] Elizabeth W. Samuels, Kim Ellis and Mary C. Durkin, *The Taba Program in Social Science*, (Reading, Mass.: Addison-Wesley Publishing Co.,1972), pp. 14-19.

The children could role play various endings in this situation and examine the consequences of each: if Lito agreed to spend the money in the purse; if Eddie sided with Benito; if Benito changed his mind. Then the questions might be raised:

Would you say that Lito's behavior could be called helping?

What about Benito's behavior?

Was he a help to Lito?

Did Eddie help Benito or Lito?

To put the children on the track of developing a general concept, ask:

What is helping?

What does helping do?

How does helping change the helper? The person helped?

Can you think of times when helping hurts?

To evaluate the effectiveness of the lesson, to check and see if the children can apply the concept of helping to a realistic situation in their lives, ask: (Don't use the names of the children in your classrooms.) "If Rosie asked Shirley for the answer to a math problem on the test, and Shirley gave it to her, whose behavior might change as a result of this?"

If the children can put into words their recognition of the interdependence of Rosie and Shirley, and then of their own interdependence with the rest of the children and the teacher, then the concept has been learned. How the children put this knowledge to work in their everyday living must be observed over a long period of time.

Interdependence and Race

The significance of human interdependence seems to evade us when we are faced with the fact of our racial diversity. We witness Black children bused into formerly white schools and permit them to remain isolated from their peers. We see Puerto Rican children and Black children sitting side by side in classrooms, yet as alienated from each other as if they were from different, hostile planets. And Chicano and Anglo children can go through school believing that they have nothing of value to offer each other. Can we teachers really believe that the separating wall between Anglo and Chicano children can have no effect on the development of empathy for children in their own groups? Is it possible for Black children to let Puerto Rican children flounder and sink and still be loving and caring in their relationships with other Black children?

Though we compartmentalize our thinking so that we often are unaware of the inconsistencies in our values and behaviors, the inconsistencies are there. The anxieties that accompany them—even when we do not recognize them in ourselves—take their toll on our satisfaction in life. A white person cannot hate Black people and still feel good about his humanity and his belief in democracy. None of us can ignore the pleas for help from our fellow human beings and still feel comfortable about our own worth. Witness the vast amounts of energy expended by bigots in their attempts to justify their bigotry: they even explain when no one is listening.

There are ways for the teacher to help his pupils see their peers through the walls of fear and distrust that separate them. And then there are ways to help them begin to assume some responsibility for helping each other survive.

One such way is what I have named, "Words and Phrases that Hurt."[3] This teaching strategy is designed especially for classrooms that have at least two racial or ethnic groups, so that children may develop empathy for different groups and practice skills in assisting each other in the face of prejudice and discrimination.

However, the list of words and phrases that hurt can be adapted for the development of interpersonal empathy and helping skills where race is not a factor.

---

[3]Taken and slightly adapted from my book, *Affective Subjects in the Classroom: Exploring Race, Sex, and Drugs* (Scranton, Pa., Intext, 1972), pp. 93-106. Reprinted with permission of Harper and Row.

Words and Phrases That Hurt

Borrow several geoboards from the mathematics teacher. (Geoboards are flat squares of wood into which small nails have been hammered halfway at intervals of one inch, so that they look something like a fakir's miniature bed of nails. They are generally used to teach children something about plane geometry by stretching rubber bands into different shapes between nails.) Stretch a rubber band from the nail in the center of the top row to the nail in the center of the bottom row. This is the starting position.

Now, divide the class into groups of eight to ten people, preferably with each group around a small table. If tables are not available, have them sit in a circle with an empty chair in the middle. Place a geoboard and a set of cards face down in the center of each table. (On each card is written an item from the list "Words and Phrases that Hurt.")

Then:

1. One at a time, each player turns up a card and reads it aloud.

2. Immediately, someone in the group extends the rubber band two spaces in any direction. (Increasing the tension in the rubber band is merely a symbolic portrayal of the tension that is built up when a member of a minority group hears the remark.)

3. The players discuss the remark, trying to understand the cause of the tension build-up. Since these items have been culled from the first-hand experiences of minority-group members, the players cannot as a group conclude that there is nothing tension producing about the remark. If no one can understand why it annoys people, then the teacher who is circulating from group to group may be called on to give additional information. During the discussion, players may extend the rubber band if they feel anger or annoyance as they begin to understand the significance of the remark.

4. When the players have some idea of the significance of the remark, they then try to determine what could be said or done to ameliorate a situation in which such a remark is made. Here players have often found it useful, without necessarily leaving their seats, to role play specific instances where such things are said, so that they may more clearly see the result of any ameliorating action. (If this game is first played after the pupils have been involved in role playing, they do this spontaneously. If they don't, it is good to get them started role playing early in the game.) The objectives of such action are to help the target of the insult come away with his self-concept undamaged, to help the insulter and any bystanders learn the significance of what has been said, and to discourage people from saying such things.

5. If the players can think of an ameliorating response, they may go on to the next card. (It is better to limit the time spent on each card to about five minutes, or the "game" feeling is lost and the group just engages in discussion that may get further and further away from the objectives.)

6. Each time a rubber band breaks (or the players are afraid to stretch the rubber band any more) add one to the group score.

7. When all the cards have been played, the group with the highest score wins.

WORDS AND PHRASES THAT HURT
(for Race and Ethnic Relations)

1. A white woman asking just about any Black woman she knows: Do you know someone who would help me do my housework?

2. A white person to a Black person: You can make your school as good as ours.

3. A white teacher about Puerto Rican children: Why should I teach them? They'll never get anywhere.

4. A teacher about poor children: If we let them take the books home, they'll just get them dirty and destroy them.

5. A white person: Some of my best friends are Negroes.

6. A white person to a Black acquaintance: You're different from most Negroes I know.

7. About any group: They *all* do that.

8. A white person to a Black person: Why do you want to send your children to our schools?

9. Upon announcing one's intention to integrate a job situation: Of course, we will make sure we hire a *qualified* Negro.

10. A white person to a Black person: Your people are so happy all the time.

11. A white person to a Black person: I don't understand what you people want.

12. To a minority-group person as he applies for a job at 7:30 A.M.: You should have gotten here five minutes sooner. We just hired someone for that job.

13. To an Italian person by someone who is not Italian: Why, you don't *look* Italian.

14. Referring to a Black man: You know the boy I mean.

15. A white person to a Black person: I know you're proud of Martin Luther King.

16. A mainlander to a Puerto Rican: I think your people should get together and agree to help each other.

17. A white person: Our old neighborhood used to be good when I lived there as a kid, but look at it now!

18. A white person to a Black person: The death of Martin Luther King was a terrible loss to your race.

19. An Anglo about Mexican people: Why don't they take care of their own, like we did?

20. To a Jewish person, by someone who is not Jewish: I didn't know you were Jewish—you don't act like one.

21. Said to a Black nurse: Do you like this better than housework?

22. A white to a Native American: I think your people have made great progress.

The game has a number of purposes in the teaching of race relations. However, with a little imagination card items can be developed for dealing with other intergroup and interpersonal relationships. The essential objectives of the game remain the same:

1. To say aloud in a safe group situation words that insult, annoy, make angry, and hurt.

2. To reinforce the idea that, though everyone does not have these feelings when hearing the words, the fact is that many people do.

3. To give opportunity for learning why people use these words and why others respond emotionally to them.

4. To develop conviction in those who are the target that there is nothing wrong with them; that it is the people using the words who are wrong.

5. To give opportunity for developing strategies for dealing with people who say these words. Such strategies are developed, not only by the potential victims, but also by others who witness victimization.

Generally, the pattern of relations between groups in this country has been such that, when a person is hurt or angered by one of these remarks, he bites his lip and says nothing until he gets back to people of his own group. He pays a price for this in unrelieved anger, frustration, and self-doubt. In the course of this game, the minority-group person who feels the sting of these remarks can express his anger in the presence of the other group. He can say in no uncertain terms how he feels about implications and assumptions—no matter how subtle—that he should be grateful for white concessions or white attempts to relegate him to a white-defined place in American society.

White people in the class also are encouraged to give voice to feelings about intergroup situations. They can express the kind of discomfort that compels them to say, in an awkward attempt to be friendly, "Oh, I envy you! You people are always so happy and carefree." And they can express outrage and anger that their good intentions are so unkindly rebuffed. Often, both Blacks and whites are surprised at the existence of these emotions. They have been talking for most of their lives about the need for mutual understanding and mutual acceptance, and they have been unaware of those very feelings that most effectively prevented any but the most superficial rapprochement between the races.

Developing Empathy

One of the objectives of education is to add to an individual's knowledge and sensitivity what other people have learned in the course of their own lives. If our life decisions are based only on what we have experienced firsthand, we are at a severe disadvantage because everything we experience is filtered through our own unique perceptions. Through the process of education, we can open ourselves to awareness of other people's perceptions. We can compare other people's perceptions with our own. Eventually we can begin to get some feeling for what other people are experiencing. In this way we broaden the basis of our perceptions and judgments.

In the course of trying to determine why these remarks are resented, students who never saw anything wrong with them get some insight into the feelings of others. They may not realize that when they say, "I don't understand what you people want," it is really not merely a confession of ignorance. It is usually perceived by the listener as a diatribe against (1) people who are separated by a wall from the speaker ("You people" are a wall away!); (2) people who appear to be demanding more than other people have; and (3) people who are already getting everything they are entitled to.

Often students are able to experience other people's anger at such a remark in the course of the game and to feel a responsive anger in themselves. When they role play various situations in attempts to find alternate ways of dealing with these remarks and with the anger they provoke, they can actually act out anger and frustration in roles they may never have taken in real life.

With these kinds of experiences, it becomes less likely that an individual will perceive one of the situations merely in terms of his own life. He will no longer respond with impatience to others who are hurt and angered by perceived snubs and insults. He will not glibly write off Black people, for instance, with the comment: "Oh, he walks around with a chip on his shoulder." Nor will he contribute to the "generation gap" by believing that it is no use trying to make adults understand. From the vantage point of other people's shoes, he will be more understanding of them even if he does not agree with them. He will be more aware also of the significance of what he himself is saying: he will no longer deceive himself into believing that he is free of prejudice and hostility.

When two ethnic groups are represented in the class, those habitually victimized by the words and phrases are surprised when the habitual insulters begin to offer suggestions for dealing with the insults. "When I say 'you people,' " one white student said, "let me know. I probably often say it without realizing it. I'd appreciate your doing that until I get rid of the habit."

One parent admitted, "When I say, 'You'll understand when you're older,' it's only because I can't seem to explain that I feel the fear and pity and sadness. I'm afraid I'll be laughed at. If I could know that young people wouldn't ridicule my feelings, I'd feel freer to talk and to listen."

Often, the victims come away feeling less victimized, more aware that the hurters are hurting too.

Once, while playing the game, some white players were insisting that the trouble between Black people and white people was primarily that Black people were too tight, too ready to feel insult where none was intended. As the discussion and role playing proceeded, a white student playing the part of a Black person burst into anger at hearing for the third time, "You have to earn your rights, and with rights come responsibilities." She shouted, "Earn our rights! Did you fight for independence? We did, too. Did you work until you dropped? We did for centuries without pay! Did your sons die in all the other wars? Ours did! What have you done to earn your rights that we haven't?"

Suddenly her face showed a look of perfect understanding. She *knew* what was making Black people angry—really knew it for the first time.

The Value of Help

Just what can we do to help children avoid the desperation of being abandoned to failure, and to help others avoid the dilemma of having to make a choice between helping a friend and being a "good citizen"?

I think we ought to remove from our classroom vocabulary the word *cheat*. This is one of those labels with moralistic overtones that does not help the child labeled or the adult who is concerned about the child's behavior. In my classrooms, I liked to spread the idea that helping each other was good, and I modeled helping behavior. Gradually, the children and I worked out a schema for validating real helping behavior, and it became a basis for many of our discussions of social institutions that went far beyond the daily interaction in the classroom.

It started one day when a pupil asked me how to spell a word he wanted to use in his composition. I had been in the habit of merely spelling a word aloud or writing it on the board whenever a child asked me for help. They often asked each other for help in spelling, and they were all equally responsive to such requests.

This time, I recalled that Johnny had asked me several times before to spell the same word. When I reminded him, he sheepishly admitted it: "I never know how to spell it! Tell me just once more, Ms. E., and I'll never ask again."

I laughed and spelled the word, just once more.

Later, when Johnny had finished one job and had not yet started another one, I pulled a chair up to the table at which he sat and said, "Johnny, we all help each other in this class, don't we?"

"Yes," he said. "We all help."

The two other children at the table looked up.

"How do you feel when you help someone?" I asked Johnny.

He thought for a minute, then shrugged his shoulder. "I don't know," he said.

One of the other children spoke, "I feel good when I help."

"Me, too," said the third child.

"Sometimes I feel good," said Johnny.

"How do you feel when you don't feel good?"

"I don't know."

"I always feel good," said the second child.

"Sometimes I feel scared."

The third child asked Johnny, "Like you think you shouldn't give someone the answer?"

"Yeah."

"Are you afraid you'll be punished?" I asked.

"Nah!" Johnny dismissed that out of hand. "You don't punish children."

"Not punished," the third child said eagerly. "But it's not good."

"What's not good?" I asked.

"It's not good to give answers."

"On a test," said the second child.

"I want to do my electric circuit," said Johnny. And he was gone before anyone could say anything more.

"Do you want to talk more about this?" I asked the other two children.

"All right," said one.

"Maybe later," said the other.

But that was the way it started. Over a period of several months, talking informally at first, with two or three children, and then more systematically working in task-oriented groups, we developed the schema:

Questions to Ask Yourself About Helping

- *Does the person want help? How do I know?*

    He asks me for help.

    I hear him ask someone else for help.

    He doesn't go back to his work after I answer his question. He sticks near me.

- *Does the person need help? How do I know?*

    He cries when he's trying to work at something.

    He squirms around a lot when he's trying to work at something.

    He won't stick with the work; he keeps walking around or sharpening pencils or going to the boy's room.

    He wants to talk to people about other things, or just fool around.

- *What kind of help is best?*

    If I help him now, will he need the same kind of help again soon?

    Yes $\begin{cases} \text{He has asked for the same kind of help be-} \\ \text{fore.} \\ \text{He asks for help very often.} \end{cases}$

    No $\begin{cases} \text{This is an unusual situation with which I} \\ \text{have some experience.} \\ \text{He usually helps himself.} \end{cases}$

    If I help him now, what will the help add to his own resources?

He'll have the answer only to this problem.
He'll be able to solve many similar problems.
He'll feel so good about himself that he'll try harder.

How does giving this help make me feel?

Good? {
Superior, because I know and he doesn't.
Happy,   because now we both know.
Satisfied, because a friend wants me to help.
Relieved, because he'll like me for helping him.
}

Bad? {
Guilty,   because it's wrong to help him.
Worried,   because someone may find out.
           because he won't like me if I don't.
           because he can't help himself.
Unhappy, because now no one knows that I didn't need the help and he did.
}

Mutual assistance, then, becomes a matter for analysis, values clarification, and sophisticated concept development. It is no longer just a matter of teacher-made rules and punishment for violation of those rules. Certainly, in the experience of both teacher and pupils, it goes far beyond the immediate concerns of classroom management.

Problem 4
A MATTER OF PROBLEM SOLVING

If schools were set up to function without teachers, all problems that arose in the classroom could be either resolved or substantially alleviated through effective communication among the pupils. Let us look at four types of problems that beset us in our schools, examine the management implications of each of those problems, and then discuss the solutions of the problems in terms of enhanced pupil-pupil communication.

Type 1

Thomas: My new pen is gone! Somebody stole my pen!

Teacher: You don't know that it's stolen. You may just have misplaced it. Why don't you look for it?

Thomas: I *did* look for it! I *did* look for it! Somebody stole it! It was right here on my desk and somebody stole it!

Jane: I'll bet I know who took it.

Thomas: Yeah! I bet I know, too.

Teacher: Stop that! You don't know anything of the sort!

Jimmy: I did not take his rotten pen! Everybody always blames me!

Teacher: Nobody blamed you, Jimmy.

Jimmy: They did so! Every time something's missing, I get blamed!

Thomas: Well, you took Bill's knife.

Jimmy: I just wanted to look at it!

Teacher: Bill should not have a knife in school.

Bill: It's my scout knife!

Teacher: We've spent the whole reading period with this. Now it's time for assembly.

Thomas: But what about my pen?! What about my pen?!

Type 2

John: The boys finished first! The boys finished first!

Jane: The girls are smarter anyhow!

Type 3

Teacher: Class, I'm going to assign you to permanent seats. Listen for your name and then come and take the seat I point to.

Bob: Aw! Can't we sit where we want to?

Teacher: I assign seats so I can learn your names more easily. I have so many social studies classes that I can't remember everybody's name.

Keith: We can put name cards on our desks. That way you'll know our names.

Teacher: We-e-e-ll. All right. Why don't we try that and see how it works.

[That afternoon, the students make their name cards, and when they come to the social studies class the following day they take the seats they prefer and place the cards so that the teacher can see them.]

Teacher: That's very good. I'm pleased at the way you came in and sat down—quietly and orderly. Very good!

[After a few days, the teacher finds that the cards are working very well and he is able to remember many of the students' names. Suddenly, however, he realizes something else: all the white students are seated on one side of the room and all the Black students are seated on the other side.]

Type 4

Sylvia: Miss Wilson, make Billy sit down. He's not letting us work!

Miss Wilson: Sit down, Billy, and do your own work.

Billy: I just want to read this part.

Sylvia: Miss Wilson!

Miss Wilson: Billy!

Billy: What did I do!

The Modification Target

Most teachers would perceive these four situations as problems that they must solve. However, if they try to do so unilaterally, though they succeed in creating order, it will inevitably be only a temporary order, and will necessitate their continuing to spend time and energy responding to the same problems again and again.

Consciousness Raising

On the other hand, if the teacher addresses himself to raising the level of pupils' consciousness and then freeing them to develop self-management skills, classroom management problems will be dealt with by the people who are creating them, and the benefits of learning how to do this will contribute materially to the pupils' continuing process of self-actualization.

One thing that is vital to raising the level of consciousness of problems in the classroom is opportunity to name those problems in a working setting. That is, though they probably talk among themselves about many of the existing problems, pupils rarely sit down as a class to name those problems with the objective of working to resolve them. Rather, their talk generally consists of complaints, gossip, pejorative observations of all kinds, and even hostile confrontations. The naming of the problems, which are written down verbatim and then systematically taken up by the class, helps give serious recognition to the concerns of the students. Such recognition, in itself, can contribute to self-concept development insofar as it implies, "Your feelings are important." It contributes also to development of self-control, since it may make some students decide to refrain from certain behaviors because they do not want to continue to be associated with them. (This is not to say that people's names are mentioned when the problems are identified. However, those students who demonstrate the problem behaviors are well aware that, in the minds of their peers, they are associated with the problem.)

Suppose all four samples of the dialogue above occurred in the same classroom, and the responses to the teacher's question, "What problems do we have in this class?" result in the following list:

- Too much noise

- Stealing

- The boys are always picking on the girls

- The girls are always saying they're smarter

(In most desegregated classes, the apparent racial problem would probably not be spoken aloud at this time. The white children may not be aware of it. The Black children may not mention it for fear of disrupting whatever surface harmony may exist or out of the belief that the white majority will not care to deal with it. However, as the children explore the problems between the sexes, it is inevitable that the problems between the races will emerge. Of course, the teacher who observes the problem can hold a separate problem census to deal with it. In that case, the question he asks must be directly related to the specific area of race relations. He may ask, "What problems are there in this class between the white students and the Black students?" Obviously, the children cannot develop all the intellectual skills they need if they are not aware that a problem exists or if they are reluctant to mention the existence of a problem.)

The Process

Once the problem has been listed, then the teacher can help the students explore it systematically and come to some conclusions about its solution. Throughout, a significant aspect of the whole problem-solving process must be the improvement of communication among the pupils so that they may express their feelings freely; share and clarify their perceptions of the problem; either reach consensus about the definition of the problem, or become aware of reasonable differences among them; and make a behavioral commitment toward ameliorating the problem, once they have identified the appropriate behaviors.

Taking the problem of stealing as an example, a sixth-grade or even a tenth-grade class might start by delimiting the problem:

- How often do things unexplainably disappear?

- Is there a pattern to the disappearances?

- Do they always occur at the same time of day?

- Is it only certain kinds of things that disappear?

- Do they disappear only from certain places?

- Are they taken from the same people all the time?

They may then begin to formulate hypotheses, looking for reasons and debunking myths as they gather information: What are the implications of the pattern? Is someone taking food at the same time every day because he is hungry? Is someone taking the same kinds of small objects every time, which seems to indicate that he is not in need of those things? Is the same person (or the same group of students) losing his things all the time, which may lead one to think that the person taking things cares more about the owners of the things than about the things he takes? Does it seem likely that more than one person is taking things that do not belong to him?

At this point they may focus on feelings: How do the people whose things disappear feel about it? (This is opportunity for small-group affective discussion. One outcome of such discussion is developing empathy for the victims.) How do people who take things feel about what they are doing? Is it possible to feel it's wrong and right at the same time? (This may be time for role playing, giving children the opportunity to live for a while in the shoes of the guilty person and/or the victim. Out of this role playing may come, not only increased empathy for others, but also ideas about what productive, useful things can be done in such situations.)

Here the focus is on values: Is stealing always wrong? Do all individuals (peoples) believe the same way about it? What do I believe? Have I ever stolen anything? (Here children may form dyads to share personal feelings in relative privacy, never being coerced to say anything they do not want to reveal. This is an opportunity to relieve individual guilt and to recognize the universality of the behavior.)

Here the focus is on behavior: What do I do when I believe someone has stolen something? What do I do when I've stolen something? What do I do when I'm tempted to steal something? How do I help other people not to be tempted?

It is in this phase of dealing with the problem that the children can commit themselves publicly to behaviors that, in effect, provide for self-management. Stealing, if it exists, may not suddenly and entirely cease. However, the children will be empathic, so they need not feel that the suspect should be executed. Nor will the perpetrators be insensitive to their victims. The children will be skilled in preventing stealing; skilled in self-control; skilled in helping perpetrators. They will be proud of themselves, their ability, and their feelings of independence and of being in control—the most significant factors in effective classroom management.

chapter 5

Solutions Based on Curriculum

Problem 1
A MATTER OF INTEREST

Teacher: Today we're going to practice long division. Most of you did not do very well on the test Friday.

Class: [Groans, Oh-no's, long division! ugh!]

Teacher: Get your workbooks out.

Linda: Why do we have to know long division anyhow? Who cares about long division?

Harley: Yeah! Long division is boring!

Teacher: Stop being silly and open your books. How will you ever get into junior high school if you don't know long division?

Linda: My brother is in junior high school, and he doesn't know long division.

Harley: Yeah!

Teacher: Open those books!

John: [Slamming his pencil down on the desk.] Why should we do long division? I'm not doing it!

Teacher: Are you asking to be punished?

Sam: No long division! No long division! [Kicks his desk in rhythm with his words.]

Teacher: Stop that this instant!

Mary: Let's have social studies, Miss Smith. That's interesting.

Teacher: Mary, leave the room!

Mary: [Whining.] I didn't do anything! I just asked about social studies! Why am I being punished?

Teacher: Out!

Mary: [Whining all the way.] I always get blamed for nothing! How come I always get blamed for nothing?

Frank: I got a good grade. Why should I have to do long division?

Teacher: Be quiet, Frank!

Frank: What did *I* say?

Bernard: Hey! Look at that kid out in the yard! What's he doing there?

Harley: [Running to the window.] Where? Where? I don't see him!

[Three or four other children run to the window shouting, "Where?" "Where?" "Who do you see?" "Is he still there?" as if they have never seen anyone in the school-yard before this moment.]

Teacher: [Distraught.] Sit down, all of you! Stop this noise! You'll all be punished for this! No recess for a week! Frank, sit down! [She rushes to Frank and forces him bodily into a seat.]

Frank: [Struggling.] This isn't my seat! I wanna sit in my seat! This isn't my seat!

John: I have to go to special class. It's time for special class!

Sam: [Fooling with his desk until he knocks it over with a crash.]

[There is a momentary lull as everyone looks toward the crash.]

Teacher: [Resuming her distraught behavior.] Mary, I told you to leave the room! [Rushes to Harley, grabs him by the shoulder and shakes him.] Sit down, sit down!

Harley: You hit me! You can't hit me! You're not supposed to hit me!

Teacher: [Strides back to her desk and picks up the yardstick. She bangs it on the table until it breaks.] Sit down! Sit down! Be quiet!!

[The principal opens the door and closes it behind him. He stands there for only a moment before some of the children catch sight of him and quiet down immediately. Altogether it takes only a minute before the room is absolutely quiet. Some of the children start to move unobtrusively toward their seats, but a look from the principal freezes them in their tracks.]

Then the usual procedure takes place. All of you are undoubtedly familiar with it.

The Modification Target

Justifying Boredom

When was the last time you sat down at the kitchen table and did twenty-five examples in long division because (a) you were just interested in doing them; (b) you thought it was important to keep practicing long division; (c) you thought it was good exercise for the brain and would help clarify your thinking on an important problem you were facing; or (d) you believed it was a good mental discipline to strengthen the brain?

Interests and Needs

No one is suggesting that children should not learn long division, grammar, dates in history, or any of the other things they find so deadly dull. The suggestion is that the teacher cease trying frantically to make dull things interesting—not often with success. Rather, the thrust should be to abandon those processes and data that are dull when they stand alone, without relevance or reason. However, at the point when the child perceives the need for a process, a piece of information, or a formula, nothing will keep him from learning it and using it. The job of the teacher is to provide opportunities for the children to perceive such needs.

Following is a transcript of another teacher's approach to long division:

James: Gee, I wish I didn't have to come in. It's so hot here!

Teacher: You'd rather be outside for this period?

Class: *Would* we! Yeah! Let's go back out!

Teacher: All right. You've been wanting to plant stone gardens along the outside fence. Let's collect some stones from the empty lot next to the school.

[You can imagine the joyful eagerness with which containers were rounded up and the children prepared to leave the room!]

Teacher: Each of you fill up your containers and bring them back here. Then we can divide the stones equally, so nobody is penalized because he couldn't carry a lot, or couldn't find many of the right size. How does that sound?

Class: Fine. Fine. Let's go!

[For half an hour, the children forage for the "right kind" of stones—something they have discussed before when talking about beautifying the area of the school. Then they are called back to the classroom. They are urged by the teacher to deposit all the containers in one place and sit down in a circle to plan the next step in the project.]

Teacher: What's next?

Bobby: I have a picture of a stone garden, and I'm going to make one just like it.

Bill: Who says it's gonna be your way?

Bobby: Who says it's gonna be *your* way?

Grace: Let's each make our own.

Several children: Sure! That's right! There's plenty of room all around the fence! Let's make our own.

Bobby: And have a prize for the best!

James: No! No best!

Ralph: A prize for everyone!

Teacher: The prize will be so many beautiful gardens!

James: OK, let's go!

Teacher: First, let's divide the stones equally.

James: You mean we have to count all those stones! It'll take a year!

Marilyn: You don't have to count them.

James: What, then?

[Marilyn frowns, not quite able to answer that question.]

Teacher: What's another way of deciding how much material we have to work with?

Marilyn: If it's paper, we can measure it with a ruler.

James: You're gonna measure the stones with a ruler?

[Some laughter.]

Grace: My mother measures flour in a measuring cup.

[Silence. Some very hard thinking is going on.]

Paula: You measure some things in a spoon.

Vita: A five-pound bag of sugar!

Marilyn: You weigh it!

James: Weigh the stones!!

Eva: Get the scale!

Barbara: Weigh the stones!

The stones were duly weighed, and it was discovered that, by long division, they could apportion them equally among the twenty-three pupils in the class. Similarly, long division was needed to divide up the available planting space, to make decisions about how much of each space was to be planted with different seeds, and how much water would be needed to keep the land suitable for growing. Interestingly enough, some of the children who had not been able to learn long division discovered new routes to the correct answers, and everyone realized that even in arithmetic there was more than one right way to be right.

In this example, the curriculum factor was retained, but it became meaningful and interesting to the children, and was even expanded in conception with the realization that they could discover answers for themselves.

Implications for Life

What are the arguments that are brought out to rationalize forcing children to work at things they have no interest in? One is invariably that this is preparation for real life: we often must do things that are not interesting—things that need to be done if we are to survive. But what evidence do we have that being bored in childhood prepares us to cope adequately with boredom in adulthood? Is boredom easier to bear because we have had so much of it in our lives?

On the other hand, it is quite possible that we have been so well trained to expect life to be pretty boring, that many of us do not consider leaving boring jobs, boring friends, or boring families, because we do not believe there are alternative life conditions.

However, more and more people are throwing off the shackles of boredom and are making their lives over into more interesting ways. There are enough alternative ways to making a living, having a social life, and living with families that we need not be forever bored with what we are doing. So too are there alternative ways to learn long division, the history of the human race, and the structure of our language. There is nothing *intrinsically* boring about English grammar—it's just a question of tying it in to a perceived need or in to an abiding interest, for it to be seen as useful, and as interestingly apropos.

Curriculum and Living

If children learn this approach to ordering their lives, they may take a hand in living their lives more fully rather than bearing their lives in boredom.

There is, moreover, another aspect of the matter of interest that needs to be treated. That involves the whole idea of the sanctity of the established curriculum. There are so many things to learn about in the world! The continuing proliferation of knowledge is phenomenal, and there is little evidence that choices of what data to include in school curriculums are incontrovertibly apt. In the final analysis, it becomes clear that children in school today will, as adults, be living by and with information that their teachers cannot even imagine. The best we can do is to help children develop skills in processing information, and the data used as a vehicle for this learning can be almost anything.

Oh, I would agree that there are some things they ought to know about because they are surrounded by them and they should be prepared to deal with them. They ought to know about the factors in effective communication; they ought to know how to read because this is still the most convenient way to gather new information; they probably ought to know how to write, though I have doubts about how long this will be considered a necessary skill. And, since people cannot learn to communicate, read, or write without communicating, reading, and writing about *something*, subjects will inevitably be a part of the school curriculum. It is far less important that we keep all those subjects we now insist on having. As a matter of fact, there are others we never mention that are probably more useful—to say nothing of more interesting to most children!

Problem 2
A MATTER OF RELEVANCE

John: Why do I have to learn French?

Teacher: Because some day you may want to go to France.

John: When I want to go, I'll learn French.

Teacher: Let's get on with the lesson.

The Modification Target

Relevance and Education

I believe that, if we never bothered to explore any topics except the ones immediately relevant to us, we could learn more than any of us have ever learned all through our years of education. When I think of the time I spent psyching myself up to tackle a subject I couldn't care less about, I bemoan so much wasted life that might have been spent on matters that had meaning and importance for me.

I could have approached Latin through the inscriptions on seals and buildings that always intrigued me. I could have approached history through historical fiction that I discovered when I was a teenager and through biography that I read when I began to think of a career for myself. In my own time, following through on what was important to me, I could have become a far better educated woman than I was when I graduated from college.

Though we often attempt to justify teaching standard subjects by arguing that they are important for specific life objectives, it appears to me that the real reason is that we must maintain the assembly-line structure and organization of mass education. To do this, we persist in teaching everyone the same things.

How many of us studied French in school because the school had a French teacher? Another school had a Spanish teacher. Did this mean that French was more important for some children and Spanish more important for others? What would have had meaning for the children themselves—those children who hated every moment they spent struggling with the meaningless syllables?

> *John*: Trin can't speak any English. How can I help him with his math?
>
> *Teacher*: Maybe if you knew some Vietnamese, you could talk to him.
>
> *John*: Do you know someone who could teach me Vietnamese?

I often tell the story of the teacher who cajoled, threatened, and stormed because her high school juniors would not learn about the Russian Revolution. When I asked her why she thought Black American youngsters from a large twentieth-century city should jump at the chance to study the Russian Revolution, she explained to me the analogy between what had happened in Russia and what was happening in the Black movement today. I asked her if she had studied the Black movement with them and she looked at me blankly. *That* was not in the junior level curriculum!

If, however, she had braved administrative dangers (often more imagined than real), she might have found a consuming interest among the children in a subject they saw as central to their lives. It would have been easy, then, to raise questions about other revolutions (including the American Revolution), and what might be learned from them by people contemplating revolution today.

Those of us who have come to a certain age grow increasingly aware of the brevity of life. Not one minute of it ought to be wasted on matters that have no meaning for us, that do not relate to the very breaths we take. Not for a second should we submit to the demands of strangers that we spend time memorizing, practicing, repeating information that touches us, changes us, or moves us not at all. Nor should we force children to submit to this.

Relevance and Curriculum

Brazil is often the topic of a unit in the fifth grade. I saw such a unit taught recently to a class of urban children, about three-quarters of whom were Black mainlanders and one-quarter Puerto Ricans. As far as I had been able to ascertain, they had never systematically studied Puerto Rico.

They learned that Brazilians speak Portuguese. No one in the class knew any Portuguese, so the information was purely academic.

Though the objective was to study Brazil in depth and make references to other Latin American countries for purposes of comparison, the references never included Puerto Rico.

At the end of the unit they were given a test, mainly on Brazil. The academic level of the class was not very high—the range of reading and writing skills was skewed to the low end of the curve, and the achievement on the test was similarly low.

Selecting Brazil as an important subject for study, and including mention of other Latin

The Puerto Rican children were currently emotionally involved with problems related to Spanish. They spoke Spanish at home. Most of them were speaking a corruption of English and Spanish, to the dismay of their parents. No one was doing anything about helping them maintain the integrity of their language.

The Puerto Rican children knew some things about Puerto Rico that, with encouragement, they would have shared. They could even have brought parents and older siblings to talk to their classmates. They received no such encouragement. It was clear to them that any mention of Puerto Rico in connection with the unit was considered irrelevant by the teacher.

countries, led easily to the inference by the children that Puerto Rico had no such importance. This may have added to the Puerto Rican children's conception of themselves as being of little worth. It may also have exacerbated the Black children's negative perception of Puerto Ricans.

The children were learning that the people of Brazil were varied in their origins, that the customs were interesting, that the country was economically in the forefront of the world. (They just skirted past the fact that the government is a brutal dictatorship, and that the subsistence level at which so many of the people live is shocking when compared to the affluence of the few.)

It was not unusual to hear the mainland Black pupils make fun of the accents and the language of the Puerto Rican pupils. The violence with which the Puerto Rican children responded to this led me to believe that they harbored some self-doubt about the worth of their language.

All the children desperately needed success experiences in school to help them see themselves as capable of achievement. The relevance of study about Puerto Rico might have provided the impetus for the Puerto Ricans to experience success.

Most of the management problems in the room directly involved the attitudes that the Black children had toward Puerto Ricans and the attitudes of the Puerto Ricans toward Black people. They called each other ethnic and racial epithets; each minor disagreement was a signal for squaring off along nationality lines and fighting. The competition between the two groups was so intense that the teacher's commendation to one group (an unwise attempt to get the children's cooperation) led inevitably to chaos as the other group vehemently protested.

The Black children were ignorant of the varied origins of the Puerto Rican people, and what evidence of customs they saw in their neighborhood was not perceived as interesting. Rather, they rejected Puerto Rican customs as inferior, laughable, and weird.

We need not argue about how long the children retained the knowledge about Brazil that had been spread out before them. That one-dimensional study of another country could not have been so vital to their education at this particular point in their lives as long as they saw no connection between it and themselves.

A small anecdote may bring into focus the whole matter of relevance—though I cannot believe that so blatant an example of irrelevance occurs often in our teaching. In Philadelphia, during the bicentennial year, a teacher came to a story in one of the reading books about Betsy Ross. He introduced the new words in the story, wrote some comprehension questions on the board, and worked with the children for more than an hour. He told them about the history of the American flag, discussed questions about Betsy Ross's real life, and even taught them how to produce a five-pointed star with one snip of the scissors. But not once did he mention that all of this was supposed to have happened not twenty blocks from where the children were sitting! Not once did he say that the house where Betsy Ross lived was open to them every day! They were diligently studying "history" while their own lives were studiously ignored!

Problem 3
A MATTER OF ANXIETY

In urban schools, suburban schools, rural schools, and small-town schools, children suffer from anxiety. (Has this era not been called the Age of Anxiety?) The various ways in which the children act out their anxiety become defined as misbehavior, because they interfere with the smooth process of the teaching-learning situation, or disrupt the normal patterns of interaction in the classroom.

Whether or not we believe that anxiety is currently more intense or more widespread than it has been in the past, we must recognize that children experience it and are often unable to cope with it productively. A parent dies, and the child is told that "Mother has gone on a trip." A substitute teacher appears who does not know that this child must be permitted to go to the toilet frequently. Father comes home for dinner and announces that the whole family is moving to California.

When mother never returns from her "trip," the child begins to believe that he has been willfully abandoned. He cannot talk about his fear, because the adults in his family are preoccupied with their own grieving. The most he can do is ask repeatedly, "When is mother coming home?" No one notices that, as time goes on, he asks less and less often. After a while someone does observe, "He's not asking any more. He has adjusted to her absence."

But has he? How does one adjust to the belief that a loved one has cared so little that she has gone away without a word? He has stopped asking the question because he has never received a satisfactory answer. The discomfort, the vague murmurings, the hugs and tears that were responses to his question (different responses from different adults) merely increased his sadness and fearfulness.

And it is the teacher who very often is the adult who experiences the results of this unresolved sadness and fearfulness. A vague, persistent, generalized anxiety—in small children as well as in adults—can lead to behavior that interferes with effective learning in a variety of ways, from overt, inappropriately disruptive and destructive acts, to withdrawal from peer interaction, to an inability to learn that resists the most persistent and sophisticated attempts of the competent teacher.

Robert is eight years old. He is afraid of many things. It frightens him terribly when his mother and father start one of their arguments, his mother shouting and crying, and his father quietly disdainful, his voice getting lower and his words more sarcastic as his mother's get louder and wilder. The fights start at night, always waking him out of his first deep sleep, and for hours he lies, curled up under the covers, whispering over and over again, "Let them stop! Oh, please, let them stop!"

He is also very much afraid of dentists and doctors. He has never been hurt by a doctor or a dentist, and any investigator would find it difficult, if not impossible, to determine when this fear started, but there it is. It moves insidiously into his head with a corresponding pang in his stomach as he sits comfortably in a warm, dark movie theater, absorbed in the posturing of a favorite hero. It appears between the pages of an interesting storybook and makes him lose track of what he has just read. It takes away his appetite, especially when a doctor's or dentist's visit is imminent, and makes him nauseated and sometimes even causes him to vomit on the morning of such a visit.

For a long time his grandmother was very sick. She lived only a few blocks away from where he lived, but he did not see her very often. Once a month or so, the whole family would go to visit Grandma, and it was clear to him that his mother (Grandma was his mother's mother) was not comfortable about the visit. Though she told him and his younger sisters over and over again to be nice to Grandma, she was irritable before each visit, snapping at her husband and the children, and looking pinched about the mouth, the way he felt when he had to go to the doctor.

Now his Grandmother had just died, and nobody would say anything about it. He had seen his mother crying, his father had told the children—almost casually—that Grandma had gone to Heaven, and after that, nothing. He had walked in on a couple of whispered half-angry conferences between his mother and father, but he had learned nothing from them. Nobody ever mentioned Grandma again. Sometimes he thought of her, of her kindness to him, of her labored breathing when she moved slowly across a room, of the powdery smell of her when he kissed her hello and goodbye. He wondered if he would ever see her again, though, in a way, he knew he would not.

In school, Robert's behavior was so inconsistent that an observer would have difficulty in saying that he had this kind or that kind of personality. There were times when he would argue dogmatically about everything anyone said:

> *Teacher*: The story about George Washington cutting down the cherry tree is just a fairy tale. It never really happened.
>
> *Robert*: Yes, it did. I read it in a book.

Teacher: It has appeared in many books, but that doesn't make it true.

Robert: It *is* true. I know it's true.

When he participated in a game with other children, this is the sort of thing that happened:

James: Robert, you're not supposed to take two turns; only if you get on the extra-turn square.

Robert: I am so. You had two turns. I'm gonna take two turns.

James: You're ruining the game! You're not playing by the rules.

Robert: Yes, I am. I get two turns.

It was almost as if he needed to assert as true, in the face of all logic, what he really knew was not true. As if he were saying that his certainty, his safety were built on very shaky foundations.

The educational implications of this behavior were of concern to his teacher. His argumentativeness during the lesson was slowing down her presentations, and often there was not time to complete what she had planned for a particular time segment.

Also, some of the other children became annoyed and irritable during these exchanges between the teacher and Robert, and they began to create irrelevant noise, slamming books and desk tops, picking and poking at each other. Quieting them down and getting their attention again also took time from each lesson. It was sometimes difficult for the teacher to remember the point she was trying to make or to help the children wrap up the lesson by letting them generalize from the ideas and experiences she had provided for them.

Robert's behavior also had social implications. The children were beginning to pass over him in their choices of partners or group and team members, and the child who needed a feeling of safety, who needed to be reassured of his worth, was slowly being isolated from his peers.

Of more direct concern academically was the fact that he was not doing good work in the various subjects. He seemed to resist learning—how to solve arithmetic problems, the explanations of historical events. It was as if he did not want to know, did not want to understand; as if knowing and understanding would be too frightening, more than he could handle.

When he wasn't arguing, he was sitting perfectly still, so wrapped around by an almost palpable misery that the people near him were reluctant to approach him.

In customary student-file terminology, Robert was an "underachiever." He was "disruptive in class." He was "socially immature" and a "loner." He "needed psychological evaluation and, likely, treatment." How neatly this file can serve to close him off completely from any help in changing his behavior! Labelled and categorized, he takes his place with the legions of forgotten children waiting for psychological evaluation and treatment. Once such children are labelled, teachers turn to the others, the majority, who can respond satisfactorily to day-to-day teaching.

The Modification Target

A Plan for Changing Behavior

The teacher, at this point, has no way of knowing what is amiss with Robert. All she can see are the behaviors that are interfering with classroom objectives. It is not a bad idea to start with what one can clearly observe.

Simply put, the plan would be to reinforce Robert's appropriate behaviors and ignore the inappropriate until they disappeared. To be able to check and see if her plan is working, and if appropriate behaviors are indeed increasing in frequency while inappropriate behaviors decrease in frequency, the teacher should first determine the initial frequency of the target behaviors. How many times during a fifteen-minute lesson or session with peers does Robert assert himself dogmatically in the face of obvious error? Also, how many times during such a period does Robert respond more appropriately: for example, by (1) admitting his error when given additional data; (2) disagreeing, but suggesting that a more authoritative source be checked; (3) admitting little or no knowledge about the point in question and suggesting that a more authoritative source be checked.

If the teacher observes after a time that he is saying nothing at all, or speaking only rarely, then something is wrong with the process, even though the results are more comfortable for the teacher and the other children. The intent of behavior modification attempts is never to make a child compliant and submissive to social and authority pressures. If this is happening, then it would seem that reinforcing contingencies are not being provided for appropriate behavior.

Each time Robert demonstrates the more appropriate behaviors (listed above), he should be provided with some clear evidence that these are the behaviors that are acceptable in the classroom and in interaction with peers. The evidence should be in a form that is pleasing to the child; the form needs to be rewarding, or it will not strengthen the desired behaviors. For example, praise should be explicitly related to the behavior: "That's a good way to disagree with someone: to say you think you should find out more about the subject." "That's good thinking, to recognize when you've made a mistake." But rewards need not be given aloud, where everyone else can hear; they may be given quietly, when the teacher is standing or sitting close to the child. Sometimes the appropriate behavior is so obvious, that a pat on the back or a warm smile and nod are sufficient for reinforcement. Sometimes, for certain kinds of behaviors and certain children, more material rewards are more useful. Thus, during a game, candies can be given for each round that is played without disagreeing in the face of the rules.

One of the problems with this procedure is what to provide for the other children so that they do not feel neglected or otherwise unfairly treated. In a classroom it seems necessary to provide the same contingencies for the same behaviors for all the children. If this is not done, it is possible that the appropriate behaviors of the other children may be extinguished.

Of course, if the other children are being systematically educated to respond to the individual needs of their peers, then they will recognize Robert's special need for reinforcement, and they will not only accept the fact that they need no similar reinforcement, but they will, themselves, provide the satisfying contingencies that will strengthen Robert's appropriate behavior.

At the end of reasonable periods of time, like a week, two weeks, a month, two months, the teacher should check again on the frequency of the appropriate and inappropriate behaviors, and compare her figures with the figures of the initial and subsequent observations. The chances are good that Robert, getting some satisfactory results from his appropriate behaviors, will less and less respond with those behaviors that are not providing satisfaction.

Knowing the Child

While she is trying to modify some of Robert's behaviors by altering the contingencies and reinforcing appropriate behaviors, the teacher also is taking steps to learn a little bit about what Robert has been experiencing outside of school—especially at home. During recess one day, the teacher stops to talk to Robert in the schoolyard. She smiles and exchanges a casual pleasantry with him, remarks on his new shirt, and comments that his mother has good taste in choosing his clothes. "I've never met your mother, Robert. I've met some of the other children's mothers, but not yours. I'd like to meet her."

Robert says nothing.

"Would you mind if I called and introduced myself to her?"

Robert shrugs noncommittally. Miss Singer remembers her own childhood and wonders if her suggestion has caused the same nervous pang in Robert's stomach that she would have felt as a child. She puts her arm around his shoulders and smiles. "After all," she says, "we both like Robert. We ought to get to know each other."

Robert essays a half smile. Miss Singer's hand grips his shoulder and she wanders off. That evening, she calls his home and talks to his mother, not alarming her with horror stories about her child's behavior, but communicating her desire to know more about Robert so she can help him to learn more effectively. His mother is interested and concerned, and they plan to meet at Robert's home and talk.

Miss Singer learns enough about Robert to feel profoundly saddened. It is no wonder that the child is in difficulties: his world is a shaky one, and, from his point of view, near-chaotic and teetering on the edge of profound and frightening mysteries:

> *Robert's mother (Mrs. Tanoss)*:　I hope Robert isn't causing you any trouble.
>
> *Miss Singer*:　Oh, no. No trouble. He's a very bright boy and really wants to do what's right. It's just that he seems to have something on his mind that's affecting his learning.
>
> *Mrs. Tanoss*:　Something on his mind? What could that be? He has a perfectly good home, everything he needs. There's nothing special happening.
>
> *Mr. Tanoss*:　He's always been a quiet kid. He likes keeping to himself.
>
> [Is there an edge of resentment in the tone? Miss Singer wonders.]
>
> *Miss Singer*:　Yes, he's quiet. Does he worry about things?
>
> *Mrs. Tanoss*:　He has nothing to worry about. Nobody makes any demands on him.
>
> *Mr. Tanoss*:　He's just a kid. What does he know about worry?
>
> *Miss Singer*:　Maybe he doesn't understand something that's happened?
>
> [Mr. and Mrs. Tanoss look at each other.]
>
> *Mrs. Tanoss*:　We-e-ll. His grandmother died.
>
> [Miss Singer says nothing, just waits to hear more.]

Mrs. Tanoss: He didn't seem to be very much affected. He didn't say much when we told him.

Mr. Tanoss: That's right. I told him. He didn't even cry or anything.

Mrs. Tanoss: [Almost defensively.] He loved his grandmother. He never said he didn't want to go and see her.

Mr. Tanoss: She was always very nice to him. She loved him.

[Tears fill Mrs. Tanoss's eyes. She wipes them away.]

Miss Singer: Sometimes the death of someone close not only makes a child sad, but it worries him. He's never said anything?

Mrs. Tanoss: No. Not a thing. I really think he's forgotten all about her.

Miss Singer: What does he do after school? How does he spend his time?

Mrs. Tanoss: Oh, the usual things children do. He plays outside. He watches television. He does homework.

Miss Singer: Does he have something he particularly likes to do? Something he spends a lot of time doing?

Mr. Tanoss: He doesn't like baseball. He never wanted to try out for Little League.

Mrs. Tanoss: Just comic books. I never see him read them, but he always wants to buy them. He has a whole stack of them in his room.

Miss Singer: He doesn't read them?

Mrs. Tanoss: I don't think so. He just collects them. He keeps them very neatly on the shelf.

Mr. Tanoss: Sometimes he looks at the cover of a new one. But he doesn't even look inside. Just at the cover.

Miss Singer: [Smiling.] He's like a lot of collectors; they like to touch the things they collect, and arrange them in some order. That's the pleasure for them.

Mrs. Tanoss: [Smiling also.] He does keep them very neatly in his room.

Mr. Tanoss: He must have about fifty dollars worth of comic books! And he never opens one!

Mrs. Tanoss: Well, it's *his* money. He has the right to use his allowance any way he wants to!

Mr. Tanoss: *His* money! *Your* money. *I'm* the one who works his tail off to make the money in this house!

[Mrs. Tanoss gives her husband a meaningful look, and he subsides.]

Anxiety and the Curriculum

Miss Singer begins to plan some additions to the curriculum to provide for Robert's needs. It occurs to her that it is wise to include those things for all the children, rather than to wait for each individual child's time of crisis. Better to help them to be prepared more adequately for the inevitable difficulties and traumas of living than to wait until they are sinking and then try to rescue them.

She must give Robert a chance to talk about his grandmother and his feelings about dying. It is clear that he has not had such a chance in his own house. His parents actually believe he has not been feeling or thinking very much about his grandmother's death!

It is likely that, in a class of thirty children, others have experienced the death of someone close. It is even more likely that they have had thoughts about dying and death, about old people, about pets who have died. It might be helpful for some of them to talk about these feelings and thoughts and perhaps realize that they are not alone with their fears and unanswered questions.

Those children who have been able to be more open in their families might be of help to the others, to children like Robert.

Miss Singer decides also to expand the unit on the family to include problems of communication and conflict between family members. The elementary school emphasis on cooperation and clearly defined (and adhered to) role behaviors is really too antiseptic and unrealistic to fulfill the educational goal of learning to deal with real problems.

Another aspect of the curriculum, she feels, should be to develop awareness of the needs of people around you, an awareness that leads to some commitment to helping others live their lives effectively. She thinks the children should realize that many people respond to others' suffering by withdrawing from them—especially if the symptoms of that suffering include unpleasant behaviors. She wants them to examine the value of caring for each other.

She reads a story about a child their own age:

THE BOY WHO WORRIED

In this city, just a few blocks from here, lives Abraham Mayer. Abraham is eight years old. He is in the third grade in public school. Every day after school he runs home. Nobody ever has to tell him to come right home after school; he just runs home to see his mother. He wants to be sure that his mother is at home, waiting for him. Of course, she is always at home, waiting for him.

When he opens the door, his heart is beating very fast and very hard. Partly it is because he has been running, but partly it is because he is so worried that this time she will not be home.

Today, as she does every day, his mother kisses him hello and asks him if he would like some milk and cookies. He smiles and nods his head. He is still too breathless to speak, even though he now feels very good.

"Why do you run so fast that you run out of breath?" his mother asks him. "Is somebody chasing you?" she teases.

Abraham shakes his head. "No," he says, "I just want to get home."

His mother smiles and hugs him. "Let's have that milk and cookies," she says. "Then you can do your homework."

When they have heard the story, the teacher may say nothing at all. Into the silence, some child will inevitably bring his own feeling or thought. But, if the teacher prefers not to let the silence extend, if that is too uncomfortable for her, she may start the discussion with a question. Gradually, she may lead the talk from the specific details in the story to the experiences and concerns of the children themselves. She does this by starting with questions concerning literal comprehension, goes on to questions that require inferential comprehension, and, finally, asks questions about the relationship of the children's own experiences to the experiences of the characters in the story.

Here are some questions that might be asked as the discussion progresses:

- What is the name of the boy in the story?

- How old is he?

- Why does he run home from school?

- How often has the house been empty when he has come home?

- What do you think he is worried about?

- Why do you think he doesn't tell his mother what is worrying him?

- Has something like this ever worried you?

- Whom did you talk to about it?

- How do you feel about it now?

- Is there anything we can do to help you feel better?

- Do you have any other worries you would like to talk about?

At another time, you can help children examine how they feel about helping others and receiving help from others. A list of statements like the following gives them an opportunity to make choices or to recognize that they have already made a choice about the value of helping. They can share their choices with each other and in the process develop reasonable expectations of each other in their everyday interactions.

1. You shouldn't help people too much. You ought to mind your own business.

2. Helping people just gets you in trouble.

3. You ought to help only people who are your friends.

4. You ought to help people only when they ask you for help.

5. You ought to help anybody who needs help.

6. You ought to ask people if they want help when you think they are in trouble.

7. You ought to help people even if they say they don't want help.

From a discussion of these statements, children might come to realize that sometimes people want help but cannot ask for it, that some people do not want others to help them, that some people are afraid to help others, and that some people insist on helping everyone. Knowledge of these basic differences in values helps the children understand each other better, and lets them know what they can reasonably expect from each other. Sharing this information about themselves may reassure some children that helping is not intrinsically dangerous, or convince others that it is worth the risk because it improves the quality of living.

Problem 4
A MATTER OF SKILL AND KNOWLEDGE

Jimmie, Earl, and Ralph have long ago concluded that there is no sense to what goes on in school, so they are running around the room trying to impress this insight on the others by pounding a back, punching an arm, colliding at maximum velocity every time they pass another body.

Alvin patiently stands at the pencil sharpener honing a pencil down to the nub. He stolidly ignores the pushing and shouting of Tyrone and Rosa 1 who also want to sharpen pencils. He will give way soon, however, when Sylvie, who stands a head and a half above everyone else in the room, approaches quietly and zonks him halfway to the windows with one blow to the small of the back. (Sharpening pencils is an understandable, goal-oriented task that produces observable results.)

Angel keeps shouting that he wants the hall pass, but nobody listens. His voice gets louder and louder as the din around him increases. How else to communicate the sense of panic that threatens to engulf him?

In different parts of the room, Mia, Janet, Rosa 2, and Arthur sit at their desks in a crazily travestied scene of good students in an orderly class: Mia struggles to write her name, but she does not have the letters to do so. Janet reads from a basal reader—at the top of her lungs. Rosa 2 carefully tears along the perforations of the pages in her math workbook; she will soon have 82 loose pages and an empty cover. Arthur writes busily in what appears to be a healthy beginning to a thousand-page journal; he does not seem to be bothered by the noise and activity around him, except for a regular concession to his environment in the form of a crayon tossed into any altercation that erupts too close to him. (His supply of crayons seems inexhaustible.)

Myrna, Lara, and Mariette are talking in the corner of the room diagonally across from the teacher's desk. For the moment, no one is bothering them.

At her desk, the teacher is in intense communication with Joan, Lauretta, Michelle, Benta, and Willie (who is a girl); they seem to be trying to explain to her what Miss Smith in the fourth grade always did to get everyone into some kind of order. What is beginning to annoy this teacher is that the children cannot be persuaded to end this discussion and go to their seats.

Ira and Bertram are lying on the floor between rows five and six, punching and kicking each other, grunting with the effort to get the first stranglehold. Bernard, George, John, Wade, Gordy, Allen, Meta (who is a boy), and Judy are enthusiastically and loudly urging them on, and occasionally getting in a kick of their own. Patrick is on his way out the door; he has almost made his decision to go home. Dennis is mindlessly banging a metal water-color pan on his desk.

This is the first day of school this year; or the fifty-third day; or the sixtieth day; or the last day.

"All right!" shouts the teacher. "Sit down and pay attention!" No appreciable abatement of the chaos.

"Settle down at once and clear off your desks!" She shouts even more loudly.

Joan, Lauretta, Michelle, Benta, and Willie breathe deep sighs of frustration, but, because they are within arm's length of the teacher and can hear better than they want to what she is shouting, they move back to their seats and prepare to suffer what comes in silence. Janet stops reading from the basal. Patrick stops at the door, visibly debating the pros and cons of giving this whole thing another chance.

"It's time for math," shouts the teacher. "We'll review sets. Ira, Bertram! You failed the quiz in sets! Do you want to spend another year in the sixth grade?!"

Ira and Bertram keep up the good fight, but the cheering squad trickle back to their seats. A groan or two is heard: "Sets!"

Dennis stops banging on the pan. Sets? It sounds vaguely familiar to him.

The teacher half turns to write a problem on the board. She does so fearfully: a full turn may lose her those children who are seated at their desks.

"Lauretta, will you come up here and show everyone how to do this?"

Lauretta approaches the board eagerly and solves the problem quickly.

"Can I do one now?" calls out Michelle.

"No, me! Me!" shouts Joan.

"Get out your math workbooks!" shouts the teacher.

"Aw-w-w," complain Benta and Willie. "Why can't we write on the board? It's not fair!"

"Not fair," yells Angel. He still needs to go to the toilet.

"Dennis, where's your workbook?" asks the teacher.

"In my desk."

"Well, get it out! What are you waiting for?"

"I don't know how to do sets!"

"Get out that workbook, Dennis, and stop arguing! You'll never learn if you don't pay attention!"

Dennis slaps a workbook out onto his desk. He slaps it three or four more times for good measure.

The teacher glares at the top of his head.

"Myrna, Lara, and Mariette, are you talking about sets?"

They look up, startled, and then begin to giggle. Multiplication might be closer to their concerns.

"Open your workbooks to page sixty-five and begin the examples."

"How many do we have to do?" yells Gordy.

"All of them!"

"Aw-w-w," from all around the room.

"What do we have to do?" from Meta.

"Be quiet!" shouts the teacher.

"I don't know how to do it!" from George.

"Be quiet!" shouts the teacher.

"I never learned sets," Judy says plaintively.

"Sure you did, stupid! We learned it last week," answers Bernard helpfully.

"Do you know sets?" she challenges him.

"Sure I do!"

"Then show me!"

"Do your own work!" shouts the teacher. "I'll fail anyone who copies!"

Joan, Lauretta, Michelle, Benta, and Willie know how to work with sets. They sit in an enclave of diligence doing example after example in their workbooks. All those answers, row on row; observable results of effort expended.

The teacher decides to tackle Ira and Bertram. She jerks one up by the arm and marches him to his seat. He sits with his head in his hands, as his red, perspiring face slowly fades to normal. The other one lies on the floor, resting from his exertions.

"Get up this instant and get out your workbook!"

He drags himself to his feet, plops himself down at his desk and begins to rummage through papers and books.

"Your math workbook! Your math workbook!" the teacher yells at him.

He gives her a slow, long-suffering look and comes up with his workbook.

"Open to page sixty-five," she mutters and begins to flip the pages impatiently. "Do these examples. Quickly!"

He stares at the examples and twiddles a pencil at his ear. The teacher flounces away to the next target.

"There will be a test on Friday. Fifty examples."

The groans are loud and long.

"Anyone who fails that test will have to bring his mother in for a conference."

Louder and longer groans.

"How do you do it?" Ira asks Bertram. Bertram shrugs. The fiery combatants are partners in confusion.

"Stop talking!" shouts the teacher.

"*He* was talking to *me*." whines Ira. Bertram punches his arm, and they are all at once again in the aisle between rows five and six. Bernard, George, John, and Wade laugh and cheer. Dennis starts banging the paint pan again.

The bell rings to end it—temporarily.

The Modification Target

Business as Usual

The problem with most professional advice in classroom management is that the advisor seems to start with the premise that the twenty-five or thirty children in the room are in a tabula rasa state. The assumption is that they are ready and waiting for the first steps in getting started with the business of learning. Ignored is the probable fact that these children come to this point in time with a background of ego-damaging school experiences: they have been subjected to physical pain, mind-boggling confusion, academic failure, social rejection, and boredom. They are not sitting there quietly waiting to be fitted with the pedagogical strategies and subject matter methods that fill the professional literature. Nor do they tamely respond to the teacher's knowledge of mental health principles or cause-and-effect psychology. They are busily responding to all the things that have been happening to them—in and out of school—for the whole of their small lives.

Merely to continue in the prescribed ways with the established curriculum is useless. Children who have succeeded in school, who are comfortable at home, who have some sense of direction, may easily respond to the teaching of long division, though it interests them not at all. If it is incomprehensible at all but the most elementary level, at least they are able—after cursory introduction—to find answers to simple problems. For these children, the teacher's "I covered sets," is virtually synonymous with, "They know how to do sets."

Academic Achievement and Self-management

For the others—the unsuccessful, the frustrated, the angry, the confused—the teacher's assumption of professional accountability is not fulfilled by her plaintive, "But I covered sets." Nor is it useful to point to the confusion in the room as an explanation of why "these children" will not learn. Though the confusion and the lack of academic learning are interrelated, I would put the weight for cause of chaos on the lack of learning. *In the classroom, motivation and skill in self-management are a function of academic achievement.*

In this classroom, the teacher is teaching what most of the children are unable to learn—probably because they do not have the skills and knowledge required to learn the new process. The most exciting presentation cannot motivate them to become involved with a concept and process that they are nowhere near intellectually. The most earnest attempt to demonstrate the relevance of sets for their lives will—if it does anything—only increase their anxiety at their ignorance. It will not help them learn what they are not cognitively prepared to learn.

Jimmie, Earl, and Ralph cannot add numbers at a second-grade level. Alvin seems forever to be searching for something that makes sense to him. Sharpening pencils makes sense. Carefully tying and retying his shoelaces makes sense. Making his desk neat makes sense: his desk is very neat. No one dares try to teach Sylvie: she looks capable of beating up any teacher who hassles her. Angel's language is Spanish: no one has tried to teach him arithmetic in Spanish.

Joan, Lauretta, Michelle, Benta, and Willie learn quickly—too quickly for the teacher. They are in charge of their own management in the classroom. They thrive on their feelings of superiority to Rosa 1 and Rosa 2, to Janet and Earl, to Bernard and Mia and the teacher.

The modification target in this management problem is the level of skill required for the children to achieve academically. The curriculum—both the content and method of presentation—is too difficult for the ones who are contributing most to the disorder in the classroom.

A Plan for Increasing Skill and Knowledge

Step 1. The teacher must relinquish the time-honored method of standing at the chalkboard and "teaching" the whole class. The children who do not understand what she is talking about will probably begin to talk to other children because they are bored; make irrelevant noises because they feel frustrated; begin to leave their seats and move about because they feel cramped and/or edgy with all that immobility to no purpose that is apparent to them.

Step 2. Put Jimmie, Earl, and Ralph to playing cards. Put Joan, Lauretta, and Arthur in with them to help them keep score. Casino is a good game for learning how to add simple numbers—

that is what Jimmie, Earl, and Ralph need. Joan, Loretta, and Arthur may learn something about the satisfaction of giving something of themselves to others. They may all learn that the sexes can work together productively. This group will need intermittent supervision so that they may observe the teacher's kind and patient teaching behavior; so that the teacher may make sure that those who can are not doing all the adding without demonstrating the process, and to exclaim enthusiastically at every instance of success—from taking the time to help someone, to protecting someone from attack, to giving evidence of learning, to playing harmoniously. Every such reward will make the children feel good about themselves: the low achievers will be encouraged to believe they can learn; the high achievers will be encouraged to believe in the intrinsic value of low achievers; and Arthur will be encouraged to see some sense outside of his frantic isolation.

Step 3. Alvin, Wade, Janet, and Mia can be given a box of tinsel by the yard and Christmas ornaments and told that they may string the tinsel around the room and hang the ornaments every three feet, to make the room look pretty. First, however, before they begin to decorate, they must determine if they have enough tinsel and decoration for the total space available. They must measure the wall space, and compute how many ornaments are needed. This gives Alvin a purpose and a recognizable goal; it gives Janet a chance to move about, so she may not need to yell every time she opens her mouth; Wade knows some arithmetic and he may be able to help the others with their computations; Mia will get a chance to write numbers, which she can do, and some letters, with help (words like feet and inch may be learned relatively painlessly in the course of this project). Here, again, the teacher will need to keep an eye on the proceedings, to see that each child is getting what he needs, and also to see that these children are not interfered with by others as they move around the perimeter of the room.

Step 4. Sylvie might be put in charge of the supply store, and "sell" the materials the other children need to do their jobs. A certain amount of "money" may be given to each one to begin with, and perhaps more money earned for appropriate behavior and completion of tasks.

Rosas 1 and 2 and Mariette might be part of Sylvie's team, planning how to store and arrange supplies, keep track of depletion, write orders for out-of-stock items, and even "go on the road" to suggest the use of items that are not moving. Heavy corrugated board could be obtained by the teacher, and, with Angel's help, a "store" could be built in one corner of the room. (Angel is good at building. With her little Spanish, the teacher has understood parts of a story he keeps trying to tell about the birdhouse he built and put on his windowsill at home.)

Step 5. The teacher will, for a while, work very closely with Keith, Bernard, George, Judy, and Meta. She has not been able to identify an area of interest or any particular skills that they have. Maybe, if the others are working more or less on their own, she can at least bring these children along on some of their basic skills.

Step 6. Gordy, she knows, can go ahead very quickly. Much of his trouble lies in the fact that he is so far ahead of the others in his knowledge of math and physics that even she cannot help him. She can provide materials for him, and a chance to speak to a college professor at the university nearby—sometimes on the telephone, sometimes in person. Occasionally, she will pull him away from his math and science to explain a process to the group she is working with or to help them read a story.

Little by little, the teacher adjusts the plan, as adjustments are needed. Children change groups. They change activities. They begin to plan—with the teacher—for the use of large blocks of time, so they can change groups and activities without waiting to be directed. Generally, they begin to feel good about themselves and what they are doing in the classroom. The teacher provides a mechanism for keeping track of each child's progress in the development of different knowledges and skills, and an aura of success permeates the group.

One day, Rosa 2 and Mariette are annoyed that Rosa 1 is "fooling around" and not taking her job in the "store" seriously. They suggest to her that she join another group and do something that she is more interested in. She refuses to move. And she continues to (1) give out supplies without collecting "money," (2) force supplies on people who don't want them, and (3) call Sylvie names when she remonstrates with her. (Amazingly, Sylvie does not resort to violence in retaliation. She leaves her loyal defense to Rosa 2 and Mariette.)

They bring their problem to the teacher, who suggests that perhaps they ought to have a system for dealing with problems like this. The store people, including Rosa 1, decide to have a meeting of the whole class to decide how such differences of opinion should be settled. This is the beginning of class meetings, rule making, and other governance decisions.

The class is well on the way to effective self-management—this class of fighters, loiterers, and diddlers. The growing number of success experiences has encouraged and provided opportunity for the practice of management skills. And growing skill in management has encouraged and promoted success experiences. These children will "cover the curriculum" eventually, with an increasing appreciation for their own ability and worth.

chapter 6

Long-term
Solutions

SELF-CONCEPT INTERVENTION

Manipulating the school setting so that the child gets from it positive reflections of himself and his worth is probably the most important teacher function in the education of the child. Even if the teacher believes that the only legitimate learning objectives of the school are cognitive ones, positive, realistic self-concepts undoubtedly contribute to academic achievement. Though it is clear from the available research that pupil self-concept development is influenced by the classroom teacher, it seems to me that we must go beyond the study of teacher effects on pupils and begin to focus on peer effects on self-concept development. The reason for this conclusion lies in some facts about our human nature.

The Teacher as a Person

Inevitably, teachers come to the profession with a variety of perceptions about themselves, their professional roles, pupils, and relationships with pupils. Not all of these perceptions contribute to effective teaching. However, taken together they represent a philosophy of life, and it is likely that many of us would be reluctant to substantially change our approach to life, even though we recognize the limiting effect of a particular facet of it on the development of the pupils. The professional books and the research studies notwithstanding, the reality is that we do not change easily, even if some of us change at all. So we are faced with an intellectual commitment to behave in certain ways, a commitment based on what we know about teaching and learning. At the same time we are confronted with our knowledge of what we are and what we were long before we became teachers. Not infrequently, the two sets of perceptions are incompatible, and we are on the horns of a dilemma.

Perhaps the answer to the dilemma lies in (1) recognizing the probable effects of our individual values, perceptions, and behaviors on pupils; and (2) developing teaching strategies that minimize these effects.

Traditionally, the child has been encouraged to look to the teacher for recognition, praise, and acceptance, as someone to depend on, as someone to be controlled by. And teachers have either provided recognition or ignored pupils; praised or criticized them; accepted or rejected them. Depending on their perception of their own roles and of the role of the pupil, they have compelled their pupils to be dependent on them; submissive to them; or they have taught them to be free, independent, self-actualizing individuals. In the process of being "educated," the person inevitably recalls this or that teacher who was good for him or who interfered with his development.

Years of professional education, reams of pedagogical literature, endless controversy in the popular media have not really changed the fact that teachers—like other people—differ in their values, perceptions, and behaviors, some of us in spite of our terrible struggles to reach some kind of ideal professional self.

A Rational Solution to a Professional Dilemma

Perhaps we are on the wrong track in trying to do with ourselves what other human beings are not called on to do—

instantly make ourselves over into some ideal image (depending on whose ideal is ascendant at the moment). Perhaps we ought to start over again and look at what is possible for us as well as what is necessary for the optimal education of children. There are some points that, it seems to me, we have never adequately considered:

1. Children will do most of the work of their lives in conjunction with their *peers*, not their teachers or those of their teachers' generation. We know that children are very important to each other. In effect, many of the "significant others" in their lives are peers. However, when we talk about the need for recognition, acceptance, behavior models, etc., we focus mainly on the adults in the environment. It seems to me that we ought to do more educationally to help the children develop relating sensitivities and skills for purposes of intragenerational living, and release them more and more from the need to look almost exclusively to the teacher to satisfy their needs. If we can educate children to interact with each other in caring, helping ways, we may contribute significantly to the solution of many problems with which we are beset in the world: intersex exploitation, racial and ethnic discrimination, rejection of the aged, abuse of children, crime and, perhaps, even war.

2. Any individual teacher comes into a child's life and, very shortly, goes out of it. What the teacher must educate the child for is continuing his life effectively when she is no longer there to control him, to tell him what to do, to guide him (though I am not sure we always know what we mean by the word *guide*). Again, he must be freed to learn how to control himself, how to make his own decisions, how to find resources other than the teacher.

3. The possibilities for learning new things are infinitely greater for the children than they are for their teachers, if for no other reason than that the children will be living for some time after their teachers have died. The corollary of

this observation is that teachers cannot teach children everything they will need to know in their lives. Here, again, the implication is clear: children must be freed to develop knowledge and skill that will enable them to continue learning long after they are released from compulsory education. They cannot do this as long as the teacher perceives his role as disseminator of information. The most that this role achieves is the limitation of the child to the parameters of the teacher's knowledge. Given the incredibly rapid proliferation of new knowledge, such limitation must necessarily be disabling.

This is not intended as denigration of teachers. The function of disseminating information has been for millennia seen as the primary function of the teacher. Perhaps it was also a useful function in relatively static societies where a competent adult with concern for the young could act as the instrument for handing down the cultural heritage to the next generation.

But the job of the teacher today is much more complicated than that, and much more difficult. She must leave the child with a heritage of commitment to life, involvement with people, and sophistication about knowledge that will serve him and his world during his whole life. It is an awesome responsibility that cannot be fulfilled by making the child dependent on his teacher.

Perhaps these three factors will help us reconcile ourselves to the necessity of freeing the children from ourselves, so that our individual difficulties with relating to others will not affect the children's conception of themselves. Though I have avoided throughout the book the listing of dos and don'ts in classroom management and teaching, perhaps it would be helpful to pinpoint some of the categorical imperatives in the freeing of children for optimal development and living, and then go on to examine some of the specific consequences for self-concept development if these imperatives are observed.

Freeing the Child to Develop

1. Provide for discussion groups in which children express their feelings without having those feelings subjected to teacher evaluation.

2. Abolish the rule—overt or tacit—that only the teacher may initiate talking in the classroom.

3. Make a clear statement that disagreeing with the teacher—or with anyone else—is not impertinence, a discipline problem, or verboten.

4. Systematically provide time for children to make suggestions and plan for their implementation—in curriculum, teaching method, use of time, and behavior change (their own and others', including the teacher).

5. Systematically provide time for critical evaluation of all communication content (including textbooks and individual pronouncements).

6. Systematically provide time to examine consequences of behavior, develop empathy, and practice communication skills.

The child's development of a sense of his physical self depends on others' acceptance of that physical self, on recognition of him as an individual. Given our idiosyncratic preferences for physical traits, it is dangerous for the child to confine him to an environment where only one person out of thirty (the teacher) has the freedom to readily respond with acceptance to his particular physical make-up. If a child's physical appearance does not conform to the teacher's standards of beauty or acceptance, and the other children are prevented from speaking freely, then that child is in danger. The alternatives many teachers see when they have such a child are to pretend to like the child (which is too often seen through) or say nothing at all to the child (which serves no good if it is clear that the teacher says positive things to the other children). Though the teacher may decide to do something specific to get her own head together on the business of physical traits, in the meantime, she continues to live in the classroom with the child. Isn't it better to arrange the setting so that people with other attitudes, likes, dislikes, and values are freed to accept that child, than to keep him dependent on a single person who is struggling to change?

The sense of self-identity is nourished by an environment that sees the potential of the person in a variety of roles, with skills in relating to others in terms of those roles. Here, again, to impose on the child the limiting perceptions of the teacher is unfair. The teacher was reared in a culture where boys invented and girls used the inventions, where children were admonished to submit to the superior wisdom of adults, where Black people were inherently inferior to white people, where foreigners were coerced into learning English, and old people forced to retire to make way for the young. That teacher has a right to live by her beliefs and values, but does she have a corresponding right to tell the girls not to play with the trucks, to tell the children that they may not make any of their own decisions, to prevent the Black children from aspiring to the intellectual professions, to refuse to recognize the importance of a child's language, or tell him that it is the immutable way of things that people retire at age 65 or 70? Better to free children to examine all the alternatives and come to their own conclusions—and their own sense of self-identity. If we and our perceptions are accurate, the children will be free to adopt them, as we did. But if—and that is fearfully possible—we are wrong, then the children will be just as free to recognize that.

Children's conception of themselves depends on their seeing themselves as capable—capable of doing things, learning things, knowing things. If they wait only on the recognition of one significant person in their school lives, they are vulnerable. That person may be harried in his attempts to reach all the children in a class. He may be so concerned with his own search for identity and self-esteem at this point in his life that he cannot give adequate recognition to others. Or irrelevant factors in his perception may compel him to withhold recognition from some children. Even given an adult who is minimally influenced in these ways, if he is the only significant person in the room, the only one to whom the children look for positive feedback about themselves, they may begin to compete with each other for the adult's attention, and in the process permit their relationships with each other to deteriorate. If it is true—and I believe it is—that peer relationships are probably more important to the effective living of the person— then we are depriving the child of a vital part of his education. For his continuing sense of self will inevitably be damaged by competitive/destructive relationships with his peers.

BUILDING TRUST

A recent article headlined, "Our Nation's Teachers Are Taking a Beating," states: "In New York City, a teacher in the high school where *Blackboard Jungle* was filmed in 1955 has been beaten by students three times since last September. . . . in rural Missouri, a third grader twisted a teacher's thumb and tore several ligaments in her hand. . . . in Los Angeles, a group of high school girls, angry over their low marks, set a teacher's hair afire. . . . according to a study just released by the Department of Health, Education and Welfare, 6,000 junior high and high school teachers are robbed at school 'in a month's time,' and over 5,000 are physically attacked."[1]

Apparently this behavior goes on in suburban and rural, as well as city schools. What does one say about the data published in an article like this when one is preparing a book on classroom management?

It is not enough to point out that this sort of thing never happens to the vast majority of teachers in the schools. If we maintain—and I do—that the value of human beings is not measured by the number of people involved in a destructive situation, then we must say that if only one person is hurt or robbed, it is a matter of vital concern to our profession and our world.

---

[1] Marguerite Michaels, "Our Nation's Teachers Are Taking a Beating," *The Philadelphia Bulletin Parade*, February 26, 1978, pp. 6-7.

Nor can we declare out of hand that the teacher who is violated by children must be doing something wrong to those children to precipitate this kind of violence. We could say this only if the teacher were the only significant other in the child's life. We might say this if all kinds of adults besides teachers were not also being attacked by children. We might say this if children were not also perpetrating all kinds of violence against each other.

In the article, a teacher is quoted as saying: "There isn't much laughter among the staff. You go in, you come home. Success is just being able to keep the kids in their rooms. We're not talking about teaching, we're talking about survival. This school is a concentration camp, and it kills morale, professionalism, idealism—everything."

Reacting to Danger

We may not be the original causes of violent behavior by children, but that does not mean that we are justified in doing nothing about that behavior except increase the number of policemen in the schools (including adding ourselves to their number) or defend ourselves when we are attacked. If we are teachers, we must make a difference; we must effect changes in children's behavior, or we lose the right to call ourselves teachers.

Perhaps it would be useful to look more analytically at this business of battered teachers and see if we can generate some creative suggestions for resolving the problem.

There are some teachers who go to schools day after day wondering when they will be attacked, fearing to walk down a corridor alone, suffering from hypertension, headaches, and other symptoms of excessive stress. Other teachers *in the same schools* suffer from none of these symptoms. The question is, why? If the situation is really dangerous, are some teachers ignoring the danger—to their ultimate sorrow? Is it perhaps that some people can perceive danger realistically and not be bothered by it, but are able to continue functioning even while they take reasonable precautions to maintain their safety?

It seems to me that we had better start, as a profession, to make decisions about the kinds of personality traits that interfere with effective teaching. It may be that some people are reacting not so much to the existence and imminent probability of violence, but to a perception of threat that is greater than the real possibility of violence. It is possible that they are also generally afraid of cities, rural lanes, and strangers, in which case, the fact that they are afraid of schools is merely incidental. If they were not teachers, this particular aspect of their personalities would not be added to the data on violence in the schools. Maybe these people would be better off not being teachers.

Overgeneralizing Fear. If whites are afraid of Blacks, they perceive every Black person as dangerous. Is it not possible that if adults are afraid of children, they perceive every child as dangerous?

It seems absurd to suggest that adults can be afraid of children, especially when they have chosen to spend the rest of their working lives in the company of children. But let us look at the process that, too often, propels people into teaching before they realize that they have chosen the wrong profession.

A student decides she would like to be a teacher because she "loves" children. How does she know this? Why, *everyone* loves children! Aren't we a child-centered culture, determined to do everything for our children? Anyhow, she has had delightful times with nieces, neighbor-children, small cousins. She knows she would love to spend her days working with children!

So she enrolls in a teacher education program in a college or university. The chances are good that she will have no contact with children in classrooms for three and one-half years, while she takes all the required liberal arts courses, and then all the required education courses, and still further, a sprinkling of electives in both areas. Finally, during her last semester, she is enrolled in student teaching, and begins to spend some time in the classroom actually trying to teach children.

If, to her dismay, she discovers that she has made a tragic mistake, that spending a whole day with thirty children is not at all like playing with a niece for a few minutes, it is probably too late for her to change her mind about going into teaching. In one semester she will have her degree. She cannot start all over again to learn a new profession! Look at the investment of time and money that would be lost! Her parents would kill her! So she becomes a teacher.

Suddenly aware that she is afraid of children and certain— if she can admit this, too—that she doesn't like them very much (thirty at a time!), she goes to her work as condemned rather than committed. And all her reactions and decisions arise essentially out of this basic fear and dislike. Perhaps she should not be a teacher.

Some Additions to Teacher Education. Perhaps, as alternatives to leaving the profession, we can provide support systems to help ourselves to work through our misconceptions and fears and become first-rate educators.

Many professionals in the field of medicine are afraid of death and deal badly with dying people. They do little or nothing to help themselves work through their fear and become better able to treat terminal patients. Recently, however, the nursing profession has begun to work systematically to deal with fears of dying. Why do we not take a leaf from the book of nurses and do something for ourselves—individually and professionally? With our knowledge of the learning process, we have an edge on any professional in discovering more satisfying ways of living—if we are willing to use all we know.

Dr. Alfred Bloch, a Los Angeles psychiatrist who has treated teachers, has recommended "[1] *Psychological and physical training*. None of the teachers . . . had been prepared for the violence they encountered. [2] *Crisis intervention teams*. They would consist of two or more teachers with mental health training who could immediately go to the aid of the battered[2] teachers. [3] *Three new R's*. Rotation, rest, and recuperation from the combat zones should be given the teachers at the end of a two- or three-year period."[3]

---

[2]Dr. Bloch uses the term, *battered*, to indicate psychological stress, not always physical attack.

[3]Michaels, *op. cit.*

While firmly rejecting Dr. Bloch's comparison of teaching to war, I think we can make something useful of some of his suggestions.

(a). There is no doubt that teachers need more knowledge of psychology than they now get in their professional training. Teachers are exposed to a smattering of the psychology of learning in their preservice training. Sometimes, they explore the psychological aspects of classroom management. But they rarely have opportunity to develop the kind of self-awareness that is the basis for effective human relationships or find answers to such questions as: What errors in perception are human beings subject to? How are our roles and our specific behaviors perceived by children?

It would not be amiss to have children in the groups where these questions are raised, so they, too, can develop awareness of their own and teachers' perceptions of each other. (This will probably be a very difficult idea for adults to accept. I remember once when it was suggested that children be part of a group of parents and teachers struggling to understand how to deal with drug use among the children. The adults adamantly refused to have children in the group. They preferred to find answers and then deliver those answers to the children. You can be sure that the use of drugs among children in that community did not abate.)

If we are clear about how we think, about the effect of our feelings and values on our perceptions, we can apply ourselves to solving specific problems with more success, since our assessment of problems and evaluation of solutions will probably be more realistic.

To suggest that teachers get physical training, presumably to enable them to counter violence with violence, suggests not only bad education but downright foolhardiness. (Even evenly matched boxers are never sure which one of them will win a match. To pit teacher against pupil physically is a bad bet under the most favorable circumstances.)

But, in such a physical encounter, no matter who wins, everybody loses. If the teacher is able to physically overpower the child, what has he taught the child about dealing with his own urges toward physical aggression? And if the child wins the fight, what has he learned about problem solving? All in all, the very nature of the educational setting is destroyed by this kind of approach. Teachers know it when they complain about violent children. They are complaining about more than just the violence: they are dismayed at the subversion of educational goals in a place where violence is an accepted mode of interaction.

(b). Not only a small team of teachers should get mental health training. If all teachers had such training there might be fewer crises in some of those crises-ridden classrooms. The psychological training mentioned above should be undertaken from the mental health point of view. If all teachers were prepared in this way, they could, in each school, systematically arrange to support each other in times of stress, come to each other's assistance in a crisis, and arrange for continual mental health learning as a part of their working lives. Here, too, it would be a good idea to involve children in the support, assistance, and learning, so that mental health becomes an objective for the total school population, not just for the adult school population. There may be some danger, if only the teachers are involved in the mental health activities, that a we/they dichotomy may be reinforced in the relationships between teachers and children, and the errors in perception and difficulties in communication may continue to proliferate.

The thread running through all of this activity to deal with violence where it occurs in the schools must be an educational one. Teachers and children, thrown together for hours every day, for such large parts of their lives, must learn to trust each other.

The Problem Class. When children have had a lifetime of experiences that have led to hostility and anger that they direct against teachers, there is no way that they can be dealt with effectively in groups of thirty and forty. What sense does it make to put all the "problem" children into one classroom and saddle one teacher with the job of making enormous changes in their behavior? Even a competent and experienced teacher will find the job impossible, but competent and experienced teachers stand by and watch new teachers getting this kind of a class, and everybody else breathes a sigh of relief because they have already been through this and need not be faced with it again.

Teachers as a profession must demand that children with many inappropriate behaviors should not all be put in one classroom.

Back to Basics.   A slogan-engineered movement like "back to basics" is not the answer to the problem we are faced with. In observing the movement, I wonder why people educated to know what is involved in teaching and learning can be so taken in by a slogan like this. I come to the conclusion that a large part of the reason must be the inability to deal professionally with the fearfulness concerning children's behavior.

After all, just what do we mean by "back to basics," and where did this slogan originate? Does it mean that teachers have not been teaching reading, writing, and arithmetic and that now is the time for them to get back to teaching these subjects? This, as we know, is arrant nonsense! Most teachers have always taught these basics and continue to do so, no matter what they teach.

Does "back to basics" imply that the only basics—the only things all people need to learn if they are to function productively in a democratic society—are reading, writing, and arithmetic? That is just as ridiculous an idea! We teachers are as aware as are most thinking human beings that children need to learn how to solve the problems of living that previous generations have failed to solve, they need to learn to think clearly and utilize the available data in their decision making, they need to learn how to order their lives and control their environment.

From what I have seen, the teachers in so-called back to basics programs continue to teach all the things they have always taught and that they know children need in order to live effectively. But what they often have, in addition, are the external threats that generate fears in the children. The expectation is that these fears will keep the children under control. Thus, the fears that the teachers have of losing control of the class are dealt with by making the children fearful.

The education of children in a free society must be done in freedom. Subjecting them to arbitrary authoritarianism and threat of punishment will not teach them to be caring, empathetic, creative at problem solving, free. To the extent that we make use of these means for facilitating the teaching job, to that extent do we *avoid* doing the job.

Teaching is opening doors for children—all the doors. How can they trust us enough to walk through those doors if we harry them along with sticks and threats? Establishing trust in the classroom—between teacher and pupils, and among the pupils—is a vital factor in teaching and learning. One chink in the infallibility of the supreme authority and all trust evaporates. Does anyone know a principal or system whose armor is inviolate?

Withholding Information

Honesty and candor are the key values that undergird educational strategies and curriculum content in any classroom where the development of trust is desired. Knowledge that is sifted through the teachers' fears of raising certain topics, their anxieties about parents, and judgments about what children should and should not know, does not suffice for most children. Sooner or later they learn what they want to know, and when they discover that they have been closed off from what is real, they conclude that teachers and school are not to be trusted.

Again and again teachers ask me how they can teach things to children when their parents are insisting that they be shielded from those learnings. "Shall I tell my third grader about death, when I know her mother doesn't want the subject mentioned in her presence?"

My answer must be unequivocal: (1) You don't tell the third grader what she should believe about death. (2) You start by giving her a chance to express her feelings, her ideas. If, at this point, you give her the usual bromides about sleeping and traveling, you will close her off from honest communication; she knows very well that grief and mourning are not appropriate accompaniments of sleep. What you are teaching her, with this kind of content, is not to trust you. (3) Then you help her to find out all she wants to know about death; you trust her enough to let her know what she wants to know.

Manipulation in Teaching

Teaching strategies, too, reflect a level of trust in the relationships between teachers and pupils. Children should be privy to the processes used to encourage their learning, otherwise those processes become manipulative. Again, sooner or later the children realize what is happening to them, and whatever trust was possible is lost.

For example, if you want to work with a group of children, all of whom are having problems with initial consonants, you may divide the whole class into groups and arrange to have the children with the problem all in the same group.

When this is done, you may ignore the protests at removing children from their friends and neighbors and just go about ordering the new arrangement. This creates unresolved animosity that may be acted out in other, unexpected ways and causes difficulties in the classroom. An element of trust is also involved here, because children may feel that their comfortable relationships are at the mercy of an arbitrary authority, and they can never know when their familiar world will be disrupted. One cannot feel trust for such an authority.

You may say to the children that you are dividing them into these groups in order to work on different projects, and each group will have a bird's name, to make it more interesting. Sooner or later, however, they will discover which is the target group, and, bluebirds notwithstanding, the "dumb" group will become victim and target.

Or you may say honestly that you are dividing them into groups for various reasons. Some groups will have a chance to work with people they don't know very well. Perhaps, in the process, they will discover that long-term friendships are not always the most useful basis for selecting co-workers. Another group, you say, needs help in reading. A third has individuals in it who have expressed a desire to go ahead of the rest in math.

They may not like being separated from their friends or identified as needing special help, but they will respect your candor and proceed to apply themselves to getting their satisfactions out of the situation. At any rate, there will be no danger of being "found out" and exposed as just another adult who, while preaching that honesty is the best policy, tells pupils something less than the truth.

FATE-CONTROL DEVELOPMENT

The Motivation for Change

Sally Kirshbaum has been teaching for three years. She is generally viewed in the school as a competent, though young and still naive, teacher. Though she tentatively talks to the older teachers in the school about small-group organization in the classroom, team teaching, and individualized instruction, she has followed the pattern in the school and has taught pretty much in the traditional ways. She plans carefully for each lesson and teaches it to the whole class. She permits questions, but mostly she asks the questions. She insists that the room be quiet and orderly, and that children speak only when they are given permission to do so.

This year, Sally received life tenure in the city school system, which means that—barring some horrendous behavior on her part—she is assured of a position until she is ready to retire. Though she feels grateful to the principal and other supervisors for appreciating her ability and has a pervasive feeling of safety now that she doesn't have to worry about being replaced, all her professional promises to herself are crowding in to haunt her. She remembers her determination to help children feel free and independent. She remembers her fascination with interest centers, where children explored the areas they were already interested in and learned to ask questions that would carry them even further in their explorations. She remembers her rejection of her cooperating teacher who tried to ignore the obvious fact that at least three of the children in her class were not learning what she was working so hard to teach. (When she could not ignore it, she found some reason to attribute it to the failure of the children and/or their parents.) As her tenure year went by, Sally began to feel more and more guilty about the way she was working.

Tentatively, she began to talk about her feelings to her family and close friends, some of whom taught at other schools in the area. Most of them argued on the side of "prudence": Why change your way of working now? You've been so successful, everyone thinks you're doing a good job. Why do it differently and risk failing? Everybody in the school conducts classes in pretty much the same way. If you start changing, you will inevitably call into question the validity of the other teachers' practices. This can only cause hard feelings. You have such a good relationship with the rest of the staff. Why spoil it? It will only make coming to work uncomfortable and maybe even unpleasant.

The experienced teachers in her circle called out the armament of educational psychology: Children are disturbed by change. All the children in the school are accustomed to working in the traditional way. They know what is expected of them and they function in school in an orderly manner. To change the procedures, to establish new expectations, would just confuse and upset them and interfere with the generally good progress they are making. What is to be gained—from the purely pedagogical view—from changing?

The scientists among them were clear and precise in their summing up of the educational knowledge: There was no hard evidence that group work and open education made any difference in the academic achievement of children. As a matter of fact, there were some data that actually indicated that children did not do as well in these settings—hence the appeal of the very strong back to basics movement. Growing evidence indicated that children learned more effectively in the traditional, no-nonsense setting.

The pragmatists among them dusted off the old "experience is the best teacher" argument. It was clear that those who had been teaching for ten and fifteen years—and had survived—knew what they were doing. And they were *not* opting for radical changes in their way of teaching. Who ought to know better what worked than those who had been on the firing line year after year?

Sally had been an interested student of education. She, too, had studied the data on the effectiveness of various teaching strategies and had learned about the practical realities in a school where much learning was going on—almost all of it incidental and of the wrong kind. She knew the risks of messing with the status quo and she was scared. But she made her decision on the basis of the commitment she had made in her senior year. Her teaching would not be a repetition of the way she had been taught as a child.

School had not been horrible for her. After all, her experiences had been, by and large, success experiences. One would have thought that this would have made her school years a happy time, a satisfying time. But her prevailing memory was one of repeated disappointments. At the beginning of each year she had set out to school filled with excited anticipation. The last few days of the summer vacation were always agonizingly slow in passing.

Days before the first day of school, she had bought the latest thing in new notebooks, sharpened her pencils, tested her pens. The excitement of anticipation was almost too much to bear, and the Sunday night before opening day she actually could not sleep.

But after spending that first day in school, she always recalled again the experience of every new semester—the dreadful disappointment of that first day, before she settled down to the unutterable boredom of the endless days stretching before her until the winter or summer vacation. She remembered the hours of lessons about things she already knew, the additional lessons about things she couldn't care less about, the enforced silence, the cramping muscles that were forbidden to move, the wordless agony of watching that same boy (every term it was another same boy) being harassed and even physically hurt by the irate teacher—hurt for transgressions she could no longer recall.

Her grades were always very good, her acceptance by her teachers was unqualified, she was praised often and sincerely for her industry, her neatness, her handwriting, her verbal skills. She took her report cards home with pride at the end of each month, and returned them, duly signed by an approving parent, on the day they were due back. She did not hate school, but the commitment to it was not her own. Adult others had committed her to it and never questioned that her own feelings about the experience matched theirs. To this day, her mother fondly reminisced, "Sally always loved school. I knew that some day she would be a teacher. Why, even before she ever started kindergarten, her favorite game was playing school."

Sally remembered and made a new commitment.

It wasn't that her children weren't learning—they were. And they seemed satisfied enough with what was happening to them. But there was no excitement in it—for them or for her. The curiosity that she saw in three- and four-year-olds was just a faint flicker in only a few of the children. The joy of asking and making and doing was missing. And, for her, the ultimate evidence of her broken promise—the children were too dependent on her. They sat passively until she gave them the nod to do something. They waited for her to say what the "truth" was about almost everything. They looked to her to settle every argument, every confrontation among them. She simply did not want all this authority; she believed that no one should be the ultimate authority in any other person's life. Though it might be expedient for classroom teachers to manage their children in such ways that they achieved divine order and unquestioning obedience, children grew older and left the benign authority of their teachers; it was dangerous to let them go believing that all people in authority were to be obeyed and all demands for order were justified. She wanted none of the blame for contributing to a twenty-first century "New Order."

She did make one concession to the pressures on her from all sides. Whatever changes she made in her teaching strategies, her classroom organization, and the amount of freedom she afforded her pupils would be made as quietly and unobtrusively as possible. She hoped nobody outside her classroom would notice what was happening until she could point to results that could allay most of the fears and doubts of the people around her.

Day One. The first thing Sally felt she needed to know was how the children really felt about what was happening to them in school. The next morning, after they had settled down in their seats and were waiting expectantly for her directions, she asked them the question, "How do you feel about school?"

Right on cue, smiles appeared on most of the morning-clean faces, and hands went up on all sides.

"We love it, Miss Kirshbaum," said Minaruth.

"It's great," said Johnny.

"It's all right," said Peter.

"My mother says I'm doing fine," said George.

"You're our best teacher, Miss Kirshbaum," said Tressa.

Sally smiled because the children obviously expected her approval of these responses, but what she felt was a momentary dismay. What prissy little teacher's pets, she thought. They didn't have an honest feeling among them.

And then she recoiled in horror from her own unfairness. The distaste she felt should more properly be directed against herself. The children were just giving her the answers they believed she wanted to hear. And who had made them so subservient, so eager to please that they denied their own feelings? Nobody, she stormed silently, could be so perfectly satisfied with his life!

"All right," she said to the children. "I notice that some of you didn't raise your hands, and others haven't had a chance to answer. Maybe we can make it a little easier for everyone to say what he really feels.

"Listen to my directions, and when I say go you will all follow those directions. The first row will take your chairs and sit down in a circle in that corner opposite near the window. The third row will take your chairs and sit down in a circle in this corner near where I am standing. The fourth row will take your chairs and sit down in a circle under the pumpkin. The fifth row will wait until all the others are seated in their circles, and then I will tell you what to do."

Some of the children started to get up and leave their chairs.

"Wait," she called to them. "Sit down and wait until I say go."

There was a sprinkling of self-conscious laughter as they settled down again in their rows.

"Now, will someone in the first row tell me where you are to form your circle of chairs?"

All the hands went up, and Thomas answered correctly. One by one she verified their understanding of the directions.

"All right. Go."

In a reasonably orderly fashion they walked to the free spaces of the room and arranged themselves. The two boys who enthusiastically swung their chairs over their heads as they walked were signaled to swing them back down again with a raised eyebrow and a meaningful look.

(Silently she thanked her stars that they *were* so obedient. There would have been chaos in any other classroom if the teacher had tried to get 35 children into small groups for their first experience in small-group arrangement.)

Very quickly she moved the desks in the second and third rows apart, leaving a cleared space in the center of the room.

"The fifth row will now take chairs and arrange them in a circle in this space, and sit down."

They did as they were told. She noticed that the children in the other groups were already buzzing to each other. This was a new experience for them, and they were probably wondering aloud what was going to happen.

"Listen, now. This is what I'd like you to do. Talk to each other for ten minutes (she pointed to the clock on the wall) and tell each other how you feel about all the things about school—subjects and teachers, homework, talking, and punishing—everything. I won't listen; you say anything you feel. You can start now."

She then turned and stepped outside the room and closed the door behind her. What she could hear was a profound silence.

Slowly the silence gave place to the sound of voices that rose and rose until there was a roar of shouting that sounded as if all thirty-five children were talking at once. She looked up and down the corridor with some discomfort, wondering when the other teachers would start coming out to complain. But she calmed herself with the thought that, by the time they bestirred themselves to open their doors and she stalled them a few minutes with vague explanations and reassurances, the ten minutes allotted for the discussion would be up and she could go back inside.

She must also make a note, she thought, to make the children aware of the problem of noise in a thin-walled building, and help them develop some skills for keeping the sound at reasonable levels. (Such awareness and skill would also be useful outside of school, in their thin-walled apartments and row houses. I'll bet they never dealt with that when they were studying the second-grade unit on community helpers!)

Amazingly, no one came out to investigate the sudden rise in sound volume, and at the end of ten minutes she ducked back into the room, smiling. Many of the children looked up at the sound of the door opening and closing, and the noise went down enough for them to hear her:

"Your ten minutes are up." (They could not in any way construe her entrance and her words as reprimand for the noise volume. She had said at the outset that there would be only ten minutes for the discussion, and, though obviously most of them would have liked to continue—some of them were still talking busily to each other—they could accept the end of the discussion period without apprehension or too-personal resentment. Most of them had learned to cope with the frustration of always having to stop things just when they were getting interesting.)

"Will each group tell us one thing you talked about?" she asked the children as they still sat in the small groups.

Group one all began to talk at once. She said nothing, just waited, and they finally sorted themselves out. "You tell, Janie," they directed. And Janie did.

"Why do we have to come here every day? Can't we learn things other places? Even my father says it's a drag coming to the same place every day."

There was some self-conscious laughter around the room.

"It's not that we don't like school, Miss Kirshbaum," broke in Jack. "But everybody needs a change," he said ponderously. She could just hear his pot-bellied father intoning this at the breakfast table.

"All right. How about another group?"

The second group had already appointed its spokesperson. Thomas ticked off three points on his fingers, "Why are we always last to go to lunch? Social studies is very interesting. Grammar is boring."

"All right. Next group."

This group seemed to pick up its discussion at the point at which it had been interrupted. One girl went on with the story she had been telling, ". . . and then I had to wait the whole math period while Emma learned the times six. I knew the times six, and I just had to sit there and listen."

Emma, in another group, was hurt. "It wasn't my fault! I knew it, I just couldn't get that one answer!"

"Oh, sure. You knew it. You knew it," some of the others put her down.

Sally intervened, "Everybody needs a little more time for some things. The question is, should other people have to wait for everyone to get every answer?

"Let's hear from the other group, and then we'll talk about all these things and see what we can do about them."

In less than twenty-five minutes, Sally learned that her apparently happy youngsters had some very salient objections to what was happening to them in school. It had not taken her long to discover that, given the opportunity, these children could take a hand in making their lives more satisfying.

She had known from reading the educational literature that low-achieving children felt they were powerless, had little or no control over their own lives and could not change them. They often felt that they were born into a bad scene and were stuck with it. Yet here were high-achieving children who also lived with frustration and dissatisfaction. Apparently they also felt that there was no use saying anything about it because they were powerless to effect any changes.

It was probable, she thought, that these children continued to apply themselves to academic objectives because they did get some satisfaction from the successes they experienced. The others who were overwhelmed by their powerlessness were those who were even more overwhelmed by the weight of the repeated failures they experienced.

However, she wanted more for her pupils than good grades in school; she wanted them to be independent, courageous and caring people who were clear about what they valued and were not afraid to live by their values.

She told them, "Tomorrow, let's plan what we will do for the rest of the week, and make time for dealing with some of the changes you've discussed in your groups."

"Are we really going to do something about always being last?" Thomas asked.

"Let's talk about it," she answered.

"Oh, sure," Thomas muttered under his breath, but loud enough for her to hear. "That's what everybody always says."

Sally made a great effort and resisted the need to defend herself. They would learn that they *could* become involved in making changes that they themselves had identified as being needed. They would learn that "Let's talk about it" was not the same as "I have no intention of letting you get what you want, but there's no point in making a big confrontation about it right now."

Day Two. Some of the children came into the room much earlier than usual. They came in with an air half-expectant, half-skeptical, and she didn't keep them in suspense.

"These are the topics we're supposed to cover by the end of the month." She pointed to three sheets of newsprint tacked up on the wall. "While you're waiting for the rest of the people to come in, why don't you give some thought to how we can plan our days so that we cover these things, and also take up the problems you discussed yesterday."

They gathered around the newsprint, reading, talking, and gesticulating. As the others came in, they joined the group and broke up into small clusters as they discussed the topics.

At 8:45, Sally asked them to push their desks to the walls and form a single circle with their chairs. She joined them in the circle and raised the question: "How shall we divide up our days so we can cover everything we want to?"

Silence. Sally said nothing, just waited. This, she thought, is going to be one of the most difficult things for me to do—just be quiet and give the children time to take hold. This is working against the professional model; we teachers feel obliged to fill every empty space with words. Well, I *am* going to leave some silence—for thinking, for mustering courage, even for day-dreaming!

Some of the children looked at each other uncomfortably. She could almost see the question written on their faces: What does she want us to say?

Others looked at her expectantly, waiting for her to break the uncomfortable silence. Still others were not uncomfortable at all; she could tell that they were applying themselves to the question she had put before them. And one of them proved her observation accurate:

Steve: I don't mind doing math first thing every day. I like to get it out of the way.

Laura: I like math.

[Catcalls and laughter.]

Laura: I really do!

James: You can do my share.

[Laughter.]

Peter: We have math in social studies, too. All that stuff about taxes.

James: Why don't we let her do the math in every subject?

Laura: I wouldn't mind.

Rita: Well, do we agree? Math first?

[General assent.]

Rita: OK. What next?

James: Something good, after that math.

Al: How about recess?

[Laughter and some applause.]

Rita: How about some of those things we were talking about yesterday?

Grace: Which ones?

Alan: Let's take the most important one first.

Janie: What our group talked about.

Laura: Why was that the most important?

Grace: Why can't each group do its own?

James: What are we gonna do?

[Perplexed silence.]

Peter: [Tentatively.] Maybe how to change those things . . .

James: Yeh! Get what we want!

Peter: I just meant when people vote and all that stuff. And sign petitions. They're trying to change things.

Laura: And get what they want.

Keith: [Derisively.] I'd like to see you vote to do away with school!

Laura: Be serious. There are some things no one can do away with.

Keith: Why not, if it's a democracy? Why can't we do what we want?

Laura: Because we're children.

[Some derisive laughter.]

Janie: Even fathers can't do what they want.

Norton: Aren't we going to do any work today? Are we just going to sit around and talk?

Sally felt a twinge of anxiety. These children were so work oriented. She didn't want them to feel they were wasting their time with all of this.

Keith: Let's do those things right now.

They all knew what he meant: they wanted to examine the possibilities for making some changes in their lives.

Joy: What about science and English?

Janie: We can do those later. Can we have the same groups as yesterday, Miss Kirshbaum?

Sally nodded and watched them arrange themselves efficiently and begin to argue about what to do first. She was not displeased at the evidences that the children were seeing connections between subject areas, and even were identifying this activity with some of the things they had been reading about in social studies. She was even more sure than before that she was doing the right thing, helping them see that school subjects were not just isolated intellectual exercises—or even just "preparation for life" some time in the future. These children were human beings and they had a right to become involved in improving the condition of their lives.

Now she began to circulate, going from group to group and listening for a while at each one. What she was doing was gathering data: identifying educational needs. In one group she realized that the children had little idea of the processes that were useful for instituting change; she would have to see that they had access to that information. In another group, she observed the children interrupting each other, ignoring each other's suggestions, pushing a single idea of their own without concern about other people's ideas, feelings, or needs. They would need to develop some awareness of what was happening in the group, some realization that there was a connection between the way they were operating and the objectives they were to achieve. They could also use skill development sessions, to become more adept at listening, building on others' ideas, expressing their own ideas more clearly and succinctly.

In the third group she heard the children efficiently identify the changes they wanted to make. She heard them volunteer to divide the job of finding out what processes were available to them in the school, and which individuals in authority needed to be dealt with. She heard one of them say that they had all neglected to finish planning their time for the whole month and had to get back to that before the day was over. She wondered how it had happened that the most knowledgeable and sophisticated of the kids all seemed to have found their way into the same group.

In the fourth group they wondered what the other groups were planning to do and if they would all be doing the same things.

The bell rang for lunch while the group discussions were still going strong, and she had to literally push some of them out of the door, reassuring them that they could go on with what they were doing after lunch.

When they returned in the afternoon, she had written two sentences on the board for them to read: (1) There are people here who want to know what the others are doing. (2) Some of you realize that it is necessary to complete the month's time schedule for covering the work to be done.

> *Rita*: Why don't we talk in our groups for fifteen minutes, and then we can share what we've decided so far?
>
> [General agreement.]

By the end of the day, the children had (1) decided on an order of priority for the changes they wanted to work on; (2) completed their time allocation schedule for the rest of the month; and (3) spent the last half-hour of the day finishing the work they started on an interesting short story. Only Norton expressed concern about not going over the work in science he had done the night before. Sally offered to read his homework and find time to discuss it with him the next day, and he left with the frown erased from his forehead for the first time that afternoon.

Sally had other things to do when she went home that afternoon. She did not scrap her lesson plans in English, science, mathematics, and social studies, but to each she began to make additions, providing the children opportunities for taking initiatives, for decision making, for involvement in self-governance. Alternately, she worried about covering the required curriculum and rejoiced that she had children who could—with so much confidence—take the ball and run with it. She attributed this to the fact that they had had a great many success experiences all their lives and they felt confident about starting something new.

She also was well aware of the probability that their enthusiasm might flag and their confidence diminish when they faced real-life obstacles to their goals. She began to plan for experiences that would help them through those times. She would have to:

1. provide opportunities for increased involvement in those activities that afforded success and feelings of satisfaction.

2. help them to consult with people who were knowledgeable and skillful in the area of socio-political change.

3. provide opportunities for expressing their feelings and learning to deal productively with disappointments and failure.

4. help them develop analytical skills that would serve them in identifying causes of failure.

5. help them identify the skills and knowledge needed to be competent change agents.

6. help them upgrade their own change skills.

Elementary education was getting more complicated, she thought to herself. And much more exciting and interesting!

SKILL DEVELOPMENT

The class hasn't even started officially yet, and James and Thomas are already squaring off in back of the room and preparing to punch each other's heads off. From past experience, Ms. Green knows that—though the causes are probably different for them—Jenny and Richard will soon be hitting each other, too.

It is rarely that any of the other children in the class get into fights. However, there is no mistaking the fact that almost all of them are emotionally involved in any fight that breaks out. They quickly surround the fighters and—according to their differential learnings—cheer one side or the other, give vehement advice on how to survive, or express disgust at such vulgar behavior. The expressions of disgust, more often than not, betray a certain amount of delight at the disruption to the established classroom routine. Though the reports are made to the teacher, the reporters are irresistibly turned back to watching the fight as soon as the report has been acknowledged.

Ms. Green does not want fighting in her classroom. No matter what is going on at the time, the minute a fight breaks out it signals the end of the activity; all concentration immediately focuses on the fight. A considerable proportion of class time is wasted in this way, and she does not like it.

In addition, there is the matter of liability. Should a child be seriously hurt in the course of a fight, Ms. Green might be considered by the administration to be legally responsible, with all the attendant report writing and rationalization to protect herself and the school system from any possible action by parents.

Actually, the chances of the fighters being seriously hurt seem far less likely than the chances of Ms. Green being hurt. More than once she has sustained bruises on various parts of her body in her attempts to separate combatants.

Dealing with Fighting

The remedy of choice for fighting in this school is punishment. Some teachers treat it like immoral behavior and lecture endlessly on the evils of fighting. The lectures are invariably accompanied by one of the established punishments, which are clearly identified in a rank order of severity. Which degree of severity to be applied depends not so much on the intensity of the fight, its cause, or the extent of the bodily damage done, as it does on the teacher's level of frustration tolerance at that moment. (An accidental kick in the teacher's shin inevitably results in the most severe punishment.)

The Sincere Lecture. This is punctuated by solemn exhortation, "I hope you understand what I'm saying to you" and "I know I can rely on you to control yourself." Though the explicit plea is for consideration of others and the desirability of self-control, the general tone is one of "How can you do this to me, when I want only the best for you?"

The Angry Lecture. This makes it clear that civilized people do not fight, and no civilized person will stand for fighting in the classroom. Implicitly and explicitly, the message is clear: "Fighting will not be tolerated."

Ostracism. Text after text written for teachers advises that children who have been misbehaving be removed from the other children and made to sit alone in a corner of the room, or in a partly enclosed space apart from the others. The only problem is that violence is usually necessary to implement this advice, because the child who is fighting—or even engaged in some other undesired behavior—is unwilling to be isolated. Consequently, he must be wrestled apart, and it is a toss-up as to who wins the match. Ostracism is used in this school and it often ends up as a fight between the teacher and the pupil.

Proximate Removal. A fight may occasionally break out between teacher and pupil if the teacher wants to put the child out of the room. However, the children seem less reluctant to do this than to be isolated within the room. One has only to walk through the corridors of many schools to see rather contented-looking children passing a pleasant time of having been sent out.

An occasional shame-faced look is seen in response to the question: "Did the teacher put you out?" But, generally, the pupil is more relieved than repentant.

Distant Removal. Exile to the principal's office may be a fate worse than death in some schools, but in others it is only mildly disconcerting. One may see seven or eight children at any time of the day sitting, lying, and fidgeting on the bench outside the principal's office. It is with a certain feeling of relief that they finally confront the principal and listen to the impatient threats of suspension. It is interesting that in almost every school I have been in for any length of time it has become evident to me that a number of the children outside the principal's office are always the same ones. No one, however, thinks to question the effectiveness of the treatment.

Telling Mother. In school after school the rule is being handed down that the classroom teacher is not to initiate contact with parents. In some schools there is a home/school coordinator who makes this contact. In others, only the counselor may do this. In still others, the principal reserves the right to screen requests for parent contact, and then makes the contact himself if he thinks the circumstances warrant.

In Ms. Green's school, only the principal may call the parents, and he is reluctant to do this unless all the preceding methods have failed and the teacher is obviously at the point of imminent explosion.

"Telling your mother" has always reminded me of the practice of those mothers who threaten a misbehaving child with telling "your father when he gets home from work." So, a person who has not witnessed the transgression, has felt none of the discomfort of the situation, and usually is loath to give credence to the possibility that the child's behavior might have been justified, is handed the responsibility for punishing him. (Few alternatives to punishment are ever considered.)

In schools, the absurdity is increased; the teacher tells the principal and the principal tells the mother. Presumably the mother tells the father. The chances are that the behavior of the child remains the same.

Suspension. Of course, keeping the child out of school is a great relief to the harassed teacher. The only trouble is that the child will probably return one day and respond to provocation the way he did before he was suspended. Now, of course, he will be more likely to respond inappropriately because he has additional troubles caused by the suspension: he is behind in his work and he's probably angry at the injustice of it all.

Expulsion. This is not generally feasible in public schools unless the child is of legal leaving age. In parochial and other private schools it is often done. In Ms. Green's school, several children have been—for all practical purposes—expelled, even though they were not of legal leaving age and they were in a public school. They were suspended with the proviso that they would not be readmitted until their parents had come in for a conference with the principal. For one reason or another, the parents had never come in, and the children's suspensions had been extended until concern about them had been lost in the press of daily school problems.

"Execution." Some children have been written off as incorrigible and been reassigned to "disciplinary" schools. These are, in effect, prisons, except that the children go to their homes each evening. The attitude of the "teachers" in these schools is that the kids assigned to them are tough troublemakers who need a firm hand to straighten them out. Some few children actually find their way back to their original schools. Most just "die" in the disciplinary school—cutting school whenever possible, tolerating the hassle, and then dropping out at the age of sixteen.

Clearly, Ms. Green's established alternatives are many—though not really as varied as they appear to the superficial perception, since the results are so uniform. She cannot help admitting to herself that the fighting throughout the school has been a problem for years and continues to be a problem.

Social Acceptance of Fighting

Do children really grow out of fighting? Ms. Green asks herself. How, then, to account for all the adult fighting that goes on in the world, and which seems to be increasing? Wife beating, child beating, fights between neighbors, fights in bars, to say nothing of wars which seem to have no end in the world. Even professionals justify fighting as a procedure for doing their jobs, rather than rejecting fighting as a nonviable approach to any professional problem. For example, police officers see the need to fight as inevitable in dealing with citizens; vice-principals are often hired for the sole purpose of hitting children; teachers advocate corporal punishment as a necessary alternative strategy for classroom management; and parents will argue that every child needs hitting sometimes. Even some professional sports depend for their attraction—to players as well as to audiences—on systematic mayhem. Witness as an outstanding example the fighting by opposing teams during professional ice hockey games.

Professionalism and Hitting

There are times when even the most even-tempered teacher feels as if she would like to whack the living daylights out of those kids. That is all right—human beings have the right to feel this way. However, I have grave doubts that the right extends to the actual act of whacking.

While it is true that the Supreme Court has decided that teachers have a right to use physical violence on children, it should be borne in mind that the Supreme Court at one time decided that it was all right to count a Black man as three-quarters of a man, and at another time that women had no property rights. Both Black people and women have been vindicated—these decisions have been reversed. I have no doubt that children, too, will one day be similarly vindicated and come into their legal own as real people with inalienable rights over their own persons.

Though the aim of Supreme Court review is to elevate the functioning of the law above the influences of current fashions of thought and keep it consistently democratic, we know that it often falls far short of this ideal. Teachers need not blindly follow in the law's failures. Unlike the legal profession, the teaching profession has for a far longer period of time based its recommended practices on the best scientific knowledge available, and we know things about the effects of physical punishment that the Supreme Court justices apparently chose to ignore.

We know, for example, that reward works very much better than punishment in helping children learn. We know that punishment—especially the inflicting of pain—may result in dislike of the punisher and, if the punisher is a teacher, dislike of school. We know that corporal punishment may intensify a feeling of powerlessness in the child, and this can have direct negative effects on his motivation to learn. We know he may displace his feelings of powerlessness and anger onto people who are smaller and physically weaker than he, and do to them what is being done to him. We know that children who are beaten grow up to be adults who beat children, adults who often rationalize that corporal punishment is the only/best way to teach them.

I can say categorically that there is no pedagogical justification for inflicting pain. Yet I have met teachers who are so intent on continuing the practice of hitting children that they blindly persist in arguing from untenable and illogical positions:

C.E.: You have no right to hit a child. Inflicting pain is not acceptable teacher behavior.

Teacher: Sometimes, you have no choice—if you're trying to defend yourself.

C.E.: How would you describe a situation calling for self-defense?

Teacher: I've had kids threaten me with knives.

C.E.: A child attacked you with a knife?

Teacher: No, not exactly. They fooled around with it and talked about what they could do.

C.E.: That hardly constitutes self-defense.

Teacher: Well, sometimes the safety of another child is involved.

C.E.: You mean you hit a child who is threatening another child?

Teacher: What would you do if someone came at you? I'd defend myself. I have a right to defend myself.

And round and round we go.

It is curious how the inflicting of pain has come, over the millennia, to be associated with teaching and learning. Perhaps when schooling was seen primarily as a way of eluding the devil, beating children might have been rationalized as beating the devil [out of them]. However, in our compendium of pedagogical theory and practical application, our carefully developed teaching strategies, and our sophisticated instruments for curriculum development, the inflicting of pain becomes an anachronism. It does not merit any serious discussion of pros and cons. The arguments in favor of corporal punishment, like the arguments in favor of war, are based on misperceptions, if not outright lies:

1. Corporal punishment—like war—is *not* used only as a last resort.

2. Corporal punishment—like war—does *not* resolve problems; it creates additional ones.

3. Corporal punishment—like war—is *not* a deterrent to disorder; it *is* disorder and it sows the seed of further disorder.

4. Corporal punishment—like war—is nonintellectual and nonrational.

5. Corporal punishment—like war—is a confession of failure in human relations.

Fighting and Teaching

Despite clear evidence to the contrary, most adults view fighting as one of those behaviors peculiar to children. It is almost as if there is some tacit acceptance of the idea that children are born with propensities for fighting and that they will somehow—through a maturing process—cease that behavior gradually.

Among some adults, there is a belief that, given certain extreme provocations, even a mature person is justified in hitting another adult. But, usually, hitting by adults is appropriate only when the hitting is done to children.

To many adults, too, it is clear that it is *often* appropriate for children to hit other children, and they urge it on children and generally encourage it. But it is never, *never* appropriate for children to hit adults, no matter how intense the provocation.

Obviously, then, before we are to deal with the children's behavior, fighting, we must be clear in our own minds what our beliefs and feelings are about this behavior. If it is natural for children to fight, then we had better save the time and energy we spend in scolding them and otherwise punishing them for fighting. The sensible thing to do in this case is to ignore the fighting and just wait for it to go its developmental way.

If the fighting interferes with the educational objectives in the classroom—and there seems to be universal objection to fighting while class is in session—then provision should be made for fighting where it does not interfere with those objectives. A ring roped off in a corner of the room or a reasonably large closet may be provided for those who cannot put off their fighting until recess time or after school. If there is some reluctance to permit children to break each other's skin and bones, we can provide protective clothing, as we do for Little League baseball and kids' football and hockey. This will undoubtedly take some of the satisfaction out of fighting, but we must weigh the needs and effects and arrive at a balance that suits us. Many people see quite clearly that there is no point in fighting if one cannot inflict a bloody nose or a split eye.

If the nature and the intensity of the provocation are to be used as justification for fighting, then we are faced with an educational problem. Children must be taught to recognize justifiable provocations. They also need practice in resisting fighting when the provocation is neither intense enough nor of the right kind.[4]

---

[4]Just in passing, we note the prohibition against a child hitting an adult also becomes a matter of education, for, although it is clear that hitting someone obviously bigger and stronger than you is suicidal and resisting it can be quickly learned, it is not always so easy to recognize the appropriate target when you are a tall, strong, teenager and the adult is about your size or even smaller. Here it is necessary to develop in the child a certain perceptual acuity that will enable him to identify adults with the smallest possible margin for error.

(How to do this will be demonstrated below.) The investment in school time is appropriate for such teaching, since it is clearly preparation for effective living as an adult. Knowing when it is appropriate to knock down another adult may make all the difference between—for example—job promotion and job failure. Clarifying values about appropriate fighting is important also if we are to educate people for community participation. Since it is now illegal to knock someone else down except in self-defense, we must as citizens either get the law changed or clarified—depending on how we define provocation.

There are some few adults who believe that any person, no matter how old he is, who responds to provocation by hitting is demonstrating behavior that is inconsistent with the reasonable expectations people in a free society have of each other. They believe that such behavior also indicates some mental health problem because it interferes with the long-term solution of the problem being dealt with by fighting. But they believe that primarily what they are observing is a developmental problem related to a gap in the fighter's education. The problem, they feel, is that the person who responds to insult and/or interference from another with hitting probably does not know any workable alternative behaviors. He either does not have in his repertory of responses suitable behaviors that will limit and/or stop the interference; or he does not believe the possible responses he is aware of will really work for him and so he does not even try them; or his knowledge of alternate responses is so casual, that, when faced with the need to respond in a crisis, he uses the behavior that is imprinted on his system, the one he has used over and over again in the past.

The solution to the problem is obviously an educational one: provide opportunity for the fighter to identify alternative responses, try them out in safety, and, also in safety, experience the consequences of each alternative. With enough such experiences, he will have practice in responding with the alternatives of his choice, and in a crisis situation he will have at quick command one of those alternatives to fighting. The educational strategy here is neither complex nor difficult, but care must be taken not to change the process as it is presented below. Certain changes in teaching strategy—though seemingly inconsequential—result in behaviors that interfere with the resolution of the problem, and the teacher is then convinced that the strategy doesn't work for her kind of children.

A Process for Skill Development

Suppose, as the teacher, you relate as a story any one of the many situations that seem to lead inevitably to fighting among the children in your class. Keep the essential factors, but change the details so that the children who were involved do not have a strong vested interest in defending the way they responded when it actually occurred. Certainly, do not use the real names of the children who were involved.

The objective in presenting this story to the children is to help them systematically examine the consequences of and alternatives to fighting. Ultimately, the decision to fight or not to fight will be theirs and theirs alone. A rational examination of alternatives as they play out the roles of the story in different ways may help them make a rational decision.

The objective is not to tell them what decision they ought to make. Telling them what they ought to do is explicit in all the punishing going on in Ms. Green's school. But the fighters obviously continue to make their own decision.

In spite of the fact that it is clear to many teachers that telling the children not to fight does not prevent fighting with a significant number, the urge, even during role playing, is to continue this hortatory behavior. In this transcript of a role-playing lesson, *identify the points at which the teacher tells the children what they ought to do, and ought not to do.*

Ms. Green gathers the children near her and lets them settle down to listen to the story:

> Allen and Evan are in the same sixth-grade class. They don't sit near each other: Allen sits in the first row, second seat, and Evan sits in the sixth row, last seat. Today is Tuesday, and it is now 1:00 P.M. Everyone is just back from lunch and getting ready to do social studies. Evan gets up to sharpen his pencil. The sharpener is at the front of the room over to the side, just as it is in this room. As he

walks past Allen's seat, Evan pops him on the head. Allen is startled, and he lets out an "Ow!" Evan laughs and keeps walking toward the sharpener.

Allen gets out of his seat and walks after Evan, catches up to him at the sharpener, and zonks him on the head—maybe a little harder than Evan popped him.

What happens now?

[There is a long silence. At the end of about three minutes, Ms. Green asks again, "What happens now?"

James: Uh . . . Allen shouldn't get out of his seat.

Ken: Evan shouldn't of hit him.

[Silence.]

Ms. Green: What happens now?

Allen: There's a big fight.

[Some laughter.]

Ken: Yeah! That Evan punches him right in the face!

Robert: That Evan started it!

Clara: Just like James and Thomas.

Thomas: James always starts it.

Ms. Green: All right. Instead of just thinking about what happens in the story, let's act it out, so we can see what happens right in front of us. Ken, you be Evan. And Robert, you be Allen.

Clara: Let me be the teacher.

Ginny: There's no teacher in the story.

Clara: Yes, there is!

Ms. Green: I didn't read about a teacher, but it does happen in a classroom, so there probably is a teacher there. All right, Clara, you be the teacher, Mrs. Simmons.

Ginny: What about the other children in the class?

Ms. Green: Well, we can have a couple of children—not a whole class. Ginny, you be Rita, one of the children. And James, you be John, another one of the children.

Now, you five who are going to act out the story, go out into the hall for a minute while the rest of us talk a while. Try to remember that other people are working in their rooms, and you shouldn't disturb them.

[The five role players leave.]

In a few minutes, they'll come back and act out the story the way they think it ends. What are some of the things we can watch for as they do that?

Harold: Ken and Robert fight.

Ms. Green: There is no Ken or Robert. You mean Evan and Allen fight.

[Laughter.]

I'll write that down so we can remember to watch for it. What else can we watch for?

Max: Evan wins.

[Laughter.]

Merry: Allen wins.

[More laughter.]

Ms. Green: [Writes both responses.]
What else can we watch for?

Keith: Maybe they don't fight.

[Some murmurs of assent.]

Ms. Green: All right, who will watch to see if they fight?

[Some hands go up.]

Who will watch to see if Evan wins?

[Some hands go up.]

Who will watch to see if Allen wins?

[Some hands go up.]

Who will watch to see if they don't fight?

[Two children raise their hands.]

Remember, everybody, watch for your thing, and take notes, so you won't forget what you saw. We'll have a discussion about it afterward.

Also watch for anything that happens that nobody thought of.

Now I'm going to call the role players in. While they're acting, don't talk to them or say anything. Remember, it's not easy to act in front of everybody. So just watch carefully and take notes.

She calls the role players in. They mill about for a while, uncertain about what to do. One or two of them look to the teacher for directions, and one of them asks, "What do we do?" Ms. Green just nods encouragingly and motions "go ahead" with her hand. Finally, one of the children directs the others, and the scene is picked up at the pencil sharpener.

[Allen slaps Evan on the head.]

Evan: [Obviously not expecting such a hard slap.] Ow!

[He hits Allen.]

Allen: Hey! That hurts! [He squares off, prepared to fight.]

Ms. Green: [Jumping into the scene.] Don't hit hard. This is just pretending.

Evan: ⎰ I didn't really hit him.

Allen: ⎱ He didn't really hurt.

Ms. Green: You hit too hard. Just pretend.

[Ms. Green resumes her seat, and the two boys exaggerate fight motions without actually touching each other.]

Mrs. Simmons: Stop fighting! Stop fighting this instant!

[The fight goes on.]

Mrs. Simmons: [Moves closer to the fighters and tries to separate them. She is elbowed to one side.]

Ms. Green: Be careful! That's the teacher! Is that what you do to the teacher?

Mrs. Simmons: Yes! You hit the teacher! You're going to be expelled!

Evan: It was an accident! She shouldn't have butt in!

Allen: Yeah. Who told her to get so close?

Mrs. Simmons: You'll be expelled for this!

Ms. Green: Well, go on with the scene, but be careful.

[The two boys clutch each other and fall to the floor, rolling over and over. Rita and John stand on the sidelines.]

Rita: [Laughing.] They're really fighting!

John: [Also laughing.] You need any help? You need any help?

Mrs. Simmons: Stop this fighting immediately! Stop it!

Ms. Green: All right. Let's stop now and talk about what happened. First, all the role players sit down, facing the rest of the class. [Then, pointing to one at a time.] How did you feel about this?[5]

Ken: I don't know. [He shrugs his shoulders.]

Ms. Green: All right. How did *you* feel about this?

---

[5]The purpose of this is to give the role players an opportunity to absolve themselves of any guilt or relieve anxiety at the way they played their roles. I call this a safety factor. See my book, *Affective Subjects in the Classroom: Exploring Race, Sex and Drugs*, for a detailed description of the whole strategy of teaching with role playing.

Robert: I didn't really want to fight, but I couldn't help it. He just pulled me into it.

Ms. Green: All right. How did *you* feel about this?

Clara: I didn't know what to do. I couldn't stop the fight; they wouldn't listen to me.

Ms. Green: All right. How did *you* feel about this?

Ginny: I felt fine.

Ms. Green: All right. How did *you* feel about this?

James: How come Clara . . .

Ms. Green: You mean Mrs. Simmons.

James: Yeah, Mrs. Simmons. How come she didn't get Mr. Josephs? How come she didn't get him to really punish them?

Ms. Green: Well, while you were all role playing, the rest of the class was watching for certain things. Who was watching to see if they fight?

Barry: Nothing happened to them for fighting.

Sam: They'll be punished. Sooner or later they'll be punished.

Cheryl: I think Evan won the fight.

Sally: No he didn't! Allen won!

Barry: Nobody won. They'll both be punished.

David: They ought to be punished for pushing the teacher.

Robert: I didn't want to fight. He made me.

Ms. Green: Could Allen have done something to avoid a fight?

Robert: I couldn't do anything.

Sylvia: He didn't have to hit Evan just for a little pop on the head.

David: Sure! Then next time he'd pop him harder. I wouldn't take a chance. I'd hit him for popping me. I'd pop him a hundred times!

Ms. Green: Sylvia, why don't you play Allen, now. And David, you be Evan this time.

Sally: I want to be Mrs. Simmons!

Ms. Green: All right. And Jane and Barry, you be Rita and John. Start right now. The rest of us will be watching to see what happens.

Allen: Why did you hit me?

Evan: Aw, I was just kiddin. Can't you take a joke?

Allen: It wasn't so funny. It hurt.

Evan: I didn't mean to hurt you! I was just passing, and I tapped you.

Allen: Well . . . well . . . Don't do it again.

Ms. Green: That's very good! I'm proud of you!

[David makes an ugly face at Sylvia.]

All right, how did you feel about this?

Sylvia: I didn't fight.

David: You're a girl! What do you know?

Sylvia: Oh, yeah! Well, girls fight! They can fight just like boys!

David: You were just chicken! That's why there was no fight.

Harold: Why would you hit her, even if she *was* a boy? She didn't do anything to you. She just asked you why you hit her.

Ms. Green: What about the rest of you? What else did you see happening here?

Harold: There were plenty of times when I didn't fight, even though somebody started something.

David: Yeah, you're chicken too!

Thomas: Sometimes it looks like fighting, but you're just kidding. And everybody gets mad.

Sylvia: Then you better say when you're kidding.

[Murmurs of assent.]

Ms. Green: It's not a good idea to fight, even if you're only kidding. Someone can get seriously hurt.

James: You mean we're never supposed to fool around?

Ms. Green: Not in ways that someone can get hurt.

[There is sudden complete silence. The discussion is over]

Besides the examination of alternative behaviors, another objective in this kind of role playing is to provide opportunity for the children to experience the consequences of the various solutions to conflict situations. Without such experience, they really do not know the basis for making one choice or another. The adult may tell them what he has learned as a result of his own experiences, but for many children this is not sufficient to convince them that what they are strongly motivated to do has undesirable consequences for them. Go back over the role-playing transcript and *identify the points at which the teacher actually prevents the children from experiencing the consequences of their choices.*

After the role playing, the children are encouraged to compare the alternative solutions and the consequences, and share some of their personal experiences that shed additional light on their own past behaviors. They may even begin to make certain commitments to behave differently in the future. They may, during this discussion express various values, either for continuing their old behavior or changing. There is nothing to be gained when the teacher tries to impose his own values on the discussants. The chances are that they know very well what he thinks of fighting, and his values have not materially affected their beliefs—or their behavior. It would be more fruitful for the teacher to listen to the range of values and use them as a basis for further teaching.

Reread the transcript and *note the points at which the teacher tries to negate the children's values by forcefully enunciating her own values.*

This one lesson has resulted in some apparent changes or—at the very least—some children are putting into words insights and opinions that they have never before revealed:

1. Some children are admitting publicly that they will not be provoked into fighting. Presumably, those listening may learn that this is acceptable behavior, even for boys.

2. Some children are admitting publicly that they may be drawn into fights against their will. Presumably, some of those listening may now be freer to admit that there are times when they really do not want to fight—that fighting per se is not always a satisfying behavior.

3. At least one child knows how to defuse an imminent fight. Presumably those watching have learned that there is a way to do this.

4. One child playing the teacher had some taste of the feeling of powerlessness that a teacher might experience when confronted with the violence of children. Those watching may have caught some of this feeling. This may be a beginning to the development of empathy with the teacher.

5. There is evidence that some of the children recognize that there are questions about cause and effect relationships in behavior. "Why would you hit her?" Harold asks. "She didn't do anything to you." (See pp. 25 ff.)

6. It is clear that fighting is a subject the children are interested in and willing to examine seriously. It is also clear that, in the face of the traditional adult exhortation, they withdraw from such examination.

It becomes clear from the role playing and the ensuing discussion that there are a number of educational needs that should be addressed by the teacher if the behavioral objective—no fighting—is to be achieved:

1. The teacher should not participate in or interfere with the role playing. (In all the years my students and I have used role playing with children, no child ever seriously hurt himself or someone else.) Even if the teacher is moved to restrain a hand or a body, he should quickly move the potentially offending part and *say nothing.*

2. What, exactly, does "winning" mean in a fight? The children at first were geared to identify the winner of the fight. However, during the discussions, though one child identified one fighter as the winner and another identified the other fighter, the rest of the children did not pick up this point. Perhaps some examination of the concept of winning can result in more rationally based values about fighting.

3. The children—quite understandably, given their experiences—rely on recognized adult authorities to intercede, to punish, to preach. Some planning must be initiated to help them become aware of the role of the noncombatants in preventing the perpetuation of the fighting.

4. Children need to learn that punishment does not necessarily—or even usually—prevent inappropriate or undesirable behavior. Just as in conflict there are more useful alternatives to fighting, in deportment there are more useful alternatives to punishment.

5. Children may need to see that, though it is, on the surface, logical to expect that behavior involves reciprocity

(he hit me, so I hit him), very often a person's perception of what constitutes reciprocity is not based on situational logic. Thus, if someone perceives himself to be maligned or otherwise attacked, he may respond with behavior that merely seems reciprocal to him. The perceived attacker then may see himself as unfairly attacked, since he did not intend his original approach to be hostile. In this way, individual perceptions may escalate violence in a situation where no one really wants violence.

LIVING COMFORTABLY WITH CHANGE

What is involved in educating a generation of children to live productively with the rapid changes that have occurred and will continue to occur in their lifetime? One may say that is not a realistic concern. It is obvious that today's children take change for granted. Look at how blasé they are about television, while we adults still marvel at the magic of movies in the home with a flick of the switch. Listen to the way they talk about moon shots and Mars probes! And their interest in science fiction is almost an expectation of shortly having in reality what now involves their fantasy. What is there to teach them about accepting change?

The thing that strikes me most forcibly is that our children do not *accept* change, they do not *understand* change, they merely absorb it and are absorbed by it. Unquestioningly they live by the changes that occur all around them, and they are as moved by them as if those changes were merely natural phenomena, like the changing seasons.

There is grave danger in this apparent mindlessness in the face of great technological change. There is danger in such casual absorption of change. It leads to relinquishing by default control of the effects of such change. Thus, for example, radio and television become the private concern of a few people who make enormous amounts of money out of the public airwaves. In addition, through advertising and control of newscasting, they manipulate us in a variety of subtle and not-so-subtle ways to respond to their own ends and advantage. The monster is appallingly frightening, but very few people seem to be afraid. Certainly, there is very little systematic involvement in the critical examination of the effects of radio and television programming.

Children's Response to Change

Is there some connection between the response of the young to technological change and their response to great changes that occur in their personal lives? There certainly seem to be some similarities between responses in both areas of change:

> 1. They do not talk much about these changes *as* changes. Rather, they respond to each change by altering their behavior in some way, but they do so without awareness of what is happening to them, without questioning the nature or the constructiveness of the accommodation they are making to absorb the change.

> 2. The accommodation they make is, not infrequently, self-destructive. It contributes to self-concept damage and generally interferes with optimum development.

> 3. The accommodation negatively alters the nature of social and interpersonal relationships on an individual level.

> 4. By implication, it probably destroys relationships on a national and global level.

Let us look at some of the changes that inevitably occur in children's lives and see how their responses conform to this model, and, inevitably, result in problems for the classroom teacher.

A child moves with his family to another neighborhood and is enrolled in a new school. He says goodbye to his mother at the office door, and the school secretary escorts him to his new teacher. In the classroom, all work stops so that the teacher may say something like, "Class, we have a new pupil. James Ellidon has just transferred here from the Blake School. I hope you'll all welcome him to his new school."

James stands there, straining away from the teacher's arm around his shoulders. He is not happy.

1. That afternoon at home his mother asks him how things went at school. He shrugs. "OK," he says, and wanders off, out of his mother's sight. For days he drags his feet around the house. In school he hovers tentatively on the outskirts of the activity in the schoolyard. In the classroom he says nothing. Every once in a while, an adult—parent, teacher, aunt—will brush past him with a broad smile, ask how things are going, pat him heartily on the back without realizing that he hasn't answered, and go on to more important things.

Slowly and warily, some of the larger white boys begin to nod toward him or direct a word to him to show they may be ready to recognize him. He, too, is a boy who is taller than most of the other children his age, and the recognition he begins to receive takes the initiative away from him: even if he would like to make friends with girls, small boys, or children of another race, he has relinquished the initiative and the choice is made for him. Nor are the children who approach him aware of how circumscribed is their own world, limited as are their criteria for choosing their friends from among the strangers they encounter.

2. Though James finally is relieved at being part of a group again, his conception of himself as timid and unenterprising has been reinforced. He believes that other people do not experience the fears and anxieties he does in these situations.

3. James feels he must go along with the decisions and activities of the group that accepted him, or he will be an outsider again. When they make sexist remarks, he does, too; when they scapegoat a boy in the class they perceive as different, he does, too, though it troubles him; like them, he flaunts his physical prowess and looks down on anyone who does not.

4. One may, perhaps, predict with some accuracy that James will not become the kind of adult who takes public stands against discrimination or war.

Teaching for Living with Change

The children of a sixth-grade class go from a teacher with one teaching style to a teacher with another teaching style—styles so different in basic orientation to human needs and human development that they actually conflict with each other in the perceptions of the children and their responses to the world. One teacher is authoritarian in her view of the world and of the way in which children should be educated. She demands that the children sit quietly in class and work at what she tells them to do. They are not to speak without permission from her. There are rules they must obey—rules they have had no hand in establishing. Infringement of rules is punished in a variety of ways, ranging from assigning extra work to inflicting physical pain. She believes the teacher's job is to teach and the children's is to learn, and those children who are not learning are lazy or rebellious or just genetically incapable of learning.

The other teacher has a more democratic personality structure. He and his children cooperatively decide on the problems they will study and the schedule for studying them. The children work independently and in small groups, coming together as a whole class when they want to deal with something of concern to all of them, or when their teacher feels the need to talk to all of them at once. They speak freely to the teacher and to each other.

The authoritarian teacher teaches them English and social studies. The democratic teacher is with them for math and science.

The children's problem lies in their response to the changing from one teacher's style to the other teacher's style. Following the model above:

1. They do not talk much about the differences *as* differences. They complain about the punishments they are subjected to in the authoritarian class when they speak out in class, talk to each other, or move out of their seats for what they feel are justifiable objectives. They respond with anger and more clearly disruptive behavior. For example, they will often point-blank refuse to submit to the teacher's demands and they will laugh with loud exaggeration at minor occurrences. Not infrequently, they seem to act out their frustration and resentment by picking on each other, and

there are many arguments and even some fights that occur at what seems like slight provocation.

2. & 3. More and more often, when they are in the democratic setting, they are demonstrating some regression in their ability to function democratically: they compete more with each other and more often refuse to help their peers who need assistance in learning and achieving success; there are more arguments in the class; the noise level is more often too high for comfort.

4. It becomes increasingly clear that this "democratic" setting will provide little encouragement for democratic functioning in the future.

The democratic teacher suggests to the children that one morning of the following week be set aside for talking about what is happening to them in the two rooms. The children acquiesce, but apathetically—they are not taking as active a part in what goes on as they used to.

On the appointed morning, after everyone is seated, the teacher raises the question:

Teacher: How do you feel about school this year?

[Silence. Teacher waits calmly, encouraging responses by making pleasant eye contact, first with one child, then with another. Finally . . .]

Pupil 1:   [Uneasy giggle.] Too much trouble.

[Scattering of uneasy laughter. Teacher just nods and waits.]

Not all my fault.

[Some low-pitched catcalls and laughter—then silence.]

Pupil 2:   Miss Percy picks on us.

Pupil 3:   Yeah!

Pupil 4:   We don't do anything and she picks on us.

Pupil 5:   We talk.

Pupil 4:   We talk here! Mr. Johnson lets us talk.

Pupil 5: You let us talk, Mr. Johnson. Why does Miss Percy pick on us?

Mr. Johnson: Why do *you* think?

Pupil 5: I don't know. She doesn't want us to talk.

Pupil 6: She lets us talk—but we have to raise our hands.

Pupil 5: Even when we raise our hands, she doesn't let us talk.

Pupil 6: She wants us to work.

Pupil 4: [Doubtfully.] We work in Mr. Johnson's class, don't we?

Pupil 6: Ye-e-s. But it's different.

Mr. Johnson: How is it different?

Pupil 6: We-e-ll. You're not strict.

Pupil 7: That's not it. Mr. Johnson is strict. We do work.

Pupil 8: Mr. Johnson doesn't give orders.

Pupil 3: Like in the army!

[Laughter.]

Pupil 8: Miss Percy always is telling us what to do and not to do.

Pupil 7: Mr. Johnson asks what we want to do.

Pupil 8: Sometimes he asks us.

[Laughter.]

Pupil 4: We always get into trouble with Miss Percy.

Mr. Johnson: What do you do that gets you into trouble?

Pupil 4: [Shrugs as if to say he doesn't know—or it's nothing important.]

Pupil 1: We fight.

Pupil 2: We can't talk so we fight.

Mr. Johnson: What has not being able to talk got to do with fighting?

Pupil 2: [Shrugs.]

Pupil 8: It makes you nervous!

Mr. Johnson: You feel nervous?

Pupil 8: When I have to ask something, I get nervous.

Pupil 2: We don't exactly fight; we sort of fool around.

Pupil 8: Sometimes we fight. They get me mad.

[Half joking.]

Pupil 2: *You* get *me* mad!

Pupil 8: What do *I* do?!

Pupil 1: See—you want to fight now!

Pupil 8: No, I don't!

Pupil 1: What are you yelling about?

Pupil 8: I'm not yelling! I don't want to fight!

Pupil 2: Miss Percy wouldn't let him yell like that.

Pupil 8: [Louder still.] I'm *not* yelling!

Pupil 2: Mr. Johnson, can you teach us English and social studies too?

[General encouragement to Mr. Johnson and agreement with Pupil 2's suggestion.]

Mr. Johnson: No, I'm afraid I couldn't do that.

[Sad cries of disappointment.]

Is there something else we can do?

Pupil 1: We can be quiet in Miss Percy's class.

Pupil 5: That's no good.

Pupil 1: Why not? Then she won't pick on us.

Pupil 5: I think we have good things to say sometimes.

Pupil 2: Sometimes!

[Laughter.]

Pupil 8: Miss Percy could let us talk if it's not too loud.

Pupil 7: If we don't fight.

Pupil 5: Maybe very low—whisper.

Pupil 8: We can ask Miss Percy.

Pupil 5: We'll ask her nicely.

Pupil 1: Maybe just talk in science—not in math.

Pupil 8: We'll ask her tomorrow.

The objectives in this interchange have been:

To provide opportunity for catharsis. The children have all kinds of feelings about what is happening to them, and they are finding some relief by harassing each other and Miss Percy. During this discussion, some of them are able to express their anger vocally and get some relief that way. There may be others who need to do it, of course, and only a single opportunity is not sufficient. Such discussions must be held regularly, so that feelings may be expressed about a variety of situations as they present themselves in the children's lives.

To raise the children's level of consciousness about what they are experiencing. Slowly, it becomes apparent during the discussion that the children are struggling to identify the differences between the two teachers and the effects of those differences on themselves. There is a growing awareness that their behaviors are caused, and as time goes on, they should become even more knowledgeable about the cause-and-effect relationship in behavior especially in this specific instance. Out of this awareness and knowledge comes a sense of power, as ways of making changes are identified and tested out.

To help them define the problem and formulate appropriate questions. The problem is not that Mr. Johnson doesn't teach everything, so it cannot be solved by having him teach all the subjects. The children readily accept Mr. Johnson's firm response to this solution—they didn't really think the solution was appropriate. They begin to see that the problem lies in the interaction of pupils and teacher, and they take tentative steps to deal productively with this interaction: drawing all parties into dealing, being ready to compromise, recognizing that a solution is possible.

To help them solve the problem constructively. If they find a successful solution to the problem, not only will they be able to live more comfortably with the continuing change from one teacher to another, but they will grow stronger in their appreciation of themselves and of their ability to make the world more responsive to them. Such a sense of strength and feeling of control can only make for higher academic achievement and more comfortably appropriate classroom behaviors.

Even if Miss Percy refuses to change her style of functioning in the classroom, or even to discuss the matter further, the process of attempting to effect change, the continuing discussions about the effects of the process, the free expression of feelings of frustration, anger, and sadness, the formulation of new solutions and the testing of those solutions all constitute a healthy involvement in one's own life, an assertion that one can take a hand in one's own fate. It is a rejection of apathy as a way of life, of submission to whatever life happens to order up.

How to deal with changes in teaching style or a change of school does not exhaust the problems of coping constructively with change. A death in the family is a change that most children are forced to deal with in isolation, primarily because adults are tied into their own grief and because they really believe that a child's involvement in the death is minimal, and can be lessened even further by avoiding the topic and telling the child to go out and play.

Divorce, also, can leave the child to grieve alone, to struggle with feelings of guilt and anxiety, to wander through his young life with unanswered questions.

Such changes can easily result in the kinds of behavior that tend to interfere with the teaching-learning process. It serves both the children and their teachers well to make concern with those problems a part of the ongoing curriculum in order to prevent such interference and to help the child deal adequately with those and with other kinds of changes throughout his life.

It cannot be too strongly emphasized that behaviors resulting from traumatic change in a child's life are not characteristic of a geographical area or an ethnic or racial group. They are human responses to confusion, fear, and grief; they occur in inner-city schools and in suburban schools, among rich children and poor children, at elementary and at secondary school levels. The solution is unvaryingly to help the children see the change and its effects clearly and realistically—to take control of their lives instead of being absorbed by the change and responding mindlessly to it.

chapter 7

The Philosophical Basis for the Solutions

THE REASON FOR TEACHING

We teachers get so caught up in the day-to-day struggle to maintain order, cover the curriculum, get supplies, collect milk money, and all the other activities and objectives that society has tossed under the heading of teaching, that we rarely have time to stop and examine the real reason for teaching. If we ever thought about it at all, it was as a junior or senior in our teacher education college, and what the heck did we know then?

The Realities of Teaching

If we insist that children come to us knowing how to function in a classroom; if we expect that those who come into our classes after the first grade will be able to read; if we demand that, at the outset, they know the difference between appropriate and inappropriate behavior and that they prefer to act in appropriate rather than inappropriate ways, then what is there for us to teach?

253

Now, we all are well aware of the fact that many children cannot function adequately in a classroom. Even high school seniors often find it difficult to read on a fifth-grade level, and we are forever faced with children who, if they know the difference between appropriate and inappropriate behavior, seem purposefully to opt always for the inappropriate. These are the realities of teaching. The error we make starts with our perception of these realities and extends to influence the process and content of our teaching.

The Errors We Make

We perceive each inappropriate behavior, each academic inadequacy, each skill deficiency as a disappointment of our expectations, as a gross defect in society, as a topic of pessimistic querulousness, instead of as a problem of teaching. Given the differential life situations in our world, what right do we have to expect that all children assigned to us will match the grade-level curriculum guide on which we base our lessons? One child is malnourished, another's parents are divorced, another has had teachers with troubles of their own, and still another has been engaged all his life in a fight to get a bit of recognition in his own home. If each one of these fifth-grade children is not at the "fifth-grade level" of mathematics knowledge, why be surprised—or even disappointed? If you believe it is important for them all to learn a certain amount of mathematics, then begin to teach them what they are equipped to learn. That is what it means to be a teacher.

What it does not mean is that you stand prepared to teach a specific curriculum, no matter who or what the individuals are in your assigned class. Even the haberdasher asks, "What size do you wear?" before he tries to sell you a suit of clothes. He does not expect that you will accommodate your height and weight to fit the suit he has decided to sell you.

To identify poverty, prejudice, and hydrogen bombs as essential causes of classroom problems is probably not inaccurate, but you must admit that it has the effect of limiting the teacher's alternatives. It seems reasonable that, if we wait until poverty, prejudice, and hydrogen bombs are eliminated from our lives, we will have lost to ignorance all the generations who come to us. And then who will be equipped to figure out how to rid the world of these defects? It seems as if the only chance we have to do this is to rear enough educated people who will apply themselves to the problems and begin to find some solutions!

The pessimism that afflicts us as a profession is an indulgence. It leaves us free to act as the agents of our profession's failures. If it is no use to teach because the obstacles preclude success, then we will not teach—and the failure will be complete. There are obstacles to teaching and obstacles to learning, but we are, by definition, committed to overcoming these obstacles and causing learning to occur. If individuals among us give up, that is inevitable in any human endeavor. The profession, however, has no moral right to throw in the sponge.

Children who are motivated to learn, ready to learn, and involved in learning need very few teachers. With all the other educational facilities we have in our country—libraries, working adults, museums, science institutes—motivated children will find their way to the sources of knowledge. The real job of the professional teacher is to find effective ways of motivating children who do not want to become involved in a systematic process of learning. *That* is the real reason for having teachers! The trick is not in motivating children who have no other problems and who wait—uncontaminated by physical, emotional, or intellectual disabilities—for us to lead them to learning. The real professional trick is to involve in active learning children who come to us wishing they were anywhere else but in school.

If we could just rid ourselves of the idea that our primary function is the dissemination of information, we would be taking a giant step toward fulfilling a purpose that society has never really defined for us. We are not vast repositories of information. Even the subject area specialists among us know very little of the vast bodies of knowledge in our own fields. Almost any computer has much more information at its terminal tips.

Our job is far more esoteric than storing and retrieving information. If children do not see the connection between sitting at a desk and learning some things, then we must teach them to see the connection. If they cannot read, we must teach them to read. If they speak aloud whenever they are moved to do so, we must help them to make the connection between fulfilling their slightest need impulsively and working in a room where other people also have many needs. If they do not care about other people, we must teach them the consequences of caring and not caring, so they can make their choices based on knowledge about human interaction.

Every obstacle to teaching and learning that we encounter in our classrooms is merely a pedagogical problem for solving. Sometimes, just the way we look at the behavior of a particular child obscures this fact. When we describe Johnny to his mother, we tell her, "Johnny is impudent." There is almost an echo of moral indignation in this label, and Johnny's mother becomes either defensive or morally outraged. When Johnny's teacher of last year tells us this about Johnny, we are compelled to respond to Johnny's behavior with wariness, if he has never been impudent to us—or with punishment, because what else can you do about continuing impudence? (Of course, there is the margin for error in understanding another adult's definition of impudence. What Ms. Blum calls impudence, Ms. Norton sees as reasonable and desirable assertiveness.)

To make our communication clearer, we may say to Johnny's new teacher, "Whenever I gave directions, Johnny refused to follow them. He actually said, 'No, I don't want to do it that way. This is a better way.' " The new teacher is likely to try to look more analytically at the behavior and examine the educational consequences of it. If those consequences seem adverse enough, she may make systematic attempts to find a pedagogical solution to those problems that the behavior is causing.

Similarly, "Daryl acts silly," sounds pejorative, and makes it seem as if Daryl is a hopeless behavior problem. However, to observe that "Daryl makes faces" and "funny" body motions when he is engaged in small-group activities, gives us a handle on what might be precipitating Daryl's behavior and encourages us to think of teaching ways to deal with it.

The purpose of teaching is to give people opportunities to

change their behavior, their styles of responding, their levels of skills, their stores of knowledge. Forcing people to change is not part of our professional function. Neither is making a pronouncement that they will never change.

Refining Observations and Changing Behavior

It is not too controversial an observation when we say that the reason for teaching is to change children's behavior. Whether we disagree on what should be taught in school, or come to consensus on teaching strategies we should use, the ultimate results of learning are changes in what we do.

If there is really pretty-near universal agreement on this point in the profession, why is there so much confusion about our approach to the children's behavior in school? If we are to be professionally consistent, then we must observe the children's behavior and make a decision about whether or not it needs changing. And, if we decide that it does, indeed, need changing, then our job is—through teaching—to effect the change we deem desirable.

To carry the illustration further, if a child's mathematics skill (behavior) is inadequate (inappropriate for his age and situation), then it is clear that we must change his math behavior to more appropriate levels and forms. Although it is true that some of us merely label the child an underachiever or slow learner and use the label as absolution from responsibility, most of us see his inappropriate math behavior as a legitimate target for change, and we proceed to devise and use all kinds of strategies and materials in order to effect that change.

Though only a few of us fail to see inappropriate academic behavior as within the scope of systematic teaching, a great many of us fail to see other kinds of behavior as a target for systematic teaching. We label children in a range from annoying to incorrigible, we blame them, their parents, their culture, and the twentieth century for what they are doing, and we punish them in a variety of ways ranging from physical violence to appeal to their consciences. What we do not do is draw on everything we know about teaching, learning, and human development to *teach* changes in behavior.

One way of convincing ourselves that changing non-academic behavior from inappropriate to more appropriate is, indeed, a problem of teaching, is to begin to observe behaviors in ways that will make it easier to deal with them. Familiar observations by teachers can be redefined in ways that make them clearly objects for classroom teaching. Let us take the cases of Kathie, Bobby, Jamie, Connie, and Janie:

(A) Kathie is emotionally disturbed: she has temper tantrums.

(B) Kathie responds to frustration by holding her breath and falling down.

(A) Bobby is immature and insecure.

(B) Bobby follows the teacher around, hanging on to her.

(A) Jamie is destructive.

(B) Jamie tears up and breaks the class supplies and materials.

(A) Connie is withdrawn.

(B) Connie doesn't speak to anyone unless she is addressed directly, and not always then.

(A) Janie is hyperactive.

(B) Janie leaves her seat many times during the day when there is seat work to do.

An "emotionally disturbed" Kathie throws the teacher for a loss. Unless he has training in Special Education, or he has reasonably easy access to the services of a professional psychologist, the observation serves merely as a label, and the implication is that little or nothing can be done for Kathie in a classroom setting.

However, a Kathie who obviously responds inappropriately

to frustrating experiences *can* be helped. The teacher can apply his teaching efforts to strengthening her resources for coping with frustration. In addition—or, if he prefers the behavior modification approach, as an alternative to teaching to her inadequate resources—he can systematically reward those instances when she responds more appropriately to frustration and encourage the extinction of the inappropriate behavior by ignoring it or by providing for uncomfortable consequences of that behavior. (For example, seeing to it that she falls down on a dirty part of the floor may contribute to the extinction for a fastidious little girl.)

Similarly, the teacher of immature Bobby may be tempted to leave him to the maturing effects of time. But the teacher who deals with Bobby's behavior will devise experiences that will wean him from the comfort and safety of her immediate environment.

If Jamie is perceived as destructive, it is easy to see him as an antisocial stereotype so prevalent in our culture. Even in universities, the argument still goes on—on somewhat more abstruse levels—about the validity of the concept, "Once a criminal, always a criminal." Certainly one of the biggest problems in our country is the difficulty faced by convicts when they come out of prison: people are reluctant to marry them or hire them, and the reluctance is undoubtedly attributable to the belief that the criminal behavior is likely to be repeated.

If we look more specifically at Jamie's behavior, we see that (1) he is destroying material things, not people, (2) he destroys things in the classroom, and he may not be destroying anything outside the classroom.

Labeling the child destructive implies that the teaching job is aborted. Global destructiveness is beyond the scope of the teacher. Noting that the child destroys classroom materials, may lead us to some clues to specific causes of his behavior that can be dealt with by the teacher. Or, again, if the teacher prefers, he may proceed with a behavior modification approach to change the child's behavior.

If it is true that he breaks up only classroom materials—and there is no reason to suppose that he is destructive outside the classroom—he may be responding to classroom experiences that are too disturbing for him to handle calmly. He may be faced with repeated failures, academic or social. Or he may be trying to communicate some great need to the teacher and finding that he is not being listened to or understood. He may be worried about what is happening at home while he is absent (a home that has been the scene of some recent upheaval). Or he may be suffering from feelings of guilt, and finding that breaking up supplies is one sure way to get the punishment he believes he deserves.

Any one of these things can be dealt with educationally, even if Jamie gets nothing more than the chance to express his feelings in more acceptable ways. The catharsis of talking about what you feel when you're throwing things around can save you from the next bout of throwing. We do generally accept socialization as a school function, and the socialization process should be more than just exhorting children to behave themselves. It should involve helping children to understand themselves and the people around them. Hearing Jamie and the other children talk about what they do when they are fearful, angry, or happy is salutary for everyone in the class.

Similarly, Connie, several years ago, may have been perceived as the ideal student, a problem for no one at all. Today we are concerned about the Connies in our classes. However, if our concern is centered on the diagnosis "withdrawn," we have fallen into a trap that looks very much like the one our professional antecedents made when they thought Connie was a model child. They did nothing for her because they believed she was in good shape. We do nothing for her because we believe that we have not the expertise or training to deal with so serious a problem. The end result for Connie is the same.

But if what we see is Connie's nonspeaking behavior, then we can try to figure out some way to make speaking a rewarding behavior for Connie. Acceptance of what she says when she does say a word or two, an approving smile when she speaks, a friendly touch when she hesitates, can all help to change her behavior.

Nor are these reinforcing consequences of speaking to be provided only by the teacher. And here we have the more extensive educational purpose: the other children also need to learn to provide positive reinforcement for their peers. The plan is not to hold Connie up as an object of pity or a target for ministration, but to help the children understand that we reinforce each other's behavior all the time, and there is great power in each of us to reinforce appropriate behavior. They need to realize that, if Connie is not speaking, or if Jamie is tearing up the art paper, or if Bobby hangs on to the teacher, it may be partly because of the way the rest of the children are responding to those behaviors. Though we are always telling children that the peoples of the world are interdependent, and the people in the community are interdependent, they are not always learning the day-to-day significance of interdependence in their own lives.

What can we do with six-year-old Jane when we observe: Jane is hyperactive? Well, we can refer her to the school nurse (who does not treat hyperactivity). Or we can recommend to Jane's mother that she take Jane to a physician. (Jane's mother resents the diagnosis; she sees nothing wrong with Jane's behavior at home.) We can tell the principal that the school psychologist should test Jane. (There is one psychologist for 10,000 students in the school system.) We can demand that Jane be put into a "special" class. (Jane's mother will not give her approval for this, and the principal will not do it without her approval.) We can keep putting Jane out of the room. (Sooner or later, Jane's noise and disruptive behavior in the halls will bring the wrath of administration and colleagues down on our heads.) Or we can take another look at Jane's behavior, and maybe save us both from a lot of grief.

Let us observe her behavior specifically: Jane leaves her seat many times during the day when there is seat work to do. Now, this is something that the teacher can deal with! We know enough about teaching and learning to make a practical attempt to reduce the number of times Jane gets up when she should be sitting down:

1. We can make the rule clear that children must stay in their seats when it is time to write. ("The rule is, everyone

must remain seated for fifteen minutes. That is the writing period—from ten o'clock until ten-fifteen.")

2. We can praise Jane and all the other children regularly when they are sitting down and doing what they should be doing. ("I see you've been sitting and working for ten minutes, Robert. Very good"; and "I see you've been sitting and working for three minutes, Jane. Very good." Obviously, Jane needs reinforcement of her appropriate behavior at more frequent intervals than the other children do.)

3. We can give Jane opportunities for getting up on many occasions when it is appropriate, and make clear to her the appropriateness of the occasion. ("This is a good time for taking a walk around the room, Jane, because you are all finished with writing your name.")

4. We can ignore Jane's inappropriate getting-up behavior. It may be that scolding her or constantly talking about it may be just the response that encourages Jane's inappropriate behavior. (It certainly hasn't caused her to reduce or stop the behavior.)

5. All these steps must be adhered to consistently and over a reasonable period of time, because the inappropriate behavior has been going on for months and Jane needs time to learn a new way of behaving. (We all know that learning takes time, and difficult things take more time to learn. We *know* it will be difficult for Jane to learn to sit for longer periods of time.)

While all this is going on, we must be providing Jane with all kinds of opportunities for experiencing satisfaction in the classroom, so that the frustration that inevitably accompanies new learning can be buffered by the good feelings that accompany success.

There have been other children and other kinds of behavior that teachers have observed with few consequences that proved helpful to the children:

(A). The whole class is unruly. They are disadvantaged children because their parents are too poor to provide all the material things they need, and often too tired and discouraged to get involved in the school behavior of their children.

(B). Most of the children in the class keep getting out of their seats when they should be working on their lessons.

The (A) observation is, to say the least, inaccurate. It is also not very helpful, from the point of view of changing the situation. First of all, it is not likely that everyone in the class is unruly. If we look closely at the most chaotic class in a school, we will see a few children who are quiet in the midst of the uproar, sitting in their seats while the others are running about, even trying to work while the teacher struggles to deal with the chaos.

In the second place, what is helpful about the observation that these children are poor and their parents tired and discouraged? Here, too, it is doubtful that the teacher knows all the parents or has accurately assessed the level of their fatigue or the intensity of their discouragement. As a matter of fact, if we are to judge by the situation in most poor city neighborhoods, the teachers do not get out much among the parents, nor do the parents often find their way to the school.

At any rate, how can a diagnosis of parents affect the fact that their children won't stay in their seats in school? At the very least, one would have to help develop a plan to get parents participating in school (but the parents are too tired!) or to get parents demonstrating enthusiasm about the value of school (but they are too discouraged!). Exhorting the children is not likely to help. Punishing them will surely not help.

If, however, we merely look at the children's school behavior, (B), we can aim directly at a target within our reach. We can set as the objective: *The children will sit in their seats when they should be working on their lessons.* Now we can proceed to lay plans to effect sitting behavior. Our plans relate to the classroom, involve pedagogical goals and educational strategies, and are logically and practically the province of the teacher. We can feel confident that we have made a diagnosis in our own area of expertise and are working to do the job we were educated to do.

Harry, who had "poor personal habits" (A) turned off a generation of teachers whose attitude toward him was a vague mixture of exasperation and moralistic repugnance. But the Harry who "combs his hair during lessons" (B) has been an object of mild amusement, and perhaps understanding of his great need for reassurance about his personal appearance.

(A)   Jimmy, five years old, is overaggressive and hostile.

(B)   Jimmy hits any child who takes a toy that Jimmy wants or disagrees with an idea that Jimmy wants to act on.

(A)   Sally has a dirty mouth.

(B)   Sally uses words the other children have obviously been taught are unacceptable.

It seems clear to me that the (B) kind of observation is one that can lead to a teacher kind of diagnosis that requires a teaching strategy for amelioration. It is not a psychologist's kind of observation, a minister's, a police officer's, or even a parent's. It is the kind of observation of behavior that leads to a teacher kind of job.

Even if, as a professional, you are more committed to a causal approach to dealing with behavior than a behavior modification approach, you must identify those causes that are treatable *by you* and proceed to teach to them. There is simply no value in determining that Johnny's inability to read is caused by the fact that his father beats his mother. It is not likely that Johnny's first-grade teacher can do very much about changing Johnny's father's behavior.

What the first-grade teacher *can* do, however, is identify some other contributory causes to the fact that Johnny can't read and teach to those. For example, the fact that Johnny can't read is—at least partly—directly attributable to the equally salient fact that he does not sit still long enough to trace a letter with his finger. Here is something that the first-grade teacher can sink her teeth into without biting off more than she can chew!

First she must decide which is more important—to keep Johnny sitting or to get him to trace the shapes of letters. If she can accept for a while Johnny's need to keep moving for whatever reasons of frustration or anxiety he has in his life, she can then concentrate on the tracing behavior that is so vital to his learning to read. (Perhaps, with the ego strength developed with success in reading, he will be better able to deal with those other problems.)

I saw a teacher solve this problem for one of her Johnnys in a rather simple way. About the room she scattered corrugated board cutouts of the letters she was currently teaching. She told all the children—not just Johnny—that they could sit at their seats and trace the letters, or they could get up and move quietly around the room tracing the letters, leaning against the walls. She also asked children—often Johnny—to bring her one of those letters: "Bring me a *G*" or "Bring me a *C*." Johnny thus did his learning, and the hassle about moving when he should be sitting virtually disappeared.

Some teachers may become concerned for Johnny, who, they fear, may never learn "self-control." However, Johnny is a happy, involved third grader today. He is appropriately controlled and successful. (Also, his father is three thousand miles away, something the teacher had no hand in at all.)

SUCCESS EXPERIENCES

All of us know very well the importance of repeated success experiences on the self-concept development and academic progress of pupils. We know that, without such experiences, children begin to see themselves as unworthy—unworthy, even, of trying to succeed. Almost inevitably, they begin to fall farther and farther behind, academically. And, from the classroom management point of view, they may withdraw from all interaction, or become disruptive, hostile, and aggressive.

When they withdraw, we generally label them underachievers (or even retarded) and gradually get to the point where we don't bother them as long as they don't bother us. When they go to the other extreme and become noisy in class, interrupt the teaching, pick on the other children, and get into fights, we go through the whole routine of disciplinary procedures, before we finally announce that this child cannot be permitted to remain in a room with children who are trying to learn. "It's not fair to the other children," we say. It is not fair to us.

Here is a conversation I had recently with the supervisor of a student teacher in one of the schools in an exurban area:

Supervisor: I was so upset yesterday, I went home early. It was just awful!

C.E.: What happened?

Supervisor: I'm at the Blank school on Tuesdays, you know. I have three students assigned to cooperating teachers in that school, and I usually spend a morning there each week observing my students and talking to the teachers when I can.

C.E.: I know the Blank School. They've had three principals in the past two years. The first one got sick, didn't he? Then they had an "acting" one. And as soon as she became familiar with what was happening and began to take hold, they sent her away and brought in another body. She's been there only two months, now, hasn't she?

Supervisor: That's right. So I really don't think she knows what's happening.

C.E.: What did happen?

Supervisor: Well, as I was walking up to the second floor, I met one of the cooperating teachers coming down with four of the kids—*all four of them had bloody noses!*

C.E.: *All* of them!? For goodness' sake, what happened?

Supervisor: They were in a fight. She was taking them to the nurse. I went on up to the room, and you should have seen what was going on there! It was bedlam! All the kids were fighting! Beating up on each other.

The student was there, and I stood and watched her for five minutes, and she wasn't getting anywhere. She yelled at them and tried to separate some of them. But as soon as she let go of one pair and went to another, the first pair went right back to fighting. It was awful!

Finally, I told her to let me try. I didn't think I could do any worse than she was doing. I tried to restore order, but it was no use. I tried to separate some, I yelled and tried to get their attention. All in vain. One Black kid yelled at me, "No honky is gonna tell me to do that!" And I walked right up and looked him in the eye and said, "Well, I *am* telling you to do that."

Finally, I got them singing a song, and this calmed them down a little for a few minutes. But this sort of thing goes on all the time in that room.

C.E.: Does it go on in the rest of the school?

Supervisor: Oh, no. The other classrooms are great. The kids are working. They're quiet. It's really a very good school.

C.E.: I wonder what the problem is in that room. Have the children been together before, or is this their first term in the same room?

Supervisor: Some of them have been together. I think they were combined from three different classes—and they were all put together in one room.

C.E.: Were they put together for some reason?

Supervisor: Well, they say they're slow. But they're *not* slow. I've talked to some of those kids, and they don't seem slow to me. I think they're just discipline problems, but they're not slow.

Homogeneous Grouping

The light broke suddenly and blindingly. They had culled all the "problems" from the other classes and put them together in one room. What could the objective have been?

Could it have been to provide more individual help for children who needed it and could not get it in the regular classroom where children were all working at the required curriculum at the expected rate of speed?

But the teacher in this room could not possibly give individual children more time, when there were so many more of them that seemed to need it. And no extra help was provided.

Could it have been that putting all the "slow" children in one room would allow the teacher to teach them all lower level material at a slower rate of speed, and so give them a chance to achieve at the level of which they were capable?

But even a superficial assessment of the intellectual capabilities of the children indicated that they were no more at the same level than any class of thirty children are ever found to be at the same level. The range from the "slowest" to the "fastest" was not even significantly smaller, so no matter what level the teacher taught on, there would be the same number of children as in every other class for whom other provisions needed to be made.

Could it have been that the children were selected for this class, not only on the basis of their not achieving at grade level, but because they were, one way or another, disrupting the classes they had been in?

Given the behavior witnessed by the supervisor every time she came into the room, and given the corroboration by both the student and the cooperating teacher that that kind of behavior was not unusual for those children, one may reasonably conclude that the children's behavior was at least a contributing factor in taking them out of their regular classrooms. I would hazard a guess that the objective would be primarily to get them out of the way; what educational objective could be achieved (in reference to changing their disruptive behavior) is not clear. What could be done if they were all together that could not be done when only a few of them were in one classroom with less disruptive children?

The Professional Responsibility

Here is an instance where all the professional education of the teachers in the school should have been brought to bear to prevent this situation from occurring. The teachers should have rallied, as a group, and presented the argument to whatever administrator made the decision to give all these children to one teacher. Every single teacher in that school knew very well that the situation was unmanageable. Or, at least, that it was so difficult that he, himself would not be able to manage it. But they all let it happen, grateful that the job did not fall to them that year, and hopeful that the problem would somehow disappear before they were asked to take such a class.

In the Philadelphia schools, where teachers belong to a very strong union, it is quite clear that no teacher is compelled to remain at a staff meeting beyond the very minute of three o'clock. At three, most teachers get up and leave the meeting, even if the principal is in the middle of a sentence. How is it, then, that teachers do not use the leverage of the union to resist having to work in a situation where failure is almost inevitable? It must be because they prefer to risk having such a class occasionally to having to put up with individual children who present problems. Anyway, usually it is the new teacher in the school who is forced to take on this job, the new teacher who must do as she is told or face losing her job. It says something about our profession that teachers with job security do not rally around the one who is vulnerable and prevent her being taken advantage of. However, the new teacher is still a union member, and, if most teachers were willing to deal with this problem professionally, the force of the union would easily prevent the formation of such classes.

Failure, Resistance, and Professional Cooperation

Certainly, any teacher who accepts such a class martyrs herself and does a disservice to the children. There is not much chance that the children in this class will have the success experiences that they so desperately need. As a matter of fact, just finding themselves in such a class brings home to them the realization that they have *already* failed—totally and without redemption.

The fact that they do not get such success experiences is a failure of the school. No matter what the causes of their behavior, no matter what the past school experiences of the children, when thirty children are not experiencing success in a major part of their lives, then the institution designed to provide appropriate experiences for them must bear the burden of failure.

Here is a series of suggestions that take some of the harshness out of this dictum by identifying practical ways of averting total failure:

1. Resist as long as possible the formation of classes made up entirely of "slow learners" or "discipline problems." Resist as individuals, as total faculties, and as union members.

2. Make sure, while the resistance goes on, that all teachers have help and support in dealing with management problems in their own classrooms. The help should be immediate and should demonstrate good success in solving the problems. The atmosphere in the school should be one in which people feel comfortable about asking for help. As professionals, the faculty knows the daily problems that need to be solved, and they should work to bring their combined knowledge to solutions without, in the process, denigrating or destroying the person helped.

3. If, in spite of all reason and all resistance, such a class is formed, then make sure that the primary objective will be to change the children's behavior, not to be satisfied with maintaining the class as a custodial device. To this end, all teachers in the school must assume some responsibility for achieving this objective. Such responsibility must be planned for and systematically implemented. Following are suggestions for such implementation:

(a) Since the children need success experiences if their behavior is to become more appropriate and more productive, the faculty might share the responsibility for providing them opportunities for success. A special lesson in one teacher's classroom might include five or six of the "problem" children. The regular children in that teacher's class will have been taught to rally around newcomers and make them welcome. And the special lesson will have been designed to afford everyone in the class the satisfaction of succeeding.

(b) In the "discipline" class, children will work on tasks that take them out of the classroom for short periods of time. One or two children may go to interview the men teachers in the school on some aspect of sexism. Appointments will have been made with the interviewees, who are committed to helping the children complete the task and feel good about what they have done.

One child may be designated the person in charge of arranging for replenishing various supplies that are kept in another teacher's room because she has more space. That teacher must welcome the child into her room and discuss seriously the rate at which supplies are used up, where one re-orders, the cost of different items, etc. She, too, has as her objective to see to it that the child succeeds at the task and feels good about himself.

One child who has something interesting to talk about may be welcomed into another room and encouraged to talk to the regular pupils. The regular pupils will have planned the questions they will ask, examining, in the process of planning, the nature of their questions and the possible effects of different kinds of questions on the self-concept and the feelings of the speaker.

All in all, the contacts between the "problem" children and the rest of the faculty will be on-going rather than sporadic, will be planned for by the teachers so that the needs of the children are provided for, will *not* include such activities as cleaning floors, which do not offer the usual legitimate opportunities for growth and development in a school.

4. The clearly stated overall objective will be to turn each child back to a regular class as soon as he and his teacher agree that he is ready to function without excessive disruption. It is possible, of course, that, in the course of a semester or so, the special class will become so productive, will make such progress academically, and will live together so satisfactorily, that the children will want to continue together as a regular section of their grade. If all this comes to pass, there will not be much point in breaking them up.

The Stereotype of the Teacher

On an intellectual level teachers recognize the vital importance to the individual's survival of repeated success experiences, yet we usually function as if providing opportunities for success were not a legitimate classroom function. How else would generations of students get the idea that teachers are out to trip you up, ask you "trick questions" to which you will inevitably give the wrong answers, embarrass you for having no answer, or demean you for answering incorrectly? Teachers may protest that this is just one of those stereotypes that feeds on itself and is encouraged by the barriers to communication between pupils and teachers, and of course they are right. Surely not all—and probably not most—teachers conform to this picture that so many students carry around in their heads.

However, how many teachers do you know who help pupils prepare for examinations by giving them questions in advance around which they can focus their reading? How many teachers do you know who never call on a pupil to answer a question unless the pupil indicates that he has an answer? How many teachers do you know who carefully design *all* the pupils' learning experiences so that the chances of repeated success are far, far greater than the chances of failure?

Even students in professional schools—dentistry, education, nursing—are very often convinced that most of their professors would far rather fail them than see them succeed. How ludicrous to contemplate a generation of professional teachers devoting their time, energy, and their *lives* to figuring out how to *fail* their students! Yet their teaching behavior can easily be interpreted this way. Why else would so many professional students continue to report that the professional school is de-humanizing and that they graduate with feelings of inadequacy that some of them never resolve satisfactorily?

You may contend that most children—most people—*do* succeed in school. You *may* contend that if you ignore all those who drop out at critical points—like the fourth graders who never learn to read at the fifth-grade level; like the ninth graders who never return to the tenth grade; like the college freshmen who never become sophomores. Tens of thousands of people among us who live their lives with a profound sense of failure cannot make for a healthy society. Several dozen children in a school who feel this way make for discipline and management problems that are only forerunners of the broader social problems they will cause.

SOLVING REAL PROBLEMS

The teacher and the children are the only ones who know what the real problems are in a classroom. Each child knows his own real problems; the teacher knows his own real problems. The real problems are not in the book that was written by someone at a distant university. The problems are not in the state curriculum guide that was written by a committee. The real problems are being experienced and agonized over by the people in the classroom.

One Classroom

Problem.   Ruth is the middle child in her family. Her older brother keeps running away from home. Her mother blames her father; her father blames her mother. Her younger sister is having some difficulty learning to read. Her parents are very concerned about this; they talk a lot about it and help the younger child with her lessons. Ruth is very quiet.

Problem.   Hilda is in love. Her father is frightened and is reluctant to let her out of his sight. Her mother keeps talking to her vaguely about ". . . you know . . . you ought to be careful . . . boys don't consider . . . you're the one who has to . . ." Hilda is unhappy and—vaguely—frightened.

Problem.   The other guys keep laughing at Ron and calling him a virgin. He believes that all of them have really had the sexual experiences they talk about. Ron is very worried about his own sexuality.

Problem.   There are times when Merle really hates his brown skin. He knows enough about the racial situation and the history of his own race to know that he shouldn't feel this way. He is a very troubled young man. Merle finds himself wishing he were white.

Problem.   Money is Bill's problem. His parents can't afford to give him a regular allowance, so he picks up a little money running errands and bagging groceries in the supermarket. But he never can make enough to compete with the other guys. The way they can spend money on girls and other things always makes him feel left out. "There has got to be some way to make more money fast," he keeps thinking.

Problem. On his way to school this morning Jules has (1) knocked over a trash can and scattered trash over a half-block area; (2) sprinted into and through a group of girls, knocking two of them down; (3) crossed the street against the light causing a motorist to screech to a stop; and (4) written an obscene word on the wall of the boys' toilet. Jules knows he has no problems.

Problem. Lisa just wishes her mother wouldn't come to parents' night at the school. Her mother doesn't speak English very well, and she dresses in a very old-fashioned way. It makes Lisa's face burn and her stomach hurt when she knows her mother is coming to school.

Problem. Arnold is just waiting until he's sixteen, so he can leave school and get a job driving a truck for $125 a week. The day Arnold breaks out of this prison, he will breathe a big sigh of relief.

Problem. Charlene's grandmother has just died. Charlene was very close to her grandmother; she lived with her for the first six years of her life. She was afraid to look at her grandmother when she lay in the casket. Charlene is wracked with guilt.

Problem. Rita's mother has suddenly taken to dressing like a teenager and wanting to hang around with Rita and her friends. Rita doesn't want to hurt her mother's feelings, but she doesn't want her mother as one of the crowd. Rita has begun to be secretive about her plans, and has taken to avoiding coming home during the day.

Problem. Evelyn hates Miss Ingers, the science teacher, and she *knows* Miss Ingers hates her. She is sure she will fail science, and this will mess up her chances for a college scholarship. She doesn't know what to do about it. Evelyn is so worried that it's beginning to affect her work in other subjects.

Problem. Pat is sick about the fact that no boy has ever asked her for a date. She's sure that she'll never have any fun like other girls. She just isn't clever or pretty or any of those other things that attract boys. The truth is, nobody could like Pat!

Problem. Arnold can't sleep or eat, and he can't concentrate on his work. He's scared out of his wits, because he thinks he's responsible for making a girl pregnant. What is going to happen?

Problem. Verne has begun to notice that her two best friends make all kinds of racial slurs. She doesn't like it. Verne doesn't know what she can do without breaking up the friendship.

Problem. Sylvia has four friends. They are very close. Three of them have decided that the fourth one is too immature for them to associate with, and they want to tell her that they can't be friends with her any more. Sylvia thinks it's terrible to hurt someone like that; she also wants to keep the friendship of the other three. She doesn't know what to do. It's making Sylvia very unhappy.

Problem. Morton thinks he is very sick. He has all kinds of aches and pains but he is afraid to tell anyone or to go to a doctor. There are days when all he can do is just stay in bed—not eating or anything. His mother and father both work, so they have no idea this has been happening. Morton's teachers know only that he has been missing school.

Problem. Everybody in the class picks on Sissie. When they aren't laughing at her answers, or snickering at the way she dresses, they ostracize her. The teacher calls her a loner. What Sissie wants more than anything else is to have a friend.

Problem. Rhoda's father has always hugged and kissed her a lot. Suddenly her mother has begun to object to this behavior, telling both Rhoda and her father to stop acting in such a disgusting way, and that Rhoda was getting too big for this kind of behavior. Rhoda feels so uncomfortable in her father's presence that she can hardly meet his eyes.

Problem. Cindy's father sometimes gets drunk while he sits in front of the TV set weekends. When he drinks too much he seems to work himself into a fury. Then he hits her mother. A couple of times he really hurt her badly. Her mother won't talk about it afterwards, though Cindy has tried to tell her that something has to be done about her father. Once her father heard her say this to her mother, and he hit Cindy with his fist and knocked her down. She didn't go to school the next day because her face was all swollen. Cindy hates her father. And sometimes she thinks she hates her mother, too.

Problem. Lonnie is about fifty pounds overweight. He tells everyone who will listen that he doesn't mind being fat, that fat people are a lot of fun, and that, anyway, he loves eating all that good food! Actually, he is feeling more and more miserable about his looks. He feels like an elephant in gym class, and is even ashamed to change his clothes in front of the other guys. They never say anything, but Lonnie knows they must be thinking plenty.

Problem. Dorothy is afraid. Everything frightens her—staying home, going out, tests, teachers, boys, other girls. Sometimes she feels she just wants to die. Dorothy is afraid to tell anyone about this, because they'll just think she's crazy.

Problem. Loretta's mother and father both work, and Loretta has the responsibility for caring for her younger brother and sister. She loves her parents and her sister and brother, and she wants to do what's right, but it's getting to be too much for her. She never seems to have time to study. She can't go with her friends after school. Sometimes she feels too tired to hold her head up in class. Loretta is beginning to feel as if it's all closing in on her.

The Curriculum

And so it goes. In this group alone—the one in which these problems were identified—there is basis for the relevant teaching of family psychology, sex education, race relations (including history), economics, self-awareness, aging and death, fate control, health education, interpersonal skills, and, of course, English and American literature that deal with all these topics.

This is not to say that the students should be concerned in their formal education only with their own problems. However, if we start with the problems that are of concern to the students, they will move out in each area to learn more about related problems, to higher and higher levels of knowledge and sophistication. Generally, we teach backwards. We start with what has been accepted as important for people to know and wear ourselves out trying to motivate students to learn those things. How wasteful, when the motivating forces are present to carry students along in their own education!

Let us take one or two of these areas of concern to the students in this group and see if we cannot devise sound curriculum even as we focus on the solving of real problems.

There are at least four students in this class who are currently in the throes of major family problems. There are also a number of others who are experiencing some discomfort, as will become apparent as the course goes on. The immediately identifiable problems are: parental conflict, parental neglect, and communication within the family.

Under each general heading, we may develop specific topics that open the general area up not only to more information, but to the development of necessary skills if problems are to be solved:

Parental conflict

Types of conflict

Feelings about conflict

Effects of conflict

The relation of family role definitions to conflict

Psychological causes of conflict

Philosophical bases of conflict

Sociological causes of conflict

Economic causes of conflict

Resolving conflict constructively

Parental neglect

Types of neglect

Feelings about neglect

Effects of neglect

Causes of neglect

Society's role in child neglect

Fulfilling neglected needs

Communication within the family

Traditionally taboo subjects in American families

Feelings about lack of communication

Birth order of siblings and communication

Parent-child communication problems

Intersibling communication problems

Effects of defective communication

Developing communication skills

There are probably no children in the class who have not been touched by many of the topics listed here. As a matter of fact, it is unlikely that the teacher himself is not personally motivated to explore some of these topics! Can you imagine the excitement of a class period that provides ninth-grade students with opportunities to work on getting some answers for themselves in these areas?

Nor is the learning only in the area of content and content skills. The process of learning is also legitimately part of the curriculum. Thus, identifying the listed topics; classifying them for relatedness to each other; discovering the available resources for gathering information; defining the problems and testing alternative solutions; even the identification and practice of the interactive skills needed to work together on all these things are legitimate aspects of school learning. The days are gone when teachers taught only facts and math processes, usually by telling them to the students, and then evaluated the effectiveness of their teaching by grading pencil-and-paper tests. We know there is more to formal education than answering one hundred multiple-choice questions at the end of each semester.

Discovering the Problems

What remains is a word about how the teacher is able to discover the problems that are concerning the students, since it is not always the case that the high school teacher is the students' confidant. The most obvious strategy is to ask the students directly.

It would be neat to be able to expect that as teachers we can, at any time, sit informally with seven or eight students and ask them what problems they are experiencing. Though this is occasionally feasible in some schools, the lack of trust between generations and between students and teachers in many schools is usually enough to debar such a suggestion.

Better, probably, to set up a more formal, systematic process for asking the question and getting the answers. Start with some consideration of the question you want to ask, for an inappropriate question can in itself cause disorder in some classrooms. At best, such a question will bring forth no answer, so the learning situation is left in worse shape than it was before the question was asked. (Now the students are wary and generally turned off, and the teacher is dispirited and even apprehensive.)

You may ask a general, broad-based question, like "What problems do you have that you would like to find some answers to?" Such a question has the advantage of being broad enough to permit the students to give answers that the teacher never dreamed were on their minds. The disadvantage is that it may be too broad. Responses may cover so many different areas that the class would find it difficult to plan effectively for learning and follow through in the limited time allotted.

It may be more advisable to narrow the focus of the question somewhat, so the scope of responses is more manageable. Thus, since it is safe to assume, from what we know about human beings, that everyone has some involvement in family problems, we may ask a question like, "What family problems do people have?"; "What are some of the problems that families have in their daily lives?" or "What kinds of family problems would you like to know more about?" Such questions would probably insure responses that cluster around family relationships, a topic that is broad enough to include the concerns of most if not all the students, and narrow enough to be planned for and studied within the ordinary time constraints of the school semester.

When planning to ask the question, the teacher should arrange the physical situation to eliminate those factors that might interfere with the process. For example, the question should be written in full view of the students as should all responses. The students should all be facing the board—or wherever the writing is. There should not be large spaces between students and teacher and students and students. It is better to ask everyone to move up close to the writing surface, so that the collective expectancy is intimately focused on the responses. It is better for the teacher to do the writing, so there is no problem about legibility, spelling, or endless time spent in getting the responses down. The teacher should not evaluate or permit anyone else to evaluate the responses but should take them down verbatim, to be classified and planned for later.

Suggesting the development of curriculum based on real student problems is made in the interest of effective classroom management. From what we know about classroom management, and about human participation in most activities, we may conclude that interest in the activity, trust in the situation and the people, and some understanding of what is going on can sustain the group. We must not look for esoteric approaches to education to take the place of interest, trust, and understanding. How long would any of us remain in a situation where none of these factors were present?

Consider, then, that when young people are forced to remain in classes even when they are not interested, they feel threatened and vulnerable, they are out of their depth intellectually. What is there left for them to do but to kick and scream in any way that occurs to them, acting out of fear, anxiety, boredom, and anger to express the turmoil inside them? This is what "discipline" and classroom management are all about.

chapter 8

Fate Control for the Teacher

ADMINISTRATIVE ASSISTANCE

Teacher: Tommy, I've had about enough of your behavior. Go and see the principal; maybe he can convince you of the error of your ways.

Tommy: No, I won't!

Teacher: Out, Tommy! Leave this room at once!

Tommy: [He sits at his desk. One can almost see his heels digging in.]

Teacher: [Goes up to Tommy and grabs his arm.]

Tommy: Don't touch me! [He pulls his arm away.] You hit me! You hit me! [He looks at his shirt sleeve closely.] I'm bleeding! I'm bleeding!

Teacher: Stop being silly! Nobody hit you.

Tommy: You did! You did! [He runs from the room, crying.]

The teacher resumes the lesson, even though she seems to have some trouble with her breathing. This sort of thing is upsetting. A few minutes later, the room intercommunication speaker crackles, and the principal's voice is heard.

Principal: Mrs. Amdur, one of your pupils is in my office.

Teacher: Yes, Mr. Merriam.

Principal: He's crying.

Teacher: Yes, Mr. Merriam.

Principal: Can you come in and speak to me about this?

Teacher: I'll be glad to. I have prep time in fifteen minutes; I can come down then.

[The intercom clicks off.]

When the teacher enters the anteroom to the principal's office, there is Tommy, sitting on the bench, his face tear-streaked. A secretary sits beside him, comforting him.

Tommy: I want to go home.

Secretary: [Soothingly.] We'll call your mother in a little while. [Cajolingly.] It's not too bad here, is it? [Coyly.] Don't you like sitting here with me? You'll hurt my feelings if you say you don't!

Tommy: [Tears welling up in his eyes.] I want to go home!

The teacher stands for a moment and listens to the conversation. Then she walks into the principal's office.

Principal: Sit down, sit down, Mrs. Amdur. Now, what happened?

Teacher: Nothing, really. I sent him to your office and he refused to go. So I took his arm, and he pulled away from me. He was probably frightened about having to see you, so he began to cry.

Principal: He said you hit him.

Teacher: I didn't hit him.

Principal: He'll tell his mother you hit him. And she's one of those women who carries a lot of weight in the community. She's a big talker.

Teacher: Mr. Merriam, I did *not* hit that child! I cannot help what he says. He has been misbehaving all year. He interferes with everything I try to do in my room. I've tried everything with him! He's incorrigible!

Principal: All right. All right. Let's not get upset about this. I'll talk to his mother.

Teacher: *I* would like to talk to her. She ought to know what a problem that child is.

Principal: I think I'd better take care of it. I'll keep Tommy here today until it's time for dismissal. I'll call his mother.

Teacher: Is that all, Mr. Merriam?

Mr. Merriam: Yes, yes. That's all. That's all.

PEER ASSISTANCE

Still later, in the teacher's room, Mrs. Amdur is speaking with Mrs. Hart, another fourth-grade teacher.

Mrs. Amdur: Oh, what a day! That Tommy Rower!

Mrs. Hart: You have Tommy Rower? I don't envy you! I had his brother for two years!

Mrs. Amdur: Did you? What was *he* like?

Mrs. Hart: A terror! If it was possible to do something wrong, that kid was sure to do it!

Mrs. Amdur: Did you ever meet his mother?

Mrs. Hart: Did I ever! She's one of these my-child-can't-do-anything-wrong ladies. And Merriam does nothing but butter her up. He's so afraid she can make trouble for him, he'll do anything to keep her quiet.

Mrs. Amdur: He wouldn't even let me talk to her about Tommy. I thought if I talked to her she could do something about him. He's ruining my class!

Mrs. Hart: Just tough it out. It's only for four more months.

Mrs. Amdur: [Laughing weakly.] I don't know if I can last four more months!

Mrs. Hart smiles sympathetically. Mrs. Amdur feels a *little* better now, knowing she is not the only one who has had this kind of problem. However, she is not at all happy about leaving the situation as it is. Surely there must be something positive that can be done—to help her, to help Tommy. Just "toughing it out" seems too much like copping out. She hated to admit that nothing more could be done to make the situation better.

PARAPROFESSIONAL ASSISTANCE

Back in her room, Mrs. Amdur waited for Mrs. Heath, the classroom aide, to bring the children back from gym. Two adults in a room, and they couldn't manage one mean little kid, she thought. She hated to give up, if for no other reason than tomorrow Tommy would be here again and at it again.

The children filed into the room and took their seats. Mrs. Heath came in at the end of the line.

Mrs. Amdur: Mrs. Heath, do you think you can stay for a few minutes after dismissal today so we can talk a little bit?

Mrs. Heath: Oh, I'm afraid not. I've got to get right home. I like to be there when my Jimmy comes home from school.

Mrs. Amdur: Yes, of course. I should have remembered. Maybe we can get together tomorrow morning before the children come in. It will be only for a few minutes.

Mrs. Heath: Can't we talk during your prep period? Or during lunch?

Mrs. Amdur: Well, I'm on lunchroom duty all week. And the art teacher wants you to stay with the class during art period. Apparently she has some problems about the way they use the materials.

Mrs. Heath: Maybe we can find time next week. Was it anything special?

Mrs. Amdur: Well, we really should have some time together for planning. I don't feel right about just giving you one or two children on the spur of the moment, without giving you a chance to make some preparation.

Mrs. Heath: Oh, I don't mind. I've been around children long enough so that I don't need any preparation. Just tell me what needs to be done and I'll do it.

Mrs. Amdur: [Doubtfully.] Ye-e-s, of course. I was just hoping we could come up with something that would work with Tommy.

Mrs. Heath: I know what would work with that one! A couple of good smacks on the bottom a few times a day will get him in line!

Mrs. Amdur: I don't want to hit the children. I just think there has to be another way.

Mrs. Heath: There's just one language he understands! You can see how your other ways have worked!

Mrs. Amdur: Well, thank you, Mrs. Heath. Maybe you

can take Janie to the math table now and help her with division.

ORGANIZING FOR FATE CONTROL

One of the things teacher education faculties have talked about for a long time is the need for continuing support of beginning teachers during their first year on the job. Though there has usually been some argument against the feasibility of instituting such supports for new graduates, the belief persists that many of the persistent problems encountered by teachers could be prevented or solved if the teachers had the support of *their* teachers during that first crucial year.

At any rate, such supports have generally not been provided for, and it occurs to me that, even if they had been, they would never have been adequate to the need. It isn't just beginning teachers who need professional support during times of stress and crisis; all teachers need this kind of assistance. Actually, all *professionals* working with people over long periods of time encounter stressful situations that require the kind of understanding and support that others in their own profession can best provide.

Physicians and nurses need the help of other physicians and nurses when they undergo the continuing stress of caring for seriously ill and dying patients. Dentists must turn to other dentists for help in coping with the fear and even hostilities of their patients. Police officers often feel that only other police officers can appreciate the fears and frustrations of daily law enforcement. And teachers know what teachers know, and they can profit from systematic attempts to help each other survive and continue to function effectively. As I once wrote about medical people who minister to dying patients, "It is those in need who will have to take the initiative for fulfilling their own needs. Those who feel the pain and the urgency are the ones who are most likely to take measures to reduce the pain. The helpers themselves must marshal their resources and systematically help each other whenever [help

is] needed . . . such help depends on a heightened awareness of the need, and on the development of helping skills."[1]

School Climates

I have found that the prevailing attitude in schools varies from community to community. In one school the attitude is revealed in the open acknowledgement that teaching there is hell, that the children are generally disruptive and the classrooms chaotic. "One does what one can" is the implicit philosophy, "but you can't really teach in this place." Though, on the surface, it would seem that the teachers in such a school have satisfactorily rationalized away the failure of teaching, the truth is that they feel frustrated in their professional commitment, unsatisfied because of a sense of personal failure, and, often, guilty because of what is happening to a generation of children who come into contact with them. The guilt alone can feed the animosity against the children, the school, and the community until the teachers in that school sound and behave more like enemies than like professional educationists, and this makes them feel even more unhappy, more guilty.

In another school, where, perhaps, the incidence of disruption is not so great, the teacher faced with it continually may feel constrained to keep it to herself, lest she be identified as incompetent. Added to the strain of trying to solve her classroom management problems that seem so resistant to solution, is the effort needed to keep quiet about what is happening, and the anxiety surrounding the possibility that other teachers and the administration will discover her secret. (Generally, however, the secret is not at all well kept. The signs of disorder are there for everyone to see: the continuous noise; the deadly silences that come after the teacher's shouting; the individual children forever standing in the corridor outside the room, apparently kicked out

---

[1] *Nursing the Dying Patient*, (Reston, Va.: Reston Pub. Co., 1975), p. 182.

for exceeding even the horrendous behavior going on inside; the teacher's harried look; the bitterness in her tone whenever she speaks about teaching.)

In other situations, there is no single teacher or small number of teachers who continuously have trouble in the classroom. However, even with the most skillful professionals, in schools that are models of supportive administration, with pupil populations that are highly motivated and incredibly well behaved, there are always *those days* that every teacher has experienced. Sometimes, those days seem to happen more and more frequently, and the teacher finds himself more than usually beset with self-doubt and fear. In any school, there are always one or two teachers who are experiencing this kind of thing at any one time.

And what of the new teacher in the school? (Though there are fewer and fewer of them these days!) She was a good student of education. Her pregraduation field experience with children was exciting and satisfying. Her cooperating teachers and her student-teaching supervisor predicted a successful career for her. But there are days when she is sure she will never make it. So many of the teaching strategies that worked when she was a student and there was an experienced teacher in the room with her are just not working now. The children who all seemed so scrubbed, bright, and responsive then, too often look scruffy and bored now. And she feels so *alone*, so vulnerable. She is afraid to say too much about what is happening lest the experienced people all around her come to the conclusion that she cannot handle the job. She is still in her probationary period, and she could find herself out of work in very short order. She cannot risk letting anyone know, so she drags herself home every day, exhausted by her unsuccessful efforts, and cries a lot in solitude. Is this what teaching is going to be like after all?

How can teachers in a school help themselves to live through the inevitable stresses they encounter in their professional lives? How do they, at the same time, get the professional support they need for maintaining the commitment to the high level of operation that they started out with?

The Plan

1. It is probably not a good idea to try to enlist the whole staff for involvement in a mutual assistance/professional support organization. If this is the initial plan of one, two, or three teachers, or even the principal, so much time will need to be spent on the recruitment and organization, that ministering to the pressing needs will be postponed to some future date when everything will be "ready" and the store will be opened for business. The important thing is the helping, not the organization. And the prevailing idea that organization inevitably leads to the desired objectives is an illusion. Organization too often becomes an end in itself, and in the exciting process of organization, the essential objectives are endlessly postponed until "the organization is complete and ready to function."

2. Do not deposit the idea in the lap of the administration and leave it to the principal and/or vice-principal to establish a process for filling the needs. Though in some circles one hears that the principal is the educational leader of the school, it is usually about as accurate a statement as the one that says the dean is the educational leader of a college of education. Though occasionally such an office is filled by a person who is professionally gifted, generally the function of the office is filling out forms, juggling budgets, listening to complaints, and keeping the lid on trouble. Professional initiatives must come from the people who daily perform the significant professional functions.

3. Start out by identifying two or three other people who think the idea is a good one and probably workable. They need not be filled with the same enthusiasm that you have for it, but they are willing to devote time to try out some aspect of it. Nor is the process of identifying a few like-minded colleagues a complicated one. During lunch, during casual conversations in the faculty room, even during staff meetings when you are not interested in what is going on, introduce the idea tentatively and watch to see who picks it up. You might keep in mind that it may not be the people who feel the greatest need who will seem immediately interested. There must be considerable trust in the situation before

a troubled person will take the risk of even *appearing* to need help.

4. Invite the interested people to talk about the idea further. An hour after school, or an early evening in your home can provide enough time to express the feelings surrounding the idea. Doubts about its practicality will surface. Obstacles to establishing it will be identified. But through it all, no one will seriously deny the existence of the need for it.

5. Perhaps the safest way to begin operating is by providing assistance as it is needed only to each other. One can assume that there is some degree of trust among the people who have gathered together initially, and that they are willing to accept—along with the desirability of the idea of helping—a certain amount of help for themselves. Perhaps they will be even more interested in *giving* help to the others in the group. Immediately to announce to the whole school that the group has set itself up as helpers is an obvious mistake: for one thing it subverts the idea of *mutual* assistance; for another, the lack of response or even the outright denigration of the idea may destroy the initial enthusiasm of the original group; and finally, any such announcement will inevitably be perceptually distorted by many people who receive it, and, even if the whole idea is laid out in detail, there will be much misunderstanding. Thus, one person will think the initiators are saying that the teachers in the school are not doing a good job; the principal will resent the implication that he is not providing all necessary leadership; some people will say, "Who do they think they are, setting themselves up as the experts"; others will resent not being asked to join the founders.

It is better to be just a group of three or four people who want to help each other over those minor rough spots we all encounter in our work.

6. Next, the problem is to decide just when people will help each other. It will not do to barge into people's lives with no agreed-upon guidelines for when helping is appropriate. The group may decide that help should be given only when it is asked for, at least at the outset, and until there is a clearer common understanding of the helping relationship. The group may decide that each person in need is free to ask only one person for help, and that the

nature of the help given should be kept confidential. There may be an agreed-upon decision to provide no individual help at all but to rely on group meetings to provide in a general way whatever help is needed.

7. While the discussions continue to establish suitable helping processes, the group should be meeting regularly to identify and refine those skills that are essential if help is really to be meaningful.

Some of the same questions that the children are encouraged to ask should also be asked by the teachers (see Chapter 4):

- What is helping?

- What does helping do?

- How does helping change the helper? The person helped?

- Can you think of times when helping hurts?

In addition, it might be useful to try out the different kinds of help that might be offered, so that the different reactions of individuals to one kind or another might be examined. For example, the teachers could role play the characters in the following situation:

> Mr. Smith has been teaching the fourth grade for five years. He is considered a very competent teacher and, if one can judge by the opinions of the children, his classrooms are happy, busy places where systematic learning proceeds with a minimum of resistance or other disruption.
>
> Suddenly, two weeks into the new school year, Mr. Smith is showing signs of being very disturbed. He does not behave in the cheerful, breezy way customary with him. He seems to have something very heavy on his mind, and, when people are laughing and joking around him, he often does not seem to hear them. Several times some of his pupils have been seen coming from and going into his classroom in ways that are unusual for his classes. For example, one boy suddenly flung open the door of the room and made as if to lunge out. A shout from Mr. Smith stopped him in his tracks, and he went back in, shutting the door behind him. Mr. Smith has never been known to shout before.

Just this morning, one of the girls in his class was observed through the glass door pane by a passerby to be sitting at her desk crying, while the other children sat and listened to Mr. Smith, who seemed to be angry about something. The children looked half frightened, half angry as they stared at him.

Miss Phillips, a friend of Mr. Smith, asked him on the way out of the building one afternoon if he was all right. "Sure," he answered. "Fine." He said nothing more, just turned and walked away. This was not characteristic behavior for him; he is a garrulous, friendly man, and responds warmly to overtures by friends and acquaintances.

Miss Phillips talks to Mrs. Ingraham about Mr. Smith, and they decide that their friend must be very worried about something. They also decide to take the initiative and do something to try to help him.

First one person, then another, may play Mr. Smith, Miss Phillips, and Mrs. Ingraham. Each time it is played, after the help has been proffered and responded to, let the person playing Mr. Smith say what he felt about the help provided, and whether or not it really was helpful. Let the "helpers" say why they chose the kind of help they did, and how they felt about Mr. Smith's reaction to that help.

By the time a number of different people have tried to work out the helping situation in different ways, some of the following questions will probably have been discussed:

- What kind of help always works?

- What kind of help never works?

- What clues should people who stand ready to help be on the alert for?

- Is the kind of help *you* prefer the most reliable criterion for what other people find helpful? What other criteria are there?

In addition, some of the following types of help will have been tried and responded to:

- *Nonverbal help*
  bodily contact
  active listening
- *Verbal help*
  explanations
  reassurances
  information
  advice
- *Action help*
  going out socially with the person
  keeping the person company at lunch, on a walk, etc.
  demonstrating teaching strategies
   in the helper's classroom
   in the classroom of the person being helped
  changing the pattern of operation—either temporarily or permanently—to help take some of the burden off the troubled teacher, while maintaining the continuity of the children's education
  combining classes and team teaching
  exchanging small groups of pupils for special activities (e.g., five or six children from the class of the person needing help may visit the class of the helper for a block of time.)
  recruiting community people (like local business and professional people) to share in the education of the children. Thus, a parent could accompany three children from the class of the person needing help to a drug company in the area, where they could learn something about its operation.
- *No help at all*
  There is great wisdom in recognizing when no help at all would be the most helpful thing to do.

When a person simply does not want help, what colleagues must weigh in the balance is the right of the teacher to continue in his own way with the rights of the children to be protected from serious harm. Generally, I think, no such grave alternative presents itself, and the teacher who wants to try to work out his own problems must be trusted to do so. If the atmosphere of the school is conducive to the development of openness and trust, if people expect from each other honesty and caring and help, and their expectations are fulfilled, then the person in serious trouble professionally will be less fearful of admitting his need. Even in those rare cases when he is beyond asking for help, the intercession of his colleagues will usually be a great relief to him.

8. As these activities of the group continue, its participants should talk freely and openly to the other people in the school about what is going on during the meetings. They should also make it very clear that everyone is invited to participate—even if it is only out of curiosity. As people understand more about what the group is trying to accomplish, more people will want to be a part of it.

9. More important than anything else is that everyone—*everyone*—who wants help gets it, immediately and unhesitatingly, and in the constructive spirit of support and reassurance. Unless people come to expect that help is always forthcoming and they are never turned away disappointed because nobody cared, such an enterprise will not sustain itself. This kind of consistency is necessary to establish trust in the idea, trust in colleagues, trust in the institution. Without such trust, people will continue to suffer alone, isolated from the concern and help of their peers.

Afterword

We are accustomed, in our attempts to acquire knowledge, to consider different subject areas as if they were discrete and completely separate from all other subject areas. Most of us have lost sight of the fact that all knowledge is interrelated, and that any approach to knowing should be a unified, integrated approach. The separate study of the various disciplines has resulted in such compartmentalization of knowledge that different languages have developed among the separated scientists, and now they must, if they want to speak to each other, spend some time first in learning the others' languages.

Similarly, we sometimes think that a specific behavior problem can be handled with a specific remedy, that each disciplinary problem can be cured by its own palliative, if we can only discover the specific medicine. But, the more we search, the more we realize that it is the total teaching-learning situation that must be dealt with for most of the management problems we encounter.

In the study of classroom management, in the struggle to find answers to problems that are interfering with learning, we sometimes have fallen into the trap of thinking we can fasten on a list of dos and don'ts that will solve our problems. I also thought, when I started to write this book, that I could develop such a list from the distillation of the years of practice of dozens of effective teachers I have known.

But there are no really short-term solutions for classroom management problems, just as there is little instant learning of important concepts and skills. Nor are there simple tricks that can effectively deal with specific disciplinary and behavioral situations. (A trick may work one time and not another time, and the teacher with nothing but a bag of tricks is left without workable alternatives when the bag is empty.) Aside from a bit of general advice that helps to reassure the working teacher and prevent some obvious errors of management, management problems—if they can be solved at all by the classroom teacher—can only be solved by more effective teaching. Even the behavior modification attempts to change individual inappropriate behaviors must be used with all the children in a classroom if they are not to increase the incidence of the target behavior in the rest of the class.

If there are processes presented here that seem to overlap the treatment of different problems, then it is because those processes are the pathways toward the educational goals we set for ourselves; and it is both the process and the goal that most often must be dealt with if the management problem is to be resolved. Often, even a particular problem may begin to look much like the other problems, once the surface manifestation of it has been stripped away. And if the problems are alike, the solutions must be alike.

It should not discourage us that we have so few instant solutions to management problems. We rarely expect instant cures from our physicians, or instant remedies from the law. Why, then, the expectation that the complex processes involved in learning should lend themselves to simple, quickly applied methods of keeping them running smoothly?

We continue to invest a good part of our lives in teaching. If the job were that easy or that quickly done, we would not forever be searching for answers.

Index